PATTERNS AND PRINCIPLES OF SPANISH ART

*Pertenecen a la pintura espa-
ñola todas aquellas obras que
lleven impreso el sello nacional.*
Manuel B. Cossío

GREGORIO HERNANDEZ:
EL CRISTO DE LA LUZ,
MUSEUM AT VALLADOLID

Patterns and Principles
of Spanish Art

OSKAR HAGEN *Fellow Royal Society of Arts and*
Professor of History and Criticism of Art, University of Wisconsin

THE UNIVERSITY OF WISCONSIN PRESS
Madison 1948

PRINTED IN THE UNITED STATES OF AMERICA

To
GEORGE & MABEL SELLERY
In Friendship

Author's Foreword

Although this little book bears the same title as an earlier one issued in 1936 as one of the *University of Wisconsin Studies in Language and Literature,* it is in no sense the same work. Except for the basic construction of the whole, the text is new from cover to cover. On every page it contains new material, new viewpoints, new definitions, and its typographical and illustrational appearance has been changed quite as much.

On the other hand, I believe that my book has continued to fill a gap in the field of studies of Spanish art. While highly specialized researches have been carried on in every province of Spanish painting, sculpture, and architecture, my *Patterns and Principles of Spanish Art* has remained the only single study of the larger connections: the uniform structure of art in Spain from the days of the Moors to those of Francisco Goya. I have not altered the title because I could think of no better one.

Thomas Eakins once called it the big problem in art to forget that things are complex and to make the beholder forget. The artist, he thought, should follow the example of the mathematician who reduces complicated things to simple things. There are problems in the history of art to which the same counsel applies. Mine is one of them. If the essential features of the Spanish style are to appear lucidly, they must be definitely discovered and tested, and much material must be subordinated or cast aside. The plan and cross-section of Spanish art which I have endeavored to distill from the scattered works of art of many centuries must be in simple lines; the simpler the clearer. I am presenting only that which, in my opinion, is absolutely indispensable. It is one thing to publish an elaborate *catalogue raisonné* of the Spanish primitive painters like Chandler R. Post's unrivalled *History of Spanish Painting,* and quite another to draw an outline of the whole of Spanish art. In the former undertaking completeness is as essential as incompleteness of factual detail is inevitable in the latter. For the same reason my readers, I hope, will not misunderstand my sobriety in the manner of bibliographical references. The structure of Spanish art which I am trying to disclose could easily be swamped in footnotes. With more annotations—and many more would have been necessary even if I cited only the most important sources—the book would have grown to twice its present size. The pictorial material, on the other hand, will be found to be evidential rather than merely illustrative.

To achieve my object I have frequently overstepped the boundaries of the plastic arts. Spanish artists, being less inclined than the Italians to speculate and theorize on their particular intentions, have produced nothing to match the treatises of Leone Battista Alberti, Leonardo da Vinci, Piero dei Franceschi, and others.* To compensate for that deficiency I have found it helpful to throw the spotlight that Cervantes cast upon

* A few Spanish treatises written in the Renaissance followed in the wake of the Italians: Diego de Sagredo, *Medidas del Romano* (Toledo, 1526); Felipe de Guevara, *Comentarios de la Pintura* (edited by Antonio Ponz, Madrid, 1788); Francisco de Holanda, *Tractato de Pintura antigua* (1538; published by the *Academia de San Fernando,* Madrid, 1921); and Juan de Arphe's poem *De varia commensuración para la Esculptura y Architectura* (Seville, 1585). The latter is a perfect compendium of classicistic doctrines. Although authentic sources flowed more liberally in the seventeenth century, they were still under Italian influence, at least in the beginning; for instance, Pablo de Céspedes, *Poema de la Pintura* (about 1604), which is contained partly in Pacheco's treatise, partly in the *Diccionario* of Ceán Bermúdez (V. p. 268 ff). Vincenzo Carducho, *Diálogos de la Pintura* (Madrid, 1633; published by Villaamil, Madrid, 1865) defends the manneristic doctrine. Francisco Pacheco, *Arte de la Pintura* (Seville, 1649; edited more recently by Villaamil, Madrid, 1865), expounding authentic Spanish realism, is by far the most valuable seventeenth-century source. The viewpoint of the late seventeenth century is exhibited in the *Discursos practicables del nobilisimo arte de la Pintura* by José Martínez (published by Valentin Cardera y Solano, Madrid, 1866). For the whole matter see Menéndez y Pelayo, *Historia de las ideas estéticas en España* (2d ed., Madrid, 1901) IV *passim;* further, Sánchez-Cantón, *Fuentes literarias para la historia del arte español* (Madrid, 1923); and Julius von Schlosser, *Die Kunstliteratur* (Vienna, 1924), pp. 246 ff., 557 ff.

the literary objectives of his age upon the field of the art of his time. For the same reason I have turned some beams from the history of music upon the history of painting.

For the reader's convenience all accents on Spanish proper names have been omitted except in the index, book titles, notes, and quoted passages. For names anglicized by long usage (Velasquez, for example) I have employed the English rather than the Spanish spelling. As regards the museums, churches, and other depositories of paintings and sculptures in Spain which are mentioned in connection with each art work, certain errors have been unavoidable because of the wholesale redistribution by the art administration, particularly of Catalonia, during and after the Spanish Civil War.

I wish to extend to Miss Livia Appel a special word of gratitude for her sensitive and untiring editing of my manuscript.

OSKAR HAGEN

Madison, Wisconsin
In the Fall of 1942

NOTE ON SECOND PRINTING

This second printing of the 1943 edition includes only a very few changes in the text, embodying corrections based upon important critical comments made by Dr. Walter W. S. Cook in the *Review of Religion* for March, 1944, for which I am deeply grateful. I regret that it is impossible at this time to comply with the suggestion of this great scholar of Spanish art that "if [the author] were to bring out a subsequent edition of this book, it would be of greatest interest if he were to expand his Book One to an entire volume, because in that approach he offers something entirely new to the criticism and understanding of Spanish art."

OSKAR HAGEN

Table of Contents

List of Illustrations

THE SPANISH
IMAGINATION

BOOK ONE

Avenues of Approach

CHAPTER ONE

THE SPANISH STYLE The art of the Spaniards, not unlike the art of other individual nations, appears to the historian in at least two different aspects: first as a single, unchanging Spanish style; and second as a succession of changing period styles. The two aspects are as different from each other as is a man's soul from his physical organism. The persistent Spanish style, independent of the changing fashions, was conditioned by the national character; more precisely, by the blood, the temper, and the idiosyncracies of the Spanish race. The period styles of art in Spain, on the other hand—changing as they were influenced by ephemeral conceptions, technical facilities, and theories of international schools—were conditioned by the laws of evolution and by the ebb and flood of European civilization in general.

The persistent Spanish style is that cluster of elements of form which is present in every genuine Spanish work of art and which, as we survey a comprehensive exposition of paintings, sculptures, and architectures of all periods, tells us instantly that this, that, or another exhibited item, whatever the period in which it was done, is of Spanish origin, even as others on the walls are quite as unmistakably French, German, or Italian. The period styles that we distinguish in Spanish works are the changing international repertories of form superimposed on the unchanging racial style. The Spanish artists of the twelfth century employed the international Byzantine repertory of conventionalized forms; the Spaniards of the fifteenth century employed the international Franco-Flemish repertory of primitive naturalistic forms; eventually the Spaniards adapted the more

3

advanced international repertories of naturalism that evolved with the Renaissance and the Baroque to the exigencies of their native taste. The last words are important. It should be borne in mind where the development of Spanish art is under discussion that in every period the repertories of period forms were assimilated to those national ideals which remained the same in the face of all other changes. I shall first deal with the unchanging Spanish style.

The art of every nation is as thoroughly impregnated with racial elements of expression as is its language. It has long been recognized that the sum total of these racial elements, whether they are encountered in the language or in the art of a nation, discloses an underlying national-psychological disposition. Experience with the several national types of English, French, German, and Italian art, moreover, has compelled historians to assume that there must be inherent in every nationally conditioned art work a number of tangible features that constitute the particular style and lead us to say with assurance that this work is English, another German, and still another Spanish. What then are the features peculiar to Spanish art? What lends to it its specific Spanish flavor?

Any search for the basic elements which give the Spanish tang to Spanish art should be made, for the sake of clarity, along two avenues of approach. Every art style springs from twin roots. First, art is *content,* the representation of ideas or impressions that may be emotional or merely visual. Naturally these ideas and impressions are tempered and colored, if not altogether determined, by the artist's temperament and general disposition. Secondly, art is *form.* Apart from being an expression *of* something, it is an expression *by* something; the artist expresses his idea or impression by means of lines, colors, light, and patterns composed of all these means. It is this second root—Spanish art in so far as it is form—that I wish to investigate before I proceed along the other avenue.

The artists of Spain, like those of the other nations, gathered the images of the phenomenal or spiritual world into visual patterns. These patterns reveal features peculiar not only to the individual but to his race and blood. It is axiomatic that in artistic creation every sense impression passes through a psychological process of molding. The finished art work is the *im*pression made over into an *ex*pression. The mold of ideation from which the expression is cast is conditioned by the artist's individuality; and if that individuality is Spanish, the artist's form of ideation is, at least in great measure, a Spanish form of ideation or, as we say more commonly, it is in keeping with the Spanish taste. What the Spanish taste is can be detected by an analytical separation of its constituent parts.

FOREIGN ARTISTS IN SPAIN Spain has always attracted artists from abroad. But in transforming these foreigners into Spaniards she has had better success with the artists of Teutonic than with those of Latin blood. The history of art abounds with examples of German, Dutch, and Flemish architects, sculptors, and painters who rapidly adjusted their native training to the Spanish tradition; indeed, many of them have been mistaken for Spaniards. With the unique exception of El Greco, however, most of the non-Teutonic immigrants found it extremely difficult to assimilate the national tradition.

The sculptors from Aquitaine, Burgundy, and North France who were active in Spain throughout the Romanesque and Gothic periods abided by their French conventions and made only very slight concessions, if any, to the Spanish taste. Master Mateo's grand *Pórtico de la Gloria*, outside the great national sanctuary of Santiago de Compostela, impresses one not at all as Spanish but as typically French of the late twelfth century. The statues and reliefs carved by masons from Bourges for the thirteenth-century cathedral of Leon—above all the tympanum over the main door— are considered among the finest specimens of their kind in *French* sculpture.

But in the early fifteenth century, when Flemings, Dutchmen, and Germans began to fill the posts hitherto occupied by the French, "these Northerners were so enchanted with the peculiar charm of the country and so fascinated by Moorish and Mudejar art works that they took quite as much from Spain as they gave her in return."* They had no difficulty in expressing themselves in the forms of the Spanish tradition, however unused they were to them. In the retables of the cathedrals of Seville and Toledo it is difficult to discern any stylistic differences between the work

* August L. Mayer, *Mittelalterliche Plastik in Spanien* (Munich, 1922), 18.

of the native Spaniards and that of Germans such as Rodrigo and Jorge Fernandez Aleman and of Hollanders or Flemings such as Diego Copin and Dancart. True, certain details betray traces of foreign training; but as regards the construction plan as a whole the Teutons obviously assimilated the Spanish taste so successfully that no vestige of their native German or Netherlandish taste remained. The same is true of the paintings of artists whose Teutonic origin is concealed in their Hispanized names: Pedro de Campaña (= Kempener); Juan de Flandes (= of Flanders); Francisco de Amberes (= of Antwerp); Antonio Moro (= Antonis Mor).

The inadjustability of the French is apparent not only in the Medieval periods; it was responsible for the Frenchification of Spanish art during the reign of Philip V, in the early eighteenth century.

A similar inadjustability to the Spanish idiosyncrasies characterized the numerous Italians who worked in Spain, particularly after the beginning of the sixteenth century. The sculptor Pietro Torrigiani (1472–1522) might pass for a Spaniard, but it would be because of his character rather than his art. *"Piu superbia che arte si vide nel Torrigiano"* (there is more haughtiness than art in Torrigiano)—this is the opening passage of Vasari's short biography of the sculptor, a passage that would apply to numerous Spanish-born artists: to Alonso Cano, for instance, and to both the Francisco Herreras, father and son. As a person, Torrigiani evinced several traits that characterize the Spaniard. When as a young student he punched and mutilated the face of his rival Michelangelo, he did so not because he was jealous of his fellow student's genius but, as Vasari explicitly states, because he resented Michelangelo's patient diligence and perseverance, his unremitting labor day and night and even on holidays. Torrigiani's resentment of that was something the Spaniards understood more readily than the Italians. Impatience and lack of perseverance were cited as a major deficiency of the Spanish character by Baltasar Gracian (1601–55). So, too, the Spanish people admired Torrigiani's *animo fiero e coraggioso* (stubborn and courageous soul), which made him trade the sculptor's chisel for the soldier's sword and fight for five years as a mercenary in several armies before he returned to his profession.

But this Florentine, although he resembled a Spaniard in so many personal ways, had not a drop of Hispanicism in his art. Torrigiani's well-known terra-cotta statue of St. Jerome in the Museum of Seville is no Spanish art work. It is a late edition of an Italian idea that originated in the school of Donatello. Bertoldo di Giovanni had fashioned it in the modest proportions of a bronze statuette (Berlin, Kaiser Friedrich Museum); Torrigiani blew it up to life size. He was rightly considered in his day the herald of the Florentine High Renaissance, in Spain no less so than previously in England.

What a contrast is El Greco! Before removing to Spain he had studied in Venice, and after settling down in Toledo (1577) he never really imitated anything Spanish. Nevertheless, from the moment he stepped on Spanish soil, his every brush stroke was Spanish.

But of course the man from the little mountain town of Phodele—his birthplace, as Achilleus Kyrou discovered—must have felt as much at home among the brown rocks of Castile as among the threatening gorges of his native island Crete. Apparently the geography and climate of the countries whence the foreign artists came had something to do with their ability or inability to assimilate the Spanish spirit. If the geographical and climatic conditions at home and in Spain were similar, as in the case of the Teutons and El Greco, the adjustment was easy. If they were dissimilar, as in the case of the Italians, the adjustment was difficult.

How vastly did El Greco's ability to absorb the very essence of Spanish art differ from the lack of comprehension of the Italian mannerists to whom Philip II unfortunately entrusted the decoration of the Escorial. Their academic altar paintings and pompous Italianate murals produce upon the beholder an effect entirely alien to the irrepressibly Spanish atmosphere of that gray stone temple to death. One senses the incongruity the moment one enters the church, though it cannot at first be fully accounted for. Then suddenly comes the realization that it is the Italian language of art which refuses to blend with the ferocious Spanish mood of the place.

The fact that a large number of native Spanish artists went to Italy for study did not destroy their Hispanicism. Exceptions are found in the fifteenth and sixteenth centuries, when medieval Spain endeavored to assimilate the Renaissance and a few artists were sidetracked by Flemish and, eventually, Italian mannerisms. But with that crisis overcome, it was one thing to see Spain with the eyes of an Italian, and quite another to see Italy with the eyes of a Spaniard. The former is exemplified by the school of the Escorial, the latter by Jose Ribera. Born in Jativa (1588), Ribera removed to Naples when he was young and never returned to Spain. In these circumstances he could not remain entirely uninfluenced by the ideas of the Italian painters, particularly those who for once were establishing values that were dear also to the Spaniards—as was Caravaggio. Nevertheless, Ribera remained a typical representative of the Spanish school.

In the fact that the land and climate of Spain have assimilated the North European race, but have not revealed their mysteries to the Latin, lies, if not the key to Spain, at any rate an important truth. If Spain has always been more or less alien to the Latin races, then she cannot be, as is widely believed, a Romanized country, just another Italy—a common error which may have sprung from the similarity between the Spanish and Italian languages. If, on the other hand, Spain has always been a familiar land, and even a second home, to the people of Germanic descent, the country and its people must be kindred in one way or another to North Europe. I consider this a problem of paramount importance.

For if in seeking the key to Spanish art one sets out from a misapprehension, how can he ever hope to arrive at the truth? To measure Spanish art with an Italian yardstick is to employ the wrong standards. That is not to say that the standards of Dutch or German art are more applicable. The only authentic standards, of course, are to be found in Spanish self-expression itself. Still, if one wants to know the authentic Spanish standards, it is well to know beforehand what they are not. They are neither French nor Italian.

RACIAL TRAITS OF THE SPANISH PEOPLE In the rough and inhospitable countrysides of Spain there is little to remind one of the sweet and endearing, classical harmony of Italy. Napoleon remarked that Africa begins on the other side of the Pyrenees. Spain is a "great detached fragment of Africa" and the Spaniard is the "first-born of the white Africans of the North." This is the view of scholars who have sounded the depths of Spanish psychology and civilization—Gomez Moreno, Havelock Ellis, Klemperer, and others.

But is it permissible to speak so unreservedly of *the* Spaniard? The Catalan is as different from the Castilian, the Basque from the Asturian, and the Aragonese from the Andalusian as are their respective tongues. Nonetheless these distinct tribal tempers intertwine like the several tunes of a polyphonous musical score. When heard separately, each of the melodies may seem quite unlike any of the others; but in the contrapuntal texture of the whole it is precisely the contrasts that make the symphony. Racially the Spanish people are, next to the English, the most homogeneous people of Europe;* their uniformity was recognized even by the ancient writers. Havelock Ellis quotes the opinion of the Greek historian Herodorus of Heraclea that "the Iberians are everywhere the same people, though they bear different names because they are divided into different tribes." And they themselves are fully aware of their African kinship. In opposition to a faction that tends to Europeanize the Spanish civilization more and more, Miguel de Unamuno advocates that the people should rather re-Africanize.

In view of the fact that Spain was once connected with Morocco by land across the Straits of Gibraltar, and the further fact that for more than seven centuries vast regions of the peninsula were governed by Arabs, it would be curious indeed if Africa had not left its indelible impress upon Spain. Havelock Ellis, referring to the Oriental fiber interwoven in the rich fabric of the Spanish folk character, calls the latter "fundamentally savage."

Yet the African component is only one of several in the enigmatic Spanish blend. Another element is the Nordic one. If the Spanish folk character were of African fiber alone, how could the North Europeans feel so much at home among Spanish scenery and Spanish art? Arabian art has always been decidedly foreign to the Europeans. It is its Teutonic

* Alfred Fouillée, "Le peuple espagnol," in *Revue des deux mondes,* 1899.

fiber that has made Spanish art more intelligible to the Notherners than Italian art, for instance. Emotionally and in their modes of expression the best-known painters of Spain—Ribera, Zurbaran, and even Murillo— were the kinsmen of their Dutch contemporary Rembrandt. And Spanish architecture, despite its long dependence on French models, eschewed the measured Latin elegance of the great French cathedrals. The Spanish Gothic is more like the German—irrational, full of dark mysticism and emotional exuberance. The mystic gloom of the cathedrals of Toledo, Tarragona, and Barcelona is as remote from the clear cool light that pervades the French cathedrals of Chartres and Reims as it is akin to the romantic dusk of the German cathedrals of Mainz, Bamberg, and Dinkels-bühl.

The most independent period of the Gothic style in Spain, the *gótico florido,* is closely related to the German *Sondergotik.* The spirally fluted columns of the north aisle in the cathedral of Braunschweig are matched by those in the *lonjas* of Valencia and Palma de Mallorca, and in the cloisters of San Gregorio College at Valladolid.

The Nordic stripe in Spanish art has been credited by the anthropologists to the early political dominance of the Visigoths. The willingness with which their influence was accepted may be explained by the fact that these East-Germanic people brought with them an Oriental form of civilization not possessed by the other Germanic tribes that were swept into Spain during the migrations of the fifth century of the Christian era. It was their Oriental civilization, also, that eventually eased the inroad of the Arabs in the eighth century.

Still, the influx of foreign races is not the whole explanation. The Nordic stripe must have been ingrained at the outset in the Celto-Iberian stock, into which, after all, the Visigoths melted even as the unexpelled Moors ultimately did. When a people mixes with immigrant tribes, the aboriginal stock usually proves the stronger in the long run and absorbs the invaders. Aboriginal racial qualities reassert themselves and submerge those that have been temporarily acquired from foreigners. This is particularly true when the underlying race is obstinate and unassimilable, as are the Spaniards.

THE SPANISH MILIEU $\textbf{A}$nother explanation of the Spanish "forms of ideation" lies in the Spanish milieu. There is in Spain only one region that
may remind one of Italy or any other typically Mediterranean country.
That is the lovely eastern coast from Barcelona down to Alicante and the
Cabo de Nao. The mild and moderately arid climate of this region, its
luscious vineyards and olive groves, the gentle, undulating skyline of the
low mountain ranges in the west, and the diaphanous blue of the Mediterranean Sea and sky—all this lends to the eastern seaboard and the adjacent
Balearic Islands a truly harmonious loveliness. The *aprica litora* (sunny
shores) of Tarragona and Valencia gave rise to the Roman saying *coelum
hic cecidisse putes*—"here heaven seems to have descended to earth."

But the traveler who knows only that narrow littoral knows less of Spain
than a visitor to San Francisco and Carmel by the Sea knows of North
America. Although two of the three main cities of the republic, Barcelona
and Valencia, are located on the eastern coast, it is the least typical part
of Spain.

The larger part of Spain is a land where Africa and North Europe
mingle, neither quite European nor quite African. As one wanders through
the stony wastes of Murcia, everything seems to tell him that Morocco is
not far off. Not a drop of rain falls in four or five years. One might as
well be skirting the Sahara when the dreaded *calina,* the life-draining
heat fog, weighs like death upon the scorched stones. For months the sun
and the moon rise like disks of purple out of the brown haze on the
horizon, and the daylight sky looks gray as molten lead. The villages in
the desert stretches of southern Estremadura are no more than rows of
round, windowless huts covered with conical straw roofs that make them
resemble African kraals. The Oriental luxuriance of an African oasis
lingers in the vast palm forest of Elche. Tropical is the vegetation of
Malaga and the sense-beclouding perfume of the Andalusian orange
groves.

Higher up, in central and northern Spain, the country is more like that
of northern Europe. With their dense woods of black pine and light-green
beech trees, the forested hills between Madrid and Avila bring the German

Harz Mountains to mind. And still farther north, in the snow-covered Pyrenees of Asturia and Cantabria, or eastward in the crags of the Catalan Mountains, one who has climbed the ragged cliffs of the Montserrat and gazes down through the rifts in the clouds into the vast valleys of Catalonia may easily believe that some magic carpet has transported him to the mythical lands of the Norse giants and sagas.

The Elements of Spanish Art

CHAPTER TWO

THE SCULPTURAL INSTINCT In what way was the Spanish artistic vision conditioned by its milieu? The answer resides in the pictorial work, the sculptures and paintings, of the Spanish masters; but if we want to get to the core of the matter we shall do well to ignore at first their content and all the representational elements that are commonly, if not exclusively, discussed in books on Spanish art and to concentrate instead upon the patterns and forms that serve the pictorial content as vehicles of expression.

The southern wastes strewn with erratic granite boulders, the highlands of Castile, and the mountain masses of the northeast tell one why the artists of Spain were particularly sensitive to space and what it contained—the jostling of cornered solid bodies; and why so many of them, even if ostensibly they wielded the brush, were at heart sculptors, like the mountaineers of Greece and the Tyrol.

Judging by popular opinion and by the role the arts have played in the cultural life of the Spanish people, the outstanding accomplishments of Spanish art have been in the domain of sculpture rather than painting. It is the carved images, not the paintings, of the Virgin and the Savior which are carried as *pasos* in the processions that march through the crowded streets of the Spanish cities during Holy Week. And even a casual glance into any Spanish church or chapel impresses upon one that it is sculpture that is the true folk art in Spain. It is for this reason that the history of Spanish sculpture does not evince the erratic ups and downs that make the history of Spanish painting so confusing. The course of

13

sculpture's development was steadier and its average level of artistic achievement higher than those of painting. Moreover, the great Spanish sculptors were much less dependent on foreign models than were the painters.

It is significant that in Spanish tradition the image of the Blessed Virgin which St. Luke, patron saint of all artists, is said to have wrought was not the painting that it was in the lore of the French and the Italians, but the statue that now stands high above the main altar in the shrine of Montserrat, carved of wood and weathered to a deep black through more than seven centuries.

Sculpture appeals essentially to the sense of touch. Spanish works of art, even paintings and architectures, stimulate the tactile sense. Unconsciously we admit this when we speak of the "chiseled" character heads of Pacheco, Zurbaran, and Velasquez. It is the painters' great stress on the projection and recession of the facial surfaces that reminds us of sculpture more than of painting. So deeply did the sculpturesque effect of Zurbaran's *Dead Christ* (Seville Museum, Fig. 64) impress Agustin Cean Bermudez, author of the first comprehensive encyclopedia of the Spanish painters, that he interrupted his short biography of the painter to exclaim, *"efectivamente parece de escultura!** ("indeed it seems to be sculpture!"). One understands why Pedro de Mena, a sculptor by profession, was led to go to one of Zurbaran's paintings for counsel when he was carving his famous statuette of St. Francis for the cathedral of Toledo. The carving reproduces the painting *St. Francis in Ecstasy,* which has recently been acquired for the Museum of Fine Arts in Boston. (Another version of the painting is in the Museum of Lyons.) Conversely, Velasquez occasionally resorted to a statue when his imagination failed him for some unusual assignment. The head of his *Virgin of the Coronation* (Prado, after 1651) is patterned on the carved *Purísima* of Juan Martinez Montañes (1631, cathedral of Seville).

This preoccupation with the sculptor's point of view accounts, at least partly, for the curious fact that there was virtually no Spanish landscape art until the nineteenth century. Landscape art is essentially of and for

---

* Agustín Ceán Bermúdez, *Diccionario histórico de los más ilustres profesores de las Bellas Artes en España* (Madrid, 1800), vita of Zurbaran in Vol. VI.

the eye. The light that eludes touch and the impalpable veil of the atmosphere were not fully appreciated in Spain until Velasquez. In the fifteenth century Italian painters of the school of Venice had studied the vaporous luminosity of the atmosphere, in which the images of all the objects become submerged and lose their appearance of bulk. As early as 1500 the paintings of Giorgione appealed to the retina rather than to the fingertips, and the culmination of that "painterly" style came with the work of Titian before 1550. In Spain, however, no signs of it appeared until a quarter of a century later, with El Greco and Francisco Ribalta; and the consummation of a retinal manner of painting by Velasquez was postponed until nearly the middle of the seventeenth century. In Italy, to be sure, there was a sculpturesque school beside the painterly Venetians: the school of Florence, composed of the young scions of the ancient Etruscans. But when Michelangelo or Sansovino expressed themselves by means of stone and volume, they did so because universal ideas could be enunciated more definitely in this medium than in designs or paintings on flat surfaces. To Michelangelo the carving of a statue was tantamount to composing an abstract symphony in terms of articulate mass and space. What particular models posed for the symbolic figures of *The Hours of the Day* in the Medici chapel at Florence was quite inconsequential. Therefore Michelangelo could afford to leave his statues unpolished and unelaborated. Giovanni Lorenzo Bernini, Italy's leading sculptor in the Baroque period of naturalism, composed rhythmically organized spatial masses, as did Michelangelo. One must compare his work with that of his Spanish colleagues, Juan Martinez Montañes, Pedro Roldan, Gixon, and others, to recognize what an enormous difference lies between what the Spaniards and what the Italians understood by sculpture.

The Spanish sculptors strove less for ideas so general and abstract. Their highly realistic and elaborate sculptures aimed at the most accurate presentation of all the particulars. They resorted to the plastic medium because the things themselves were plastic; and their chief interest was in the things rather than in the images. The Spaniard Ignatius Loyola urged faithful Christians, when picturing to themselves the Lord, or His Divine Mother, to call every individual feature tangibly before the mind's eye. This was quite consistent with the opinion of Spanish sculptors that the divine or earthly figures could be rendered convincingly only if every ridge and cavity were recorded so keenly and palpably that the beholder could test it, if he so desired, with his own groping fingers.

SOMATIC REALISM The Spaniards are worshippers of the somatic world. The treasuries of the larger Spanish sanctuaries are replete with the arms, hands, and fingers, the heads or the teeth of saints; with elephants' tusks; or with whole stuffed crocodiles presented at one time or another by some caliph to some Christian sovereign. The people inspect with awe the money chest of the Cid which is exhibited in this church, the dresses of the Cid's wife which are shown in another, and the trappings of the Cid's war horse which are displayed in a third. This appreciation of material things for their sheer reality, quite in keeping with the Spaniard's material-istic outlook on the world, helps to explain the peculiar realism of Spanish art.

Thousands of years ago the Iberian cave-dwellers, adorning the walls of their rock shelters, simulated elephants, does, and buffaloes with such realistic exactitude that even an experienced hunter mistook the painted images for the animals themselves. Theirs was the same materialistic frame of mind that eventually impelled Francisco Pacheco to debate whether St. Sebastian did or did not wear whiskers, arguing that the saint, having held a captaincy in the army, must have been over forty and should therefore have worn whiskers. That kind of materialistic evidence satisfied the Spanish Church, and for his cogent reasoning Pacheco was appointed state censor of painting—*alcalde veedor del santo oficio de pintores*. The craving for what is palpably real accounts for the old Spanish practice of making statues after the fashion of manikins with moveable arms, and clothing them with genuine materials. Even the most distinguished Span-ish sculptors found it in no way degrading to transform the altars in the Spanish churches into what reminds one of waxworks. Sometimes the statues of the saints that stand upon and around the altars wear wigs of real hair, precious rings on their fingers, or brooches on their costly gar-ments. Of late this make-believe has been further enhanced by illuminat-ing the figures with magic spotlights and by many other illusionistic contrivances of the theater. I have frequently heard it remarked that such lighting tricks as well as the wigs and the real vestments are merely manifestations of poor taste. But we should not rashly pass such judgments upon the age-old habits of a great nation.

To the same Spanish predilections the world owes a number of master-works of sculpture and painting. Everybody savors the quaint charm that emanates from the *Repenting Magdalen* of Pedro de Mena in the Prado, even though some of the barriers are lacking which, according to doctrine, should always separate art from nature. Many a visitor to the Prado has been fooled into the illusion that the colored wood carving standing in the corner of the hall is a live woman, that her clothes are of real bast fiber, and that her hair is real.

Two world-famous portraits of Francisco Goya would perhaps never have been painted save for his aristocratic patron's strange affection for sensational make-believe tricks. These are two "portraits" of the Duchess of Alba in the Prado, more politely known as *La Maja Vestida* and *La Maja Desnuda*. The two pictures, identical in size, show the duchess in the same posture, reclining on a couch. The only difference between them is that in the one she is dressed, in the other she appears in the nude. We are credibly informed that the two canvases were superimposed and connected by a mechanical contrivance so that the clothed figure could be made to disappear and the nude suddenly disclosed as a surprise to the amazed beholder. The implication is that certain people in Spain who, according to our taste, should have known better, had yet to learn that a painting is not identical with the person it depicts.

The Spanish materialism does not admit those stricter demarcations which the French, for instance, draw between the material reality and its pictorial sublimation. In the world-famous painting *The Maids of Honor* (Fig. 71) Velasquez represents himself in his studio. Stepping back from behind a large canvas, the artist is seen focusing his models, the king and the queen. Everyone else in the room is looking at them too, from the chamberlain who is leaving by the rear door to the little princess in the foreground. But the royal couple is not included in the picture, save for a faint reflection of their faces in a mirror hanging on the rear wall, which indicates that they are assumed to be standing this side of the canvas. By virtue of this perplexing make-believe, the spectator, who at first overlooks the image in the little mirror, gets the impression that all the painted people are gazing at him, and so he invariably associates the painted reality with the actual reality of which he himself is a part. But even this pictorial illusionism did not satisfy the administration of the museum of the Prado. To make it into a more illusionistic make-believe they have placed opposite the picture a mirror that reflects all of it except the frame. By this device the painting is transformed into an illusion of a real room occupied by real persons. A fairly barbaric thing to do, one may say. But nothing could reveal more clearly the deep-rooted somatic realism of the Spanish mind. Both the arrangement of the painter and the added trick of the director were conditioned by the same, typically Spanish, conception.

For in the Iberian mind every individual destiny and occurrence is connected as by a thousand threads with the fluctuating life on earth and with eternity. Everything is interwoven into a larger fabric; nothing is separate or isolated. During Holy Week, throughout Spain, the statues of the Madonna and the Savior are removed from their shrines in the churches, placed on wagons, and exhibited to the multitude in processions that move through the streets of the city day in and day out. It is at such moments, when the art works actually become part of the crowd, that the true nature of Spanish art is revealed most clearly. It then becomes manifest that every work of Spanish art seems to crave its interassociation with the reality of the day.

"SCULPTURAL" ARCHITECTURE The sculptural instinct has also influenced Spanish architecture. As regards the structural clarity and the organization of space, the builders of the cathedrals of Barcelona, Tarragona, Seville, and others are commonly deemed inferior to the French architects who created the models in Chartres, Paris, and other places. Proof of their "tectonic deficiency" is seen in the fact that after the close of the fifteenth century they built right in the center of the nave of almost every great Spanish cathedral a so-called *coro,* that is, a special compartment for the clergy, walled in on all sides in such a way as to block the passage toward the altar. One who enters from the main door in the west finds his view

obstructed precisely at the point where he should be able and encouraged
to abandon himself to the eastward rush of the nave and the aisles. This
Spanish tradition should not, in my opinion, be condemned unintelli-
gently. The recent removal of such additional interior structures from the
cathedrals of Palma de Mallorca and Granada has not been an improvement. The Spanish architects of the fifteenth and sixteenth centuries knew
exactly what they wanted when they incorporated a separate body of architecture within the already existing one. Basically this was an expression
of their sculptural instinct. Their rugged mountains taught them that
"space" is conceivable not solely as the French and Italians see it—as an
ample hollow clearly defined and articulated between its bounding walls—
but quite as well, or better, as *a sum of bulky bodies,* a composition of
solids jutting, receding, overlapping, and intersecting. In the more ra-
tionally esthetic view of the Frenchmen and the Italians, architectural
space signified something at once dynamic, roomy, and easy to survey.
The Spanish conception is more mystical. To those who walk in the
valleys, the cliffs and crags overhead are confusing and oppressive, but to
those who have climbed to the mountain heights and gazed upon the succession of countless impassive solids, space is revealed in its full glory.
The Spanish cathedrals are architectural realizations of this experience.
Viewed from the floor, their plastic life is perplexing: thick piers, choir
walls, pulpits, jutting crucifixes; tombstones emerging in a jostling con-
fusion; choir stalls and lecterns projecting at every point. Viewed from
the galleries above, the rich interaction of all these bulky components of
space speaks clearly and reveals its eloquent plastic pattern.

THE MYSTIC STRAIN The artistic sensations conveyed by such typically
Spanish buildings as the cathedrals of Seville and Barcelona imply another
feature peculiar to Spanish art—a lack of structural logic, a want of tectonic
sense. It is most unfortunate that our language has no affirmative terms for
this characteristic. Whenever a critic is forced, by the dearth of adequate
words, to define something in the negative the reader invariably mistakes
the definition for an adverse criticism, even though the matter under
consideration is positive and valuable.

If the plan of the cathedral of Barcelona is compared with the plan of a French cathedral, let us say Chartres, certain deviations are noticed and, having none but a relative approach, we define them by negations. We say the Spanish cathedral lacks this, that, or the other attribute, because the other possesses them: the surging French Gothic is active, the ponderous Spanish Gothic is impassive. If such a characterization is made without any critical implications, merely to describe the thing by enumerating its properties, what it has and what it has not, well and good. But what is a mere definition must not be interpreted as a derogation. To evaluate Spanish architecture according to French architectural standards is like criticizing an oak for not being a fir.

The indefinable mood of the Barcelona cathedral stirs my emotions as no French cathedral ever does, although its proportions are less determinate and the crossing of its nave and transept is less lucid. The nave is less well articulated by a succession of sharply defined bays. Nor does it leap to the east like a single torrent, being less severely divided off from the attendant aisles and being halted in its advance toward the altar by the added *coro*.

And yet its different effect was unquestionably the conscious purpose of the school of architects that constructed the cathedral of Barcelona and elaborated it throughout the centuries. They disliked the keen rationalism of the French mind in general as much as they disliked the clear-cut functionalism of the French churches in particular. In the mysterious gloom of these halls of self-contemplation no one was to become aware of the architectural machinery by which the thrust and push of the soaring vaults was managed. Therefore the huge piers were not to be sharply outlined and articulated from bottom to top. Rather they were to give the impression of being vaguely sketched into the gloom. The total effect was to be enigmatic. The irrational has always been on good terms with the picturesque. The Barcelona architects have done their level best to surprise the vision of the faithful into unexpected vistas at every turn. One of their devices for achieving a mood of mystery was to shield the windows by jutting walls and overlapping piers. In addition, the apertures were closed by stained glass of a very somber coloration. As a result, the colored light flows inexplicably through an unexplained space.

LA TRISTEZA ESPAÑOLA The Spanish milieu has influenced not only the forms but the content of Spanish art. The oppressive and sinister moods preponderant in Spanish pictures and sculptures reflect the ferocity of the Spanish country. It is something more than a curious accident that, as Hugo Schuchardt says, the only Iberian word to survive in the modern Spanish language is *izquierdo,* "sinister" (as opposed to *dexter*), with its familiar connotation of the adverse and ominous.

I shall not recount here what has already been told so often in other books on the art of Spain. I shall not scan the illustrational range of Spanish painting and sculpture to point out its stark and often sanguinary subject matter, its predilection for what is unbeautiful, weird, and gruesome. I shall concentrate on a few features that seem important to me because of their obvious connection with the milieu.

Life was never easy for the inhabitants of Spain, a land seared by the sun, whose climate is "mingled of fire-and-ice." It is only natural that the hardy Spanish race preferred the depiction of keen character to that of suave beauty.

The fatalism and pessimism of the Spaniards—*la tristeza española*— is mirrored in their passionate adulation of death and its horrors. The Montserrat library possesses among its curious treasures of ancient music what is in all likelihood the oldest dance song having death for its theme.* Besides God and the Blessed Virgin, death is the only power the Spaniards really believe in. No people speak more often of death than they. To face death—that is the bullfighter's profession. Death triumphs even over the Church. *Hic jacet pulvis, cinis et nihil* (here lie dust, ashes, nothing) is written on the grave of their archbishop.†

Macabre subjects were represented on every occasion and in all periods: the "Dance of Death," the ordeals of the saints, the horrors of the sepulcher, and so on. But what concerns us beyond this constant preoccupation with death is the Spaniard's impassiveness toward death, his unemotional reference to it in art, which implies the underlying recognition that death

* Gregorio Suñol, in *Analecta Montserratensis* (Barcelona, 1918), I.

† Inscription on the bronze plate covering the grave of Luis Manuel Fernández de Portocarrero outside the *Capilla de la Virgen del Sagrario* in the cathedral of Toledo.

is something unalterable and therefore something about which no one should worry. Here speaks the stoicism of the Orientals. Its presence in Spanish art becomes manifest when we contrast the impassioned interpretations of the theme of death by the other European artists.

Hans Holbein's *Dance of Death* is a mordant satire on social institutions and classes, spiced with moral comment and imbued with personal bias. As Death, depicted as a skeleton, approaches each individual, he makes no secret of his frightful whims. Death is shown as a common highjacker making his prey leap with convulsions as he runs his spear through the back of *The Knight*. As a hooting jester he drags *The Queen* away from her ladies-in-waiting. Death is an affectionate hurdy-gurdy man when he leads *The Old Man* gently to his grave, and a trustworthy nurse when he lures *The Infant* out of its mother's kitchen. The Germans and Italians could not think nor speak of death without an implication either as to its ruthlessness or its mercy. Michelangelo and Signorelli, in their murals of *The Last Judgment,* show their personal sympathy for the happiness of the chosen and the distress of the damned as well as the wrathful indignation of the heavenly judge. Such an ardent manifestation of fellow feeling is alien to the Spaniards. For them death is kismet. Whenever they mention or contemplate death it is with an undercurrent of fatalism.

In the Byzantine murals and frontals of Catalonia, the Pantokrator who has come to judge the dead and the living bears the impassive features of fate (Fig. 32). He may inspire dread or fear in the beholder, but in his pose and facial expression there is nothing of wrath nor benignity. The Christ of the Spaniards is Himself the embodiment of stoical indifference. Even in the highly realistic images of the dying Christ, carved or painted in the seventeenth century, the represented agony never implies either struggle or resistance on the part of the Crucified (Frontispiece; Fig. 64). He suffers death stoically, and if He manifests any personal reaction it is ecstatic bliss. Matthias Grünewald's vision of Christ, the "dying lion," would have been unimaginable in Spain, where every individual was in some way or other another Seneca.

Ordeals and executions were depicted time and again by the Spanish Primitives as well as by the Classicists and the painters of the Baroque:

the sawing through of a martyr (Fig. 33), his decapitation (Fig. 46), his burning, either at the stake or on the grate. But all these martyrs suffer without complaint; they neither protest nor defend themselves. And if they open their mouths it is only to praise God.

The approach to such subjects was of course different in the Baroque period from what it was in the Classical, the Primitive, or the Medieval. But however developed or undeveloped may have been the manual skill and the visual observation, the stoical attitude toward death remained the same. Valdes Leal depicts the horrors of the sepulcher in his *Hieroglyphs of Death* (Seville, La Caridad, Fig. 77), going into veracious details that send shivers up the spine of an impressionable spectator; but the picture as a whole is nothing but a more or less disinterested statement about two corpses in a tomb.

SOSIEGO This stoical frame of mind is inseparable from the Spaniard's reticent behavior. Even a short visit to Spain makes one realize that this behavioristic component outweighs the differences of temper by which the tribes of the south are distinguished from those of the north, the east, and the west. If one knows all of them well enough, the nonchalant and cheerful Andalusian, the stern and dignified Castilian, the unstable Basque, the showy but progressive Catalan, and the modest but ultraconservative Galician, they all merge in one's mind into a single race of men characterized by superior austerity. This is the true meaning of what the Spaniards call *grandeza* and *sosiego*.

Sosiego is as untranslatable as its practice in life is inimitable. "Tranquillity," "composure," "restraint"—these suggest only vaguely its overtones. *Sosiego* is the keynote in the ethics of Seneca, the archetype of the Spaniard. "Never surrender to anything that is extraneous to your mind and spirit. Whatever favorable or adverse may happen to you, remember that you bear in you a mother-force, something strong and indestructible, an adamantine shaft around which the petty events of daily life revolve." The walk of a Spaniard manifests *sosiego*, that is, dignity; he salutes his fellow men with *sosiego*, that is, with circumstantial solemnity. His somber dress is an expression of *sosiego,* and so are his speech and action, neither of which is ever rash or uncontrolled.

Frenchmen and Italians make quite another exhibition of their characteristic liveliness. They are actors, even if they do not happen to be on the stage. When they talk they seem to do so with every part of their bodies. It is not by chance that Michelangelo, the epitome of the Italian, expresses his artistic messages through the rhythm and the movement of athletic bodies. Spanish art, on the other hand, disliked the display of gesticulation or dancing poses—except, of course, in those periods when it fell temporarily under the Italian influence.

The tensest moments in the Spanish bullfight are the least spectacular. Motionless the matador stands in front of the angry bull. For long minutes he may look death in the face, but he never stirs. Holding the *espada* and the *muleta* with one hand in front of the bull's eyes, he rehearses the *pases naturales;* that is, he evades the spasmodic attacks of the infuriated animal by a slight movement of the hips, a short step to the side or back. He leaves the commotion to the onlookers. They may shout enthusiasm and leap to their feet. But the *torero* remains imperturbable. The audience is boisterous, the performer is mute.

Spanish folk dances are electric with quick rhythm, but they can be performed on a spot no larger than a square foot. The characteristic feature is the constant interruption of the movement, the fixation of static poses in the dynamic flow. Moreover, the dancer does not move through space. Nor does her torso participate in the evolutions of the dance. Her arms and legs come fully into play (generally the arms more than the legs), but the expressiveness of the limbs is the greater for the complete repose of the trunk.

The Spaniard's favorite color of dress is black. That austere color was not autocratically made fashionable by Philip II. Black best expresses the restraint of the race even as does the Spanish *capa,* almost the only piece of national clothing surviving today. It is a long cape made of heavy, stiff material, which falls in rigid folds. You could not, even if you wished, disport your limbs freely in such a robe.

The reflection of such stern behavior in Spanish art is too obvious to require much comment. Spanish portraits reveal *sosiego* through a want both of gestures and stagy postures. The models adjust their pose to a simple frontal view, and the inflexible angular outline as well as the reticence of the coloration do the rest (Figs. 59, 72, 82).

Sosiego and *grandeza* are also reflected in the predilection of the Spanish artists for a solemn symmetrical composition. Bartolome Bermejo's *San Domingo de Silos,* now in the Prado, illustrates this characterstic particularly well. To be sure, the work of Bermejo epitomizes Spanish dignity in the form-language of the late Middle Ages; which means in terms of rigidity coupled with magnificence. But even the more fluent naturalistic paintings of the sixteenth and seventeenth centuries, such as El Greco's *Great Inquisitor,* in the Metropolitan Museum, and Velasquez's *Pope Innocent X,* in the Doria-Pamphili Gallery at Rome, bring to mind the tradition embodied in Bermejo's medieval effigy: its stern frontal pose, the excessive symmetry, the ponderous ornamentation of its vestments and its throne, and what other elements of expression were assembled in it to inspire the Spanish worshipper with holy awe.

No doubt this code of extreme formality was the counterbalance of the extreme individualism that is congenital in the Spanish race. Without it the Spanish individualism, bearing within itself the germ of anarchy, would have been a constant menace to the nation's social equipoise.

INDIVIDUALISM $\int$ pain has always been a bulwark of individualism. Her history teems with solitary heroes, hermits, and eccentrics. Spain invented the guerrilla. Spanish individualism had its share in delaying landscape painting for at least a century in the history of Spanish art; for in a landscape the individual is subordinated to the comprehensive unities of space and atmosphere.

Individualism in Spain was fostered, if not originally caused, by the geography of the country. The surface formation of the peninsula has splintered it into countless dissimilar regions, in each of which the conditions of life are different. Thus every Spaniard has been compelled to react to the isolation into which he is born by standing on his own feet and fighting for himself. In the ancient Celto-Iberian Spain the nucleus of every individual polity was the town and its citadel, not the clan upon which political communities pivoted in the purely Celtic and Germanic countries. The clans played a comparatively insignificant part in Spain. The numerous remnants of Iberian castles and turrets scattered over the entire peninsula bear witness that Spain was made up, originally, of a multitude of independent petty communities. A craving for political independence has governed the history of the country. A later expression thereof is the reluctance of the sovereigns to adopt the inclusive title of King of Spain. They preferred to be known as rulers of their separate possessions—Castile, Leon, Aragon, Navarre, and so on.

The geographical isolation of the Spaniards accounts for that unparalleled disdain of any higher authority, which, in the opinion of Angel Ganivet, runs like a red thread through Spanish literature. Here lies the explanation of the Spaniard's readiness to make merry over the oddities of their neighbors. Here lie the roots of the Spanish fancy for satire— the pleasure in ridiculing every imaginable social, religious, and moral institution. Here originated that "common lack of interest in what is going on at home" on which Perez de Guzman commented, the measureless admiration for everything foreign that was branded by Jose Ribera,* and "the unending national controversies with their attendant self-belittlement" to which more recently Americo Castro† blamed the ultimate decline of Spain.

ART AND INDIVIDUALISM There is also a relation between the Spaniard's individualism and his conspicuous want of talent for planful organization, to which I have already referred in connection with Spanish architecture. This want is, in a sense, the reverse side of the medal. Unquestionably Spanish individualism is partly responsible for the sluggish development of Spanish art. Not that production itself was slower in Spain than else-

* "España es madre piadosa de forasteros y cruelísima madrastra de los propios naturales." (Quoted by J. Martinez in Discursos practicables, 34.)
† Corona (Munich and Zurich), July, 1931.

where. The Spanish painters were quite as prolific as the Italians, but every one of them had his eyes so fixed upon his own particular ideas that he could not visualize a common goal. Where there is no common goal ahead, there can be no strong evolutionary current.

No other country produced so few leading schools. Think of Italy for a contrast. What a vast train of pupils followed Raphael or Giorgione. What an enormous influence emanated from Rubens and his school in Flanders, and from Rembrandt and his school in Holland. But no schools were founded in Spain by Juan de Juanes, Morales, El Greco, and Velasquez. They could not do so. They were solitary adventurerers on lone roads, improvisers of personal manners.

This absence of schools in Spain had detrimental effects upon the course of the national art. The developments of medieval art in France, and of the Renaissance in Italy, advanced rapidly like mighty single streams because of the united efforts of the respective centralized schools. Spain simply could not keep pace with the cooperative advance of the other nations, shredded as she was into many independent regional units. She was further hampered by the rigid conservatism of the Spanish patrons, who insisted that certain old-fashioned conventions be continued indefinitely.

The Italian studios discontinued the cumbersome habit of painting on wood toward the close of the fifteenth century. Spain's painters at that time were still under contract to use wooden panels instead of the more modern canvases. Moreover, they were told to gild the backgrounds of their panel paintings and richly engrave them with ornaments after the Gothic fashion—this at a time when the gilt backgrounds had long gone out of fashion elsewhere. This unyielding conservatism was the more remarkable because canvas had been a common medium in those primitive Spanish paintings that did not qualify as "monumental art." The *guarda-polvo* (dust guard) by which the altar screen was covered during Holy Week was usually painted on ungrounded canvas, as were the organ shutters and certain tapestry-like wall hangings in palatial rooms.

The far-reaching significance of this retardation will be recognized if one considers that, except for the alfresco, the use of canvas was the *sine qua non* for any truly monumental style of painting. Not until canvas was used was it possible to produce paintings of considerable size and with large figures. For a canvas may be of any size, whereas a picture on wood cannot exceed the limits of a normal panel. A panel painting hardly admits of life-size figures. It was not until the end of the sixteenth century that Juan de las Roelas dared to use canvases for his monumental paintings.

The Spaniard's conservatism, of which this is but one illustration, is inseparable from another strain in the pattern of the folk character—*el sentir caballeresco,* the "gentleman-spirit."

CABALLEROSIDAD This aristocratic vein has manifested itself in the indifference of artists to the more menial tasks of their profession. The tardiness with which the Spanish styles developed during the late Middle Ages as compared with the rapid progress made in Italy and France was partly due to the widespread distaste of the masters for manual labor and painstaking craftsmanship. Underestimation of the technical difficulties has made of many a Spanish painter a second-rater as compared with the foreigner whose work he was imitating. Lluis Dalmau, whose teacher was Jan van Eyck, is one of several examples that could be culled from the long list of Franco-Flemish Primitives. Another was Juan de Juanes, who was active in the second half of the sixteenth century. Some of Juan's paintings coincide in time with the masterworks of El Greco, but his old-fashioned polished coloration would lead an unsuspecting student to infer that he had lived a hundred years before El Greco. The more grandiose conceptions of the seventeenth-century painters were rarely matched by an adequate manner of execution. Peter Paul Rubens commented on the incompetence of the Madrilenian artists whose assistance he refused during his first visit to the capital in 1603.

In that later period perhaps the most remarkable result of *el sentir caballeresco* was the regulation that a *pintor caballero* should not work for gain. Before he was knighted Velasquez had to present evidence that he neither practised painting as a profession nor offered his nor any other artist's paintings for sale. Velasquez declared under oath that he painted only at his sovereign's bidding and for his own entertainment.

Another typical *caballero* was Alonso Cano, who preferred to be fined than march in the Easter processions—as was his duty as a member of the Brethren of Our Lady of Sorrows—along with the rabble of magistrates and artisans. Cano had a decided aversion to actual painting, preferring theoretical discussions; the critic Jose Martinez was amazed to find only two canvases in his studio when he visited him in Madrid. In fact, the gentleman's ideal was a job that involved no labor at all. Cano accepted the position of a chorister of the cathedral of Granada *para vivir y trabajar con algún descanso* (to make a living without working too much).* The understanding was, indeed, that he be given a studio free of charge and be excused from singing in the choir; in return he was expected to paint something for the cathedral. Before long, however, the artist asked to be excused from this obligation too because of the unfavorable weather, which was either too hot or too cold for work. Cano was then dismissed by the Chapter, but the king spoke for him. On still another occasion he relied on the chivalrous intervention of his sovereign to save him from pleading guilty to the indictment of having murdered his spouse so he could marry another woman.†

There is perhaps no better example of the "gentleman-artist" in all Spanish history. In his biography, which reads like a cloak-and-sword novel, Cano displays all the traits of an aristocrat as opposed to the vulgar traits of the lower classes. In Madrid, whither he withdrew in 1637 after having assaulted and wounded a fellow artist in the streets of Seville, he parried all the objections to his frequent plagiarisms by declaring that, for all he cared, others were welcome to take as much advantage of his own paintings as he had taken of those of Correggio, Veronese, and Ribalta. As a true Spanish *caballero,* of course, he hated to be bargained with. Once, when an auditor of the Granada Chapter tried to beat down the price that

---

* Ceán Bermúdez, *Diccionario,* I, 211.

† Ceán Bermúdez questions the whole story (for which Palomino is the source) because he failed to find any record of the lawsuit in Madrid. Still the strange fact remains that the pope was approached and requested to absolve Cano from the sin of bigamy.

Cano asked, the artist reached for an ax and reduced his statue to smithereens, knowing full well that this offense would cost him his pension. Not even in the face of death did his haughtiness wane. Though a pauper, Cano refused to accept the last communion from the hands of a priest in charge of prisoners. And when another priest rushed to his bedside as a substitute and gave the dying man a crucifix to hold, Cano flung it angrily to the floor because of the mediocrity of the carving.

El sentir caballeresco also signifies that fearless personal gallantry which ignores not only the consequences of a heroic act but every consideration of its usefulness or even its feasibility. Don Quixote attacking the windmills is a good illustration, and so is Charles V challenging the king of France in order to restore peace in the Christian world. I am alluding to a letter written in 1536 by the king of Spain to the pope, Paul III*: "Inasmuch as the King of France does whatever he does out of hatred and animosity against my person . . . , he should demand satisfaction only from me personally. Therefore, if the King of France agrees to fight man to man with me, I solemnly swear before your Holiness, the Sacred College, and all the Nobles present that I shall meet him wherever and however he says: single-handedly, armed or unarmed, in my shirt, with sword or dagger, on land or sea, on a bridge, on an island, in camp, or in the presence of our armies. I give him twenty days to establish peace." That kind of chivalry has been a national ideal ever since the wars with the Moors instilled in the Spaniards the romantic conviction that they were the chosen champions of Christianity, the gallant defenders of the women and the weak.

Chivalry has always been closely allied with romanticism. Together they have evoked in Spain ventures so vast that more than human power would have been needed to carry them out. Throughout her national history Spain has suffered from a lack of balance between her heaven-storming projects and her inadequate means of realizing them. From the day that Spain became a unified kingdom the Spanish rulers have attempted the impossible: the Colonial Empire, the Pan-European policies of the House of Hapsburg, the unsuccessful plans of the government for a reform of

* Fernando de los Ríos, *Religión y Estado del Siglo XVI* (New York, 1927), 46 ff.

the state administration, for the exploitation of the nation's mineral resources, for an improvement of public education, and many more. No
other nation has devised plans more high-flown and nowhere else have so
many plans collapsed because those who made them were unmindful
of their impractability. Yet such utopian enterprises, attempted repeatedly, have made the Spanish nation appear at once more interesting and
more youthful than many another. It is only sad to reflect how much
human energy has been wasted because of incompetent organization and
neglect of the indispensable minutiae, both of which are offsprings of
el sentir caballeresco.

Ludwig Pfandl* has culled more illustrations from Spanish scholardom.
Florian de Ocampo's idealistic failure is an early example from the era
of Charles V, which was repeated time and again. Single-handedly Ocampo
attempted to write a Universal History of Spain from the earliest antiquity
to his own day, but gave up before he had arrived at the middle of ancient
Roman history, leaving almost ninety-five per cent of his plan unexecuted.
In the eighteenth century, a History of Spanish Literature was planned
by the two Mohedanos but was never finished, and the same sorry fate
eventually befell the Critical History of Spanish Literature by Amador de
los Rios, which comes to an untimely end after the first half of the Middle
Ages.

Similar tragic failures in the field of the fine arts and architecture can be
cited. The Templo de la Sagrada Familia, planned in 1882 by Antonio
Gaudi of Barcelona on an incredibly large scale, is an example of the
Spanish romantic idealism in our own days. The church has not been
completed and never will be, for the funds are to come exclusively from
alms, and it is only too well known that alms today will never build a
cathedral with twelve steeples, each three hundred feet high, a central
dome of four hundred and eighty feet, and four lateral domes of three
hundred and seventy feet. Antonio Gaudi himself knew that it could not
be done. But there is a thrill in aiming at the impossible which perhaps
only a Spaniard can fully appreciate. When the cathedral of Seville was
planned, in 1402, the Chapter decided it should be on a scale so magnifi-

* Ludwig Pfandl, *Spanische Literaturgeschichte* (Leipzig, 1923), I, 3.

cent that all the coming generations would believe the builders to have been mad.

This, and other examples from the history of Spanish architecture, warns me, however, not to carry my generalizations too far. After all, mad or sane, the architects did complete the cathedral of Seville. And Philip II completed the gigantic Monastery of Saint Laurence of the Escorial, though, heaven knows, he had all the odds in the world against him.

The Allover Pattern

CHAPTER THREE

ALLOVER ORNAMENTATION The moods and sentiments we have been considering do not fully answer the question, what is essentially Spanish in the art of Spain? For these emotional predispositions of the Spaniards govern the content of their art much more than its form. What remains to be considered are the visual patterns that govern the forms of a people's art as grammar and syntax govern its language; they are those *schemata* of expression that are valid within the national borders. For an understanding of the Spanish visual patterns it is imperative that the imitative and illustrative aspects of their art be disregarded even more consistently than has been done heretofore.

Let us begin with the crux of the matter. The artists of Spain have always shown a predilection for a special manner of ornamentation. In a Spanish interior, whether it be a church or a palace hall, a profuse interlace of ornaments covers every square foot of wall space. It spreads from the floor to the ceiling, over the piers and vaults of the basilica, over the walls of the *antecoro* and *trascoro,* over the retable, and over the iron trellises that enclose the *capilla mayor* and the smaller chapels. The ornamental web may be incised, carved in bas-relief, wrought in metal, painted, woven, or embroidered; but whatever the medium, it extends as an allover pattern on every available plane.

In the course of time, as one period style was superseded by another, the individual motifs changed, but the system of the pattern remained the same. From the delicate Islamic-Moorish ornaments of the Alhambra of Granada to the Christian-Moorish (Mudejar) ornaments of the Alcazar of

Seville, through the *gótico florido* and the *plateresco* decorations of the Renaissance and the flamboyant *churrigueresco* of the eighteenth century, the tradition remained alive; the unending planar ornamentation always exhibits certain characteristics which are found nowhere except in Spain. Let us summarize its chief features.

Fig. 1.—Details of Moorish Wall Decoration in the Alhambra

The nucleus of the wall decoration in the Moorish Alhambra is a single pattern elaborated with geometrical regularity and fine precision. An entire wall pattern is composed of variations of one or several basic patterns juxtaposed after the fashion of an oriental rug. These are spread over the entire surface like water lilies upon a pond.

It is characteristic of the Moorish decorative system that, although every detail is executed with keen precision (Fig. 1), the general effect of the wall pattern is a glistening mass from which no detail stands out. The appeal to the eye is twofold. The details are there for close inspection; the total effect is there for a long-range view. As regards the latter, the quintessence of the ornamentation is its unintermittent movement. The sparkling variety of the interlace is presented without any visual accent or punctuation. That does not signify, however, that the whole is without order. On the contrary, the rippling movement is con-

Fig. 2.—Moorish Wall Decoration, Torre de las Damas, Alhambra

trolled by rigid borders of geometrical shape, as is illustrated by a section of the wall decoration of Torre de las Damas (Alhambra, Fig. 2). Here the total pattern (which at close range resolves itself into countless lozenge-shaped ornaments) is held in order by the more deeply incised square

Fig. 3.—Frieze and Fenestration in the Sinagoga del
Transito, Toledo

bands above the prayer niche (*mihrab*) and beneath the arched window with the central pillar (*ajimez*).

The survival of this plan of decoration after the expulsion of the Moors is illustrated by the interior of the Sinagoga del Transito in Toledo, which was built in 1357 for Samuel Levy, Jewish treasurer of the king of Castile. Here not only the walls but even the windows were decked with planar ornaments—first by the Mudejares, the Moorish artisans employed by the Christians and the Jews, and ultimately by the sixteenth-century practitioners of the *estilo plateresco* (the "silversmith's manner"). Naturalistic botanical motifs have replaced the abstract arabesques in the stucco frieze below the upper range of windows (Fig. 3), but the fine leaves and twigs have been fashioned, according to the old tradition, into an unending dainty lace pattern, and the universal glint of the movement is visually more important than the component part-forms. Its mobility, moreover, is controlled as strictly as that of the arabesques of the Alhambra by the horizontal borders above and below the interlace. In the plateresque ornamentation of the carved stone portal on the south wall and that of the adjacent embrasure of the wall tomb, the traditional decorative principles have undergone no fundamental change, although the motifs are the candelabra and *grotteschi*, belonging to the Renaissance repertory of forms. All the characteristic Spanish features are there: the available surfaces are spun over as with filigree; no emphatic accents arrest the flow of the interlace, yet nowhere does the billowing ornamentation overflow its banks; rigid borderlines confine it within the surfaces of the lintel, the attica, the lunette, and the pilasters.

Another example of the *estilo plateresco* is the great star that crowns the vaults of the crossing of the cathedral of Burgos (Fig. 4). Since in this

instance the decoration had to emphasize the central culmination of the nave and the transept, any such limitless expansion of the pattern as is found in the wall decorations would have been out of place. Nevertheless the geometrical precision of the entire design and the rigid dominance of certain larger patterns over smaller ones testifies how highly the ancient Moorish principles were still honored in the mid-sixteenth century. The large eight-rayed star controls the smaller one inscribed within it, and each of the triangular areas delineated by the two stars dominates a variety of finer geometrical lattice patterns. It is illuminating to compare this typical product of the Spanish imagination with the star-shaped decorations that were applied to the vaults of the Late Gothic churches in England, France, and Germany. In none of these countries were the inscribed forms either so strictly geometrical or so absolutely at the mercy of superordinated patterns.

Fig. 4.—Vaulting above the Crossing in the Cathedral of Burgos

This contrast reflects the different world views of which the contrasting decorative systems were the expressions. An analyst of form may, indeed, interpret the star of Burgos as an appropriate symbol of the unyielding hierarchical order of things in Spain, where the Universe as well as the State was rigidly divided into three separate realms between which there was no possible transition: the Universe into Heaven, Earth, and Hell; the State into Church, Throne, and Plebs.

In the Sacristy of La Cartuja of Granada (Fig. 5), a work of Luis de Arevalo (1727–64), the individual motifs are again different, and the plasticity of the decoration is much more forceful than it was in the early periods. Yet the Moorish principles are still effective. Every one of the ornaments on the pilasters and the walls "knows its place"; for they are kept there by the stern enframing borderlines. Those stressed geometrical edges which so severely rubricate all the decorative details also account for the fact that the *estilo churrigueresco* never grew so extravagant as did the

Fig. 5.—Sacristy in La Cartuja, Granada

German Rococo of the same period, for instance, in which the architectural, the sculptural, and the pictorial components of any palace or church seem to have turned liquid until they fused in the white heat of passion.

GEOMETRIC DESIGN The most characteristic expressions of the Spanish fancy for ornament are the line-and-color patterns of the tiles (*azulejos*) with which the walls of the Spanish homes are adorned, particularly in the patios. This tradition can be traced back to Mesopotamia, where, in the shadowy past, the mud walls of the houses were protected against the weather by mats or, later on, by slabs of terra cotta, and ultimately by glazed tiles. The enframing borders of rosettes frequently used in the design of the Spanish azulejos still remind one of the tack heads with which the woven mats, and eventually the terra-cotta slabs, were nailed to the walls. The age-old tradition passed from the Sumerians to the Egyptians and Assyrians and thence to the Persians and the Moslems, who finally imported it into Spain. The azulejos take one right to the roots of the decorative imagination of the Spaniards. Without the ancient Oriental tradition there would be no glazed tiles in Spain; and without them, I dare say, neither the particular character of the Spanish ornamentation nor the particular Spanish color taste would have come to be what they are. Once one has come to realize their far-reaching influence, one cannot help recognizing the underlying tile designs in the paintings of the Spanish Primitives, of El Greco, and of Velasquez.

In the tiles we have the purest and most abstract manifestation of the linear filigree design coupled with flat color areas of great beauty. They form the nuclei of the decorations of the Alhambra, the Sinagoga del Transito, and the Cartuja of Granada, and they persisted, in the face of many other changes in style, from the epoch of the caliphs to the epoch of the Bourbons.

The tile-designing tradition is sensed in the wiry geometrical patterns by which, in the Late Gothic period, Pedro Millan organized the surface composition of his *Pieta* (Fig. 10), and by which, in the Baroque period, Ignacio Vergara froze into arabesques the liquid sprays that form his grand decoration around the portal of the Dos Aguas palace in Valencia (Fig. 24). In the fifteenth-century paintings the lacy ornamentation of the walls, the tiled floors, and the brocaded raiments (Figs. 14, 44) all testify to the influence of the azulejo tradition. El Greco's flashes of lightning foregather in a tile-like pattern of color-flats (Figs. 6, 18) and the crisscross filigree of Goya's etched hatchings weaves a spiderweb over each of his impressions (Fig. 94), just as the linear ornaments of the tiles do over every wall of the Alhambra.

The reader who has followed my discussion thus far should recognize the identity of the inbred decorative imagination which relates the Spanish art works to other forms of Spanish self-expression, even though they may have no other conceivable relation. The same decorative proclivity is present in the perforation patterns of the alabaster window shades of the Sinagoga del Transito (Fig. 3) as in the capricious flourishes with which every Spaniard is wont to grace his personal signature. A more revealing comparison, however, may be drawn between the pictorial and the literary forms of Spanish self-expression.

THE VARIATIONAL FORM It is obvious that poets and prose writers have one thing in common with painters and sculptors: the narrative is a vehicle of the one as it is of the other. It is less obvious, but quite as true, that authors and artists have in common certain basic problems of artistic form: how to organize the plot, how to divide the story into chapters or other component units, and how to comprise these in a total pattern of construction. In this regard the numerous authors of the romance of *Amadís de Gaula* faced much the same problems as did the sculptors and painters of the Spanish storied retables—those huge screens composed of infinite carvings or paintings (or both) which tower from behind the altars to the very vaults of the sanctuaries. Since each was in its way a unique Spanish flower in European culture, the one in literature and the other in art, I shall compare the famous romance with a typical retable, the enormous altar screen of the cathedral of Seville (Fig. 7).

Fig. 6.—El Greco: *The Interment of Count Orgaz*, Toledo, Santo Tome

The latter clearly shows that the Late Medieval artists of Spain set their affections not only on a design that produces a smooth and continuous allover pattern, but also on a protracted narrative that meanders unceasingly across the vast expanse of the surface. A kindred pleasure in the spinning of an infinite yarn is revealed by the Spanish epic literature of that time—as a result not of any reciprocal influence but of a common predilection, deeply rooted in the Spanish creative imagination.

The genesis of the romance of *Amadís de Gaula* and its eventual culmination in Cervantes' grand parody may be compared to the formation of new cells and their agglutination into others of the original shape. The four books of the first version of the novel, written in the early fifteenth century, were augmented in 1492 by Garci Ordoñez de Montalvo, who very appropriately called his fifth book *sergas* (derived from *serica*, "tapestry"). The subsequent increase of the five books to an ultimate twelve

Fig. 7.—The High Altar in the Cathedral of Seville

was indeed like the weaving of additional square feet to a carpet already covered with similar motifs. An innate desire to prolong in the imagination a life of monotonous adventures was the psychological source not only of the unending novels but of the unending patterns as well. In no other way can one explain why, in the Amadís novel, the subject of the "tapestry" and the design of its pattern should have remained exactly the same—the sons, the grandsons, and the great-grandsons of the hero experiencing virtually the same adventures as had their ancestors.

Incidentally, here is something else which, while it does not warrant an exhaustive inquiry, deserves mention in a discussion of the Spanish taste in matters of form. This is the fancy for incessant repetition of a theme which is made palatable by slight variations of its basic pattern. The Spaniards have been particularly fond of the variational form in their musical compositions; in fact, it was among the nation's contributions to the instrumental music of seventeenth-century Europe. The old Spanish folk music was founded almost entirely upon such variation. *La Folía* and *La Chacona,* the original Spanish dances that Cervantes mentioned in addition to *La Zarabanda,* are variations to be sung or played to the accompaniment of a *basso ostinato,* that is, a short musical statement which serves for a bass and is monotonously repeated over and over again.

Every type of audience in Spain relishes the steady repetition of the same basic motif or, rather, the shimmering coat of variational ornaments that the poet, the musician, or the pictorial artist weaves from it. The reader enjoys the rippling literary similes, sentences, and words that vary the theme. The musical listener enjoys the modifications of melody and rhythm that are embodied in the variational form. The spectator enjoys the variations given to the lines and the colors that intertwine in the wall decorations and the retables. The glistening lacework in the carving of the great retable of the Seville cathedral speaks to the eye more incisively than does the narrative it contains. It is the variational fabric of the orna-ment that transcends the shrine, continuing in the boundless interlace that covers the arches, the spandrels, and the ribs of the vaulting above.

INFLEXIBILITY The retable is a good illustration of another principle of the Spanish surface pattern, the principle of inflexibility.

We have seen that the filigree of the Spanish ornamentation is generally articulated by superimposed geometrical borders. So, too, the storied reliefs and the purely decorative carvings of the retables of the cathedrals of Seville and Toledo are subordinated to a scaffolding of rigid horizontal and vertical moldings. These enframing moldings do not admit of any effect of flexibility. They do not function as joints or hinges upon which the component squares may move or by which they may be separated into dominant central and subordinate lateral wings, as was the rule with French and Italian retables, whose beauty depended to a large extent on the apparent detachability of their component parts. Rather, the rigid Spanish molding functions as a reinforcement, a superimposed framework of inflexible ties which makes the retable indivisible. In Toledo, where the horizontal bars are arranged on varying levels, the intentional avoidance of a pliable effect is even more patent than in Seville, where the bars cut uniformly across the entire width of the surface. There, with the whole fashioned as a triangle, inscribed in a square, it is quite impossible, esthetically speaking, to take the body of the retable apart and separate its members in accordance with its horizontal and perpendicular lines of articulation.

This inflexible surface pattern is not peculiar to the retables in the Seville and Toledo cathedrals; with rare exceptions it is found in all Spanish retables, Medieval, Renaissance, and Baroque, carved and painted. The parts are always so dovetailed into the rigid pattern of the scaffolding that none could be removed without detriment to the logical structure of the whole. (I leave it to the reader to correlate the Spanish dislike of any flexible effect with their racial traits of reticence and *sosiego* which have been discussed previously.)

This angularity and inflexibility is a universal feature of the Spanish style. It is not limited, as in the art of other countries, to the archaic phases of the several period styles. In ancient Greek, Medieval, and Western art after the Renaissance the angular styles of the "archaic" phases were supplanted, during the subsequent "classical" phases, by a fluent curvilinear style. The "liquid" style of the sculptural decoration of the Parthenon of Athens evolved from the "glaciated" style of the sculptural decorations of the Aphaia Temple of Aegina; the "undulating" style of the figures adorning the west façade of the cathedral of Reims evolved from the "rigid" style of the sculptures of the west façade of the cathedral of Chartres; and the rotund and fluent design of Michelangelo from the stiff and angular design of Masaccio and Piero dei Franceschi. And so on for the period of the Baroque. But throughout the entire history of Spanish art, except for the short periods during which the influence of Italy displaced the native ideals, angularity and rigidity have been the distinguishing properties of its surface patterns.

We are speaking in general terms, of course. In a long-range view of the whole of European art the student will observe that Spain was subject in a measure to the same evolutionary forces that transformed the stiff and austere style of the non-Spanish Primitives into the liquid and serene style of the High Renaissance. Thus Spanish painting and sculpture were more rigid in the archaic phases of the various period styles than in the more developed phases. Even the paintings of those Spanish cinquecentists who did not imitate the Italians, but maintained their national independence in stylistic matters, were less "wooden" than their precursors in the quattrocento. Alejo Fernandez, Luis de Morales, Pedro de Campaña, and El Greco had a fluency of line and chiaroscuro unknown to Martorell, Huguet, Bermejo, and other Spanish masters of the fifteenth century. The design of Francisco Ribalta, with whom the "national renaissance" of the seventeenth century opened, was more angular than the design of Velasquez, in whom that "unornamented" style culminated; indeed, the design and the light in the paintings of Murillo, with whom the development of the seventeenth century began to decline, were, relatively speaking, liquid. But when these Spanish artists are viewed not in relation to one another but side by side with their non-Spanish contemporaries, their style can only be described as uniformly angular and rigid.

Fig. 8.—*The Entombment of Christ, Santo Domingo de Silos*

With our attention trained on this particular feature of the Spanish style, let us survey a few characteristic paradigms of sculpture, painting, and architecture culled from the more important periods from the early Middle Ages to the age of Francisco Goya. We may begin with one of the twelfth-century reliefs in the cloisters of the Monastery of Santo Domingo de Silos, near Burgos.*

* The storied capitals and reliefs of the cloisters of Santo Domingo de Silos have been regarded in the learned literature almost exclusively with an eye to their possible dependence on the Early Romanesque sculptural decoration of St. Pierre at Moissac. I would not be sidetracked here into another discussion, though I question the conclusion commonly drawn that the sculptors of St. Pierre were Frenchmen. The presence of any number of Moorish motives makes it seem more likely that the stonemasons who worked at Moissac came from Moorish Spain. However this may be, the fact remains that the reliefs in Santa Domingo de Silos evince unmistakable features of Hispanicism. If the masons came from elsewhere, the independent creative strength of their style makes their "translation" all the more praiseworthy.

Even in the light of the well-known severity of the Byzantine-Roman-esque style, could anything less flexible than *The Entombment* (Fig. 8) be imagined? The forms are set into the shallow niche as if the assignment had been a pattern in terms of plane geometry: strict perpendiculars, horizontals, and diagonals joined together by right angles, acute angles, and obtuse angles. The body of Christ, horizontally extended, with one

Fig. 9.—Tomb of a Bishop in the Cathedral of Tuy

rigid uplifted arm parallel to the diagonal lid of the sepulcher, yields the main angular motif from which all the other figures and directions receive their visual significance—the four parallel perpendiculars formed by the three Marys and the angel; the two pointed angles formed by the men stooping to lay Christ's body at rest; and the several watchmen (in the lower section) rising from the apex of an inverted triangle as four unbending parallel diagonals.

The wall tomb of a bishop, in the fortified cathedral of Tuy (Fig. 9), was erected about 1300 and therefore belongs to the Gothic period. But there is no vestige of the well-known Gothic undulatory design. The geometrical Mudejar interlace forming the decoration of the wall of the sarcophagus strikes the key, as it were, in which the music of the whole requiem is composed. In the drapery of the figure prostrate upon the lid the sculptor confined his expression to what could be said in the stiff language of geometry. The episcopal robe, particularly where the drapery falls from the forearm, is patterned in triangles keen and pointed as spearheads, and the cushions under the bishop's head are fashioned like steps. Granted that so radically "cubistic" a style was somewhat exceptional even in Spain on the verge of the fourteenth century, it is significant that it was at all permissible at a time when elsewhere draperies were being designed in pliant and rotund folds, and when, moreover, the naturalistic portrayal of life had reached a stage that made any stronger stylization difficult. In contrast to the near-naturalism of the Gothic funerary statues of France, of which there are several admirable examples in St. Denis, the bishop's tomb at Tuy is an early paradigm of that ever-recurrent "union of the highest possible realism of detail with

Fig. 10.—Pedro Millan: *Pieta,* at one time in Aracena
Monastery near Seville

the utmost schematization of the general design" which Chandler R. Post recognized as one of the chief characteristics of Spanish Medieval art.*

Pedro Millan's *Pieta* (Fig. 10) removes us by almost two hundred years to a period concerned less with stylization and more deeply with realistic expression than any previous period. But despite the stylistic changes that had occurred by the end of the fifteenth century, the compositional pattern still seems to have been percolated through an imagination that was impervious to pliant lines and gliding transitions. The rigid schematization has been intensified quite as much as the realism of detail. The heads of the three mourners, filling the vertex angles of so many triangles and forming so many parallel diagonals, tilt angularly from the shoulders, not in relaxed curves as a head normally would, but as a stick breaks. The same is true of the Lord's head. His outstretched body is likewise represented with "wooden" joints; note the rectangular position of the left arm.

* Chandler R. Post, *A History of Spanish Painting,* V, 154 (Harvard University Press, 1935).

The puckered drapery crackles with keen edges and acute angles. Each of its countless oblique ridges runs parallel to one or another of the enframing triangles. There is nothing coincidental in this highly schematic composition; it is a *tema con variazioni,* the "theme" being stated by a bit of stuff projecting like the barbed head of a harpoon at the right shoulder of St. John.

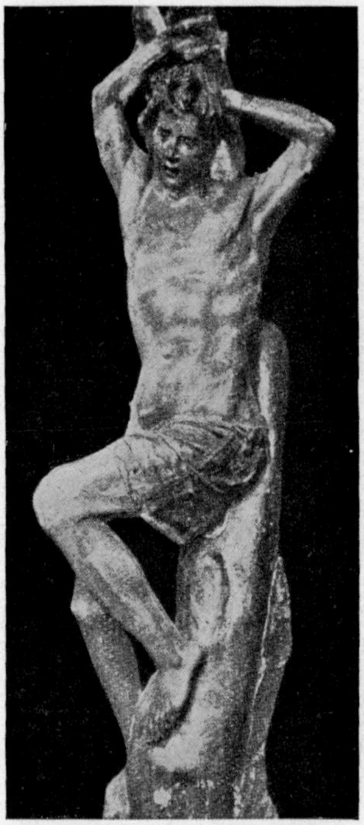

Fig. 11.—Alonso Berruguete: *St. Sebastian,* Valladolid

With Milan's *Pieta* that period of art in Spain was entered when the native stylistic proclivities were—or had been for some time—deflected by the influence of foreign art; in the fifteenth century it was more the Franco-Flemish, in the sixteenth more the Italian influence. The one strengthened the Spanish proclivity for stiff design, the other weakened and even destroyed it. As early as the second half of the fourteenth century the Serra workshop in Barcelona had yielded to the influence of the graceful curvilinear design of the school of Siena. In the fifteenth century the characteristic angularity of Roger van der Weyden, Dirk Bouts, and other Flemish "Archaics" of naturalism helped to restore the traditional rigid patterns, but they were once more abandoned in the early sixteenth century by such wholesale imitators of Leonardo da Vinci, Correggio, and Michelangelo as Ferrando de los Llanos, Ferrando Yañez de l'Almedina, Juan de Juanes (Figs. 48, 56), and others, whose undulating design would hardly be a good illustration of the Spanish inflexible style. Yet even in that exceptional period of vassalage the native idiom was not entirely relinquished. The painter and sculptor Alonso Berruguete, another disciple of Michelangelo, can be distinguished from any contemporary Italian by the peculiar jaggedness that he gives to a body outline, particularly at the bend of an elbow or a knee. The joints of Michelangelo's *Prigionieri* (of the projected tomb of Pope Julius II) do not "creak" as those of Berruguete's *St. Sebastian* seem to do (Fig. 11).

The less an artist was swayed by foreign influences, the more conspicuous the native idiom of his art. The *Pieta* of Luis de Morales (Prado, Fig. 12) embodies all the typical qualities of a "Spanish" composition. By dint of the illumination the group of Jesus and the Virgin is frozen into a stiff geometrical pattern suggesting an ace of diamonds. The angles at the four points are very pronounced, and the visual effect is the more severe because the diamond is not allowed to expand within the given surface, but is constrained within an ideated narrow vertical strip. The constraint is made al-most painful by the fact that the group is not even permitted to expand depth-ward. In defiance of the contorted limbs and hands of the Lord, the overlapping of the ear by the right shoulder, and other data of a third dimension, every form seems flattened as though pressed between two panes of glass. This effect of rigidity is enhanced by the pointed elbows, the twisted wrists, and the con-vulsed fingers; by the angular configura-tion of the nose and the eyebrows in the face of Mary; by the way her face so joins the face of Jesus that the noses compose a triangle; by the mother's excessively

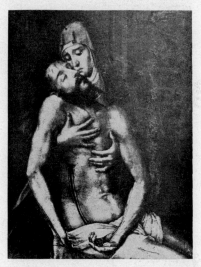

Fig. 12.—Luis de Morales: *Pieta,* Prado

straight and parted fingers, which lie in front of her son's chest; by the shaping of all the areas of light as diamonds, triangles, squares, pentagrams, and so on.

So, too, Pedro de Campaña's *Descent from the Cross,* in the Musée Fabre at Montpellier (Fig. 61), could be identified as typically "Spanish" merely from the severe effect produced by a few geometrical lines and angles which the artist selected for visual accentuation. The rigid left arm of Christ, emerging vertically from the strict angle formed by the cross and the one ladder, is silhouetted against the bright horizon at the most im-portant point of the composition.

We generally think of El Greco as an exponent of the flamboyant mannerism that stems from Tintoretto, but actually the outstanding feature of his mannerism is angularity. In his *Portrait of a Young Painter,* in the museum of Seville, every important area of light is patterned as a triangle: the head and the harsh-cornered ruffled collar; the right hand and the other one holding an oblong palette and a triangular fan-like display of brushes. Even in such an apparently sinuous composition as *The Pentecost* (Fig. 50), the lights are so many pointed flashes of lightning. If there is a curve here and there, it functions only as a contrast to intensify the zigzag design near by. Sometimes El Greco seems actually to have been seeking

Fig. 13.—Fray Juan Sanchez Cotan: *Still Life,* Madrid,
Alphonse of Bourbon Collection

a way to translate natural roundness into pictorial angularity. Follow the contour of the arms of the boy in the foreground of *The View of Toledo* (Toledo, Greco Museum); see how far the painter has succeeded in using angles and lines that might have been drawn with the aid of a ruler.

The inflexible pattern became most conspicuous toward the end of the sixteenth century, when there arose a general antagonism toward the overflowing sentimentalism of the Mannerists. The Spanish artists working for the reticent and awkward King Philip II made rigidity and angularity the backbone of the so-called *estilo desornamentado.* It marks the petrified likenesses by Alonso Sanchez Coello (Fig. 59), the granitic still life of Fray Juan Sanchez Cotan (Fig. 13), and the legends of St. Buenaventura painted by Francisco Zurbaran and Francisco Herrera *el Viejo* (regard the un-bending horizontal line of the friars' heads in Fig. 56). The great example of the new style is the square mass of the Monastery of the Escorial. Completed in 1584, that grand stone temple of the dead kings of Spain was the embodiment of the doctrine of its builder, Juan de Herrera: the hexahedron with its six square faces and twenty-four right angles is the ideal figure in art.*

I believe that Juan de Herrera was bowing to an ancient national ideal which had slowly fallen into oblivion after the Moors had been expelled. He aimed at an *estilo nacional.* The pure hexahedron stripped of any ornamental articulation had been the architectural nucleus of the Mohammedan buildings. Like numerous other ancient castles and settlements in Spain—in Alcala de Guadaira, Niebla, and the hill town of Mochagar—the Alhambra of Granada was fundamentally an agglutination of cornered geometrical solids. Herrera's Escorial, then, was this ancient Spanish "architecture of geometry" reborn in the Renaissance. Certainly it had nothing in common with the architecture of the Italian Renaissance. Had the four stories of the main building been set off reciprocally by marked cornices after the Italian fashion, or at least by something more emphatic than the thin ridge which divides the façades into two transversal sections, the effect would have been more flexible and therefore more comparable to the contemporary style of building in Italy. But even the windows have been blocked out of the imperturbable mass of the masonry with next to no enframing moldings. In brief, Herrera employed every available means to enhance the unyielding impression of the whole.

A similar want of suppleness characterizes the paintings of Francisco Zurbaran. His *Dead Christ* (Fig. 64) is an illuminating example. Another is his double portrait of *Pope Urban and St. Bruno* (also in the museum of Seville); not a single undulating line graces the square and triangular surface areas that constitute the pictorial pattern, which looks like an early experiment in abstract cubism.

* Juan de Herrera's *Discurso sobre la figura cúbica* (while it is linked with certain ideas expressed in the *Ars magna Lulli,* the *opus magnum* of the thirteenth-century Scholastic, Ramón Lull) is probably the earliest treatise on cubism. Compare Menéndez y Pelayo, *Historia de las ideas estéticas en España* (Madrid, 1901), IV, 38 ff.

Jose Ribera, one might think, would not stand the test. But an analysis of his *Santa Ines,* in the gallery at Dresden (Fig. 63), reveals that the composition depends almost entirely on the consonance of straight lines and keen angles. Rectangles are formed by the trap door in the foreground and by the relation of the upper body to the Saint's knees. Acute angles are formed by the arm and most of the folds of the blanket. The piece of cloth cutting across the plain background in a harsh, unalleviated, diagonal mass must have given something of a headache to the Italian customers of Ribera in Naples.

Velasquez, while he required none of his models to pose in quite so stony an attitude as that selected by Zurbaran for his *Likeness of a Doctor of Salamanca* (Gardner Museum, Fenway Court, Boston), also liked pictorial constructions that were straight-lined and angular. In his *Portrait of the Infanta,* of 1660 (Prado, Fig. 72) he avoided all pliancy in the pose and general outline of the figure; note the tenacious articulation of every surface by emphatic geometrical lines: the dark horizontal from shoulder to shoulder, the semi-circular edge of the bodice, and the dark perpendicular bisecting the area of the square-shaped skirt.

Lest I fatigue the reader, I shall refrain from carrying this chronological inquiry into another age of decline under foreign influence. In the second half of the seventeenth century, whose central artist was Murillo, the departures of the sixteenth century were repeated. Suffice it to say, however, that when the tide of foreign influences had subsided, toward the end of the eighteenth century, the Spanish "inflexible pattern" was once more honored, indeed brought to its final culmination, by Francisco Goya. We may let the matter rest until it comes time to speak of that last of the old Spanish masters.

Planarity in Spanish Art

CHAPTER FOUR

THE SURFACE PATTERN Inasmuch as the allover pattern and its inflexible design apply to plane surfaces, the artist's attitude toward the surface proper constitutes a separate problem which must be the object of our next investigation.

The planarity (*el planismo*) of the Spanish style is more easily recognized in painting than in sculpture, which is concerned with the effect of bulk, and in architecture, which is concerned with the effect of space. Painting is surface art par excellence. Every vehicle is a flat surface, whether it be a wall, a window pane, a panel, a canvas, or a sheet of paper. In its infancy Spanish art, like the art of every other Western and Eastern country, was governed by the desire for planarity. Therefore the apparent flatness of the Catalan murals of the twelfth century, most of which are now in the museum of Barcelona (Figs. 29–32), was not in the least exceptional. The mural painters of the time were following the Byzantine conventions and the Byzantine artists, aiming at a symbolical expression and giving no heed to the three-dimensional appearance of the phenomenal world. Exceptional only was the *excessive* planarity of the Spanish-Byzantine paintings, which any comparison with the Byzantine wall decorations of Italy will impress upon one.

The "magian" gold ground around the figures in the Italian mosaics of the twelfth century evokes, after all, a mild sensation of spaciousness. In the gilded apse of the cathedral of Torcello the Madonna appears to be floating in an infinity of space. Although there is no specific definition of either recession or bulk, the beholder inclines to interpret the impalpable

hue from which she emerges as something extended. The Catalan mural-
ists, on the other hand, were anxious to avoid even the slightest intimation
of plasticity. The flatness of their backgrounds is always emphasized by the
devices of tapestry-weaving, such as star patterns, many-colored horizontal
borders, meanders, and so on—devices, in short, that by no stretch of the
imagination suggest depth. This excessive planarity was an early manifes-

Fig. 14.—Rafael Vergos: *Saints Sebastian and Thecla*, Barcelona, Museum of Catalan Art

tation of a stylistic feeling that was to
remain a characteristic feature of Spanish art throughout its entire history.

But not until the depiction of reality
became the ultimate objective of Western painting did the native preoccupation with planarity fully manifest
itself. Not that the Spaniards evaded
the problem of representing rounded
objects in tangible spacious settings
when naturalism, cropping up everywhere after the mid-fourteenth century, made the perspective delineation
of space and spatial recession imperative. But they found means of achieving the desired planar effects in spite
of the new naturalistic manner.

This is illustrated by the panel of
*Saints Sebastian and Thecla with the
Donor, Juan Sors,* from a retable
attributed to Rafael Vergos, in the
cloisters of the cathedral of Barcelona, dated 1501 (Fig. 14). Except for
the foreshortened design of the floor, there is almost no indication that
the figures are supposed to occupy an extending space. They are seen fully
from in front, side by side like flat paper dolls. Moreover, Vergos has done
everything in his power to counteract what little there is of tridimensionality. The surface against which the Saints are projected is spun over with
flat ornaments from corner to corner. Obviously the then-prevalent, more
naturalistic conception did not impair the decorative tradition that had

been valid four hundred years earlier in the Catalan murals. The floor is as profusely covered with patterned tiles as the background is with tracery. Modeling shadows have been reduced to a minimum. Prominent outlines are treated as though they were linear ornaments. The unforeshortened halos and robes are rendered board-like by means of planimetric embroidery. All this is designed to arouse in the beholder an esthetic surface-consciousness and to detract his attention from the depth of the space.

This enforcement of the unwritten laws of Spanish taste in protest against the illusionistic innovations of the Italians, this conscious avoidance of such foreshortenings and other perspective tricks as were detrimental to the Spanish ideal of decorative planarity, dates much farther back, of course, than this Vergos picture. It can be traced back to the fourteenth century. Speaking of one of Pedro Serra's Madonnas, Chandler Post says: "The frank acknowledgement of the formal designer is carried to the point of baldly representing the floral figures of the brocade of the Virgin's mantle always in absolutely frontal view, as if they were seen on a flat surface, without regard to the foreshortening and partial disappearances that they would naturally suffer in the rounding and undulation of the garment."*

For a fuller evaluation of the attitude of the Spanish painters, their pictures should be viewed in the light of the contemporary situation in Western art. At the time Vergos painted his retable of *Saints Sebastian and Thecla* the Italians had been stunning the eyes of the world for nearly a half century with their feats in perspective design. In his alfresco decorations of the Eremitani Chapel at Padua (1454) and of the Castle of Mantua (1474), Andrea Mantegna had succeeded in transforming every wall into an illusion of a deep stage upon which his figures moved into distance. Antonello da Messina, in his *St. Sebastian* (about 1470, Dresden Picture Gallery), produced a similarly surprising effect of perspective recession, less by linear means than by the gradations of light and color. Leonardo da Vinci combined linear, luminaristic, and coloristic means in the most amazing depiction of figures in a deep room, the *Last Supper* mural in St. Maria delle Grazie at Milan (1498).

To such "modernistic" Italians the paintings of their contemporaries in

* *Op. cit.*, II, 258.

Spain must have seemed primitive and provincial beyond words. But were they really? Was it merely lack of knowledge that made them lag behind in the general progress of the European art of the fifteenth century? Did not, more likely, the Spaniards refuse to join in the naturalistic advance because they regarded their native decorative tradition as something too sacred to be thrown overboard for the advantage of faster sailing?

PLANARITY IN PAINTING In Spain, as elsewhere in Europe, the original stage for the exhibition of religious art was the altar and the space around it. On that account the peculiar construction of the Spanish altar screen was largely responsible for the compositional forms and patterns peculiar to Spanish art. Not only was the retable one of the most typical creations of the Spanish mind, as has been remarked, but it is the most revelatory of the native taste for surface expression.

Everywhere in the Europe of the Gothic period the furniture used on and about the altars was made into impressive showpieces, each country favoring a type of its own. The Italians, beginning with the Renaissance, replaced the unwieldy medieval polyptychs by so-called *quadri*—single paintings on panel or canvas, of which Raphael's *Sistine Madonna* and Titian's *Assunta* are exceptionally large examples. The Gothic North, on the other hand, made out of the relatively simple traditional polyptychs much more elaborate affairs; wood-carved architecture, sculpture, and painting all contributed to the production of huge multipartite shrines with numerous revolvable shutters attached. Thus the *Wandelaltar* became a favorite of the German church. These German Gothic polyptychs were not only more involved and of greater dimensions than the Italian *quadri;* they were also part of the architecture of the whole choir; indeed, indispensably so, being so fitted in that their silhouettes re-echoed the pointed arches by which the chancels usually open toward the transepts. Nevertheless, the northern altar screen was never so large as to obstruct the architectural setting. Laterally and above there was ample room for the vision of the congregation to roam through the choir and enjoy the colorful light that poured in from its tall windows.

The Spanish *retablo* is something essentially different from both the

Italian *quadro* and the German *Wandelaltar*. Its nearest kin is the *icono-stasis* of the Greek and Russian Orthodox Church, which, it should be remembered, originated in the Byzantine East. The Spanish retable is one enormously tall screen towering from the *mensa* to the lofty heights of the roof and covering the entire eastern choir wall (Fig. 7). Esthetically, the retable transmutes what in the churches of the other countries was an open choir space into one colossal surface which intercepts the gaze that seeks the depth of the chapel. When it consists, as it often does, of numerous painted panels juxtaposed and superimposed in several tiers, the total effect is much like a wall sealed with azulejos. This is particularly true when the panels blend in a single ex-panse of gold—the visual sum total of the several gilt backgrounds.* But even when the retable was carved throughout—in the Gothic, the Plateresque, or the Churriguer-esque manner—the visual effect produced by the whole was nevertheless planar. More-over, as will be elucidated later, the trellis through which the altar becomes visible, as through an enormous veil, aided in reduc-ing, optically, its plastic projections to a

Fig. 15.—The Chapel Royal in the Cathedral of Granada

flat surface image (Fig. 15). The retables grew ever richer until the eight-eenth century, when the influence of French classicism wrecked the native tradition; but however mysterious or pompous the glowing coloration, the retable never ceased to resemble a huge stiff carpet.

Since most Spanish ecclesiastical paintings were made for the flat retable, they had to take orders from it, so to speak. Depictions of forceful reces-sion did not fit into this wall-like structure. Any attempt to replace the original planarity by the perspective effects that suddenly came into vogue

* The prominent role the retable played in the ecclesiastical art of Spain was un-doubtedly responsible for the persistent practice of gilding the backgrounds of the paintings at a time when elsewhere the gold ground had long been superseded by realistic landscapes and interiors.

with the rise of naturalism would have been tantamount to an attack upon the decorative essence of the retable. That realization made the Spaniards from the first almost immune to the infections of tridimensional illusionism in painting. This is not a mere figure of speech. It stands to reason that a conservative people who for centuries on end had crowded their churches from morning to midnight, day in and day out, became so attuned to the surface nature of the ever-present altar screen that their artistic imagination could not be seriously affected by those concussions which the new science of perspective at first caused among the other Western schools of painting. To elucidate what I mean by the "concussions" of which Spain kept clear, let me recall what happened in Europe on the threshold of the Renaissance, when the pictorial conventions of a thousand years were suddenly challenged by a new style.

The plane surface had been the chief medium of pictorial unity throughout the Middle Ages. Suddenly, with the introduction of perspective, the plane surface was abandoned. Hitherto "composition" had meant the art of balancing one planar mass against another. Now, with the stress on the third dimension, the flow of the lines and the size of the objects in a picture were controlled by the rearward pyramidal convergence of the visual rays toward a vanishing point. So long as paintings had been composed of flat unmodeled areas of pure color and ornamental outlines, it had been comparatively easy to make them blend harmoniously. But when projections, recessions, overlappings, and similar devices to portray plasticity came into play, it was necessary to employ shadows, highlights, and foreshortenings. All these imperiled, if they did not nullify, the purity and the balance of the extended color planes, the harmonious antiphony of the dominant linear motifs, and the countless other requisites of the medieval planar counterpoint. How far the novel perspective approach upset the age-old conventions of surface unity in the non-Spanish countries may be gathered from the Flemish polyptychs painted during the fifteenth century.

In the reredos of St. Peter's at Louvain, painted by Dirk Bouts in 1464, each panel picture was perspectively designed and each perspective view conditioned by its own vanishing point; there is no single perspective for the whole. As a result, the aggregate of the panels does not form an esthetic continuity of interdependent decorative flats after the medieval fashion, but a multiplicity of disconnected peep-show stages. No further proof is needed to show that the new approach caused repercussions that nearly wrecked the whole structure of art.

In Spain the old convention of decorative unity did not deteriorate to any such extent. This was true in part because the Spanish studios were too slow to adopt the new approach unresistingly; in part, however, because they had too much respect for the plane as the authentic vehicle of pictorial unity. Some sort of compromise between decorative planarity and illusion-istic depth was of course inevitable when naturalism invaded art. Only a few artists ignored the new issue completely. But nothing quite so lacking in perspective design could be found outside of Spain so late as 1396 as the large altar screen with episodes from the *Life of the Virgin,* the *Passion of Our Lord,* and the likenesses of the donor's family which Don Pero Lopez de Ayala, chancellor of Castile (and author of the *Rimado de Palacio*), ordered for his family chapel in that year (the whole has entered the Charles Deering Collection in Chicago). The Catalans were more in-clined to make the necessary compromise, but their work, too, shows that what in Italy and Flanders was a compromise in favor of depth became in Spain a compromise in favor of planarity. How deftly the Serras, in *The Resurrection,* deterred the gaze from wandering off into distance (Fig. 38): a flat of scalloped clouds is lowered from above; planimetric hillocks and bushes are shifted in from the right and the left like cardboard wings on the stage of a doll's theater. The early Catalans, however, do not illustrate the situation so decisively; they were still in the thrall of the school of Siena, known for its allegiance to the Byzantine traditions and, more par-ticularly, for its Oriental surface-bound design and coloration.

The point is better illustrated by those Spanish painters who reflect the influence not of the Sienese conservatives but of the progressives of Flanders—Lluis Dalmau, student of Jan van Eyck, for example. As is evidenced by *The Virgin with the Councillors* (1445, Barcelona Museum, Fig. 42), Dalmau imitated van Eyck as well as he could. Not only did he in-clude some barely concealed single figures and whole groups from his master's altar screen in St. Bavo at Ghent—the Singing Angels in the right-hand background, the Saints standing in the left and right corners, and the kneeling Councillors—but he purloined the idea and the pictorial construction of his painting from van Eyck's *Madonna with the Canon van der Paele* (1436, Bruges, Fig. 43), which was at the time the most baffling painting of figures in a tridimensional interior. Yet what a difference there is between the Spanish imitation and its Flemish model. In the latter the figures were made to look bulky by submerging them in the luminous atmosphere that fairly floods the enclosing space. By comparison Dalmau's figures are neither bulky nor integrally a part of a unified atmosphere. Dalmau translated van Eyck's aerial perspective, which obviously he failed to understand, into that planar decoration which was intelligible to Spanish eyes. The floor is viewed from above, which makes it look quite flat. The apertures in the backdrop do not lure one's attention into the depth behind the Councillors. The vista is shut off by the Gothic tracery of the wall, which in turn is a part of the unending lacework of the patterned vestments and floor tile that ministers to the planimetric effect of the entire picture.

The Spanish Primitives, even as they became better acquainted with the principles of perspective and learned that bodies appear to diminish as they recede from the beholder, continued to make compromises to save the integrity of the planar surface pattern. Bernardo Martorell, in the *Transfiguration* altar of the Cathedral of Barcelona, went further than any of his contemporaries in suggesting the spaciousness of the stage set for his dramatic interpretation of the miracles of the Lord. Yet occasionally his method differed radically from the familiar Italian method, which annihilated the pictorial plane by piercing it with receding lines converging somewhere near or below the middle of the composition. The individual figures in *The Miracle of the Loaves and Fishes* (Fig. 41) are reduced in scale in proportion to their distance from us, but being spread out from the bottom of the panel to its uppermost edge, the superimposed flat faces, halos, and garments constitute a continuous surface which is nowhere perforated. Though all the spatial relations are clarified, the total effect is that of a carpet rather than that of a "peep show."

After this it became almost habitual in Spain to raise the horizon line to the top of the picture, so that, in spite of an intellectual obeisance to the depth of space, visual illusion was absent. An illustration is the *St. Michael Fighting the Dragon*, a painting, now in the Prado, by an unidentified master from Estremadura (about 1480, Fig. 16). In depicting the same subject, van Eyck and Petrus Cristus made the gigantic Archangel contrast with a deep vista across land and sea, as is illustrated by *The Last Judgment* of the former in the Metropolitan Museum and that of the latter in the Kaiser Friedrich Museum in Berlin. The Spaniard, however, suggests

Fig. 16.—Unknown painter from Estremadura: *St. Michael Fighting the Dragon,* Prado

the vastness of the space only in so far as it does not impair his two-dimensional plane. A welter of little angels and demons enframing the tall fighter coalesces in a single plane that extends from the bottom to the top molding, exactly like smaller ornaments enframing a large central pattern upon a woven rug.

With one's consciousness once aroused to the planarity of the Spanish Primitives, one cannot help observing the same quality in the work of the Mannerists of the sixteenth century, and of Velasquez in the seventeenth. The characteristic stylizations of Luis de Morales, Pablo de Cespedes, and El Greco have no parallel in the art of the Italian Renaissance but many parallels in the indigenous art of the Spanish Middle Ages. So surface-conscious were these artists that they preferred to ignore the natural tridimensional expansion of the lines and the illumination rather than permit it to disturb their closely knit surface patterns.

Unfortunately our approach to these Spanish paintings is often warped by the Central European mode of seeing. A manneristic painting such as *The Last Supper* by Pablo de Cespedes in the museum of Seville (Fig. 17) makes no pretense of being a "reasonable" representation of tangible persons and objects in a tridimensional interior. Rather it is a paraphrase of reality into the artificial language of tapestry design. Everything is schematized to meet this end: the table viewed from aloft, the exceedingly narrow stage with its occupants superimposed in two tiers, the flamboyant grain of the marble, the niches with the putti, the bottle-glass window panes, and all the other ornamentation which breaks up the walls into small flat areas; finally, the Disciples themselves with their garments so faceted that they reflect the light in a hundredfold glitter.

Fig. 17.—Pablo de Cespedes: *The Last Supper*, Seville, Provincial Museum

Least of all Spanish paintings should those of El Greco be approached as if they were the work of Michelangelo or Tintoretto. True, this late-born scion of the Byzantines undertook to paint dream-spaces more expansive than anything within empirical experience. But it is the fanciful planar expression in which the artist shrouds his visions that gives them their dream-like effect. As a poet makes his message out of the stuff that is peculiar to a poem—the meter, the rhyme, and the sound of words—so El Greco made his pictorial messages out of the stuff that is peculiar to a flat canvas. For all its emotional reference to the expanse of vast spaces, his *Thunderstorm over Toledo*, in the Metropolitan Museum, is nevertheless composed of an infinity of flat areas of yellow, green, black, and gray which join in a glinting mosaic not unlike the patterns formed by a multitude of varicolored bits of glass in a kaleidoscope. True again, this particular pattern expresses a storm that bursts over the ancient hill town above the Tagus, but that does not make it revelatory of either El Greco or Spanish art. Others have represented the spectacle of an electric storm. All that is revelatory in this instance is the primordial scheme of ideation through which the subject has passed. To ignore that would be quite as bad as to ignore the verbal structure of a poem by Luis de Gongora.

But wait a moment! All along it has been our thesis that planarity is the distinguishing feature of the Spanish style. And El Greco was neither by birth nor by training a Spaniard. He was twenty-six years old before he relinquished the Greco-Byzantine atmosphere of his native Crete for the Renaissance atmosphere of Italy. There he spent a whole decade, perfecting his craftsmanship in Venice and making his reputation as a finished artist in Rome. When at last he removed to Spain, he was a man of thirty-six. How can the style of an artist with such antecedents reveal the peculiarities of the style of Spain?

Let it be said, first, that none of the stylistic peculiarities I have been discussing was apparent in El Greco's art before he came to Spain in 1577. Further, let it be said that without the happy circumstance that we know the antecedents, El Greco's determined divergence from the Italian style of his youth, which becomes increasingly apparent after 1577, would not be, as it is, absolutely conclusive evidence that its most characteristic features were Spanish, conditioned by the tradition and the milieu to which the artist was exposed for the last thirty-seven years of his career.

His manner, after he removed to Toledo, changed from the tactile realism of Titian (Fig. 49) to the ornamental surface stylization of the Spanish school. *The Expulsion of the Usurers,* as El Greco painted it about 1570 (Richmond, England, Sir Frederick Cook, and the Minneapolis Institute of Art), shows the event credibly, as it might have happened. The same subject, as he painted it later, about 1613 (Cofradia del Santisimo

Fig. 18.—El Greco: *The Expulsion of the Usurers,* Madrid, Cofradia del Santisimo Sacramento

Sacramento, Madrid, Fig. 18), gives very little, if any, illusion of reality. This stylized surface pattern, suggestive of an exploding bomb, could not be re-enacted, as the early version indeed could be, by real actors on a real stage.

Arranged chronologically, El Greco's several depictions of *The Annunciation* appear as so many phases in the transformation of the illusionistic manner of Bonifazio Veronese or Jacopo Bassano into the planar Spanish style. The deep tridimensional setting of the picture in the Prado

Fig. 19.—El Greco: *The Annunciation,*
Prado

Fig. 20.—El Greco: *The Annunciation,*
Cleveland, Collection of Ralph M. Coe

(about 1577, Fig. 19) has been abandoned in favor of a planar composition of great coloristic charm in the version owned by Mr. Ralph M. Coe of Cleveland, Ohio (about 1604–06, Fig. 20). It is not by accident that the unspatial Byzantine miniatures of about 1000 A.D. are more closely akin to El Greco's Spanish style than are the paintings of his contemporaries in Italy. Compare the book illumination from the Sacramentary of St. Gereon (Paris, Bibliothèque Nationale, Fig. 21).

The Byzantine tradition, which in an earlier period had influenced the
entire art of Spain, was also one of several sources of the spiritual expression of El Greco's art. It was flowering anew in Crete during the artist's
youth. Its early formative influence, temporarily neutralized by the new,
quite different, style of the Italians of the Rennaissance, was revived by
the kindred mystical strain of the Spanish art of the late sixteenth century,
particularly by that of Luis de
Morales. The Spanish art encouraged El Greco to disregard more
and more the natural proportions of
the human figure and to emphasize
the abstract patterns of color and
light and the unrealistic surface
rhythm. In short, Spanish art added
to the Byzantine tradition all those
means which enabled El Greco to
express what lies beyond the images
of the material world and thus carry
the spectator away to the realm of
the undefinable and the mystical.

Now planarity does not necessarily imply the abolition of illusionism or of a realistic representation of the third dimension of space.
Francisco Ribalta and his seventeenth-century following, up to Zurbaran and Velasquez, rejected the

Fig. 21.—*The Annunciation,* from the Sacramentary of St. Gereon, Paris, Bibliothèque
Nationale

manneristic trend of which El Greco was the central figure, but they continued to employ surface patterns, using them as a serviceable vehicle for
their more realistic expression.

It was a preponderant sensitivity to the surface qualities of their sitters
that distinguished the Spanish portrait painters of the closing sixteenth
century from their Flemish colleagues abroad. Any of a hundred likenesses
painted by Sanchez Coello, Felipe de Liaño, or Pantoja de la Cruz will
serve as an illustration. The contemporary Flemings painted the dress of

their subjects in the same rigid fashion; but whereas they stressed its bulges, the Spaniards stressed its flatness, particularly by concentrating on the floral surface ornamentation woven into the stiff silk and satin materials. Sanchez Coello's *Alexander Farnese* (?) in the National Gallery of Dublin is an example (Fig. 59). Again, in the early seventeenth century, it was the inbred respect for planarity that caused Jose Ribera to paint *The Apotheosis of St. Magdalen* (1626, Madrid, Academia de San Fernando) "not whirling to heaven as was traditional with the followers of Tintoretto, but floating calmly as a flat cloud in the pale sky."[*] Finally, it was the persistent Spanish tendency to reduce round objects to planar images that made Velasquez the true creator of impressionism.

Popularly speaking, impressionism presents things not as they *are,* but as they *appear.* An impressionist distinguishes the image as he sees it from the object as he knows it. His painted "impression" is a record in brush strokes of the image that registers on his retina. Since the retina is, organically, a plane surface and sense data register on it as flat color patches, planarity is essential to an impressionistic painting. As a matter of fact, the more the impressionists learned to forget that the objects they painted were round and bulky, and the more they made the beholder forget it, the more consistently did they elaborate a repertory of flat pictorial symbols by which the retinal impression could be correctly expressed.

Whether Velasquez or his Dutch contemporary Frans Hals was "the father of impressionism" is an open question. The answer depends upon which of the hallmarks of impressionistic painting is deemed more important: the broad, sketchy brushwork or the reduction of bulky objects to planar images. As regards the latter, there can be no doubt whatsoever that Velasquez antedates Frans Hals. All the more interesting is the fact that his approach stemmed directly from the Spanish tradition.

Velasquez, to be sure, arrived at those conclusions which made him "the father of impressionism" only after a long struggle with the repertory of forms which he had inherited from the older realists, above all from his teachers in Seville. At the time when he composed his earliest dated picture, the altarpiece with *The Adoration of the Magi* (1619, Prado, Fig. 65), the true retinal impression of the whole mattered far less to him than the

[*] Valerian von Loga, *Die Malerei in Spanien* (Berlin, 1923), 204.

plastic palpability of the separate bodies. To intensify it he employed a concentrated light which falls obliquely from the left into a nearly black stage, as was common practice in the school of the *tenebrosi*. With such an arrangement he was able to achieve a forceful effect of space, but he could not have obtained the effect of a plane composed of collocated luminous color surfaces even if this had been his aim. The illumination, piercing the darkness at odd points, prevents what planes there are from consolidating into a continuous surface. In fact, the colors become part of the pictorial texture only where they happen to protrude into the beam of the lateral spotlight: the white veil upon the head and shoulders of the Virgin and her pale purple blouse and blue mantle, the coffee-colored cloak of the king kneeling in front, the black velvet tunic of the Moor, and his white collar and scarlet cape.

About a decade later, when Velasquez painted *The Topers (Los Borrachos,* 1628, Prado, Fig. 67), an advance toward a more coloristic construction became evident. Here, instead of making the figures jut forth from a dark cavity, he has lined them up as a relief-like strip in front of a uniformly bright landscape; and instead of considering each local color area separately, he has attempted an even spread of interrelated chromatic values across the entire canvas, allowing the more important colors to interwine in the pictorial texture like varicolored threads in a woven fabric. Expressions of this technique are the interlocking browns and grays near the man who is smiling broadly from under his large hat. The deep fudge-brown of his right shoulder is set between two shades of gray, the iron gray of his shirt and the somewhat bluish gray of the meadow behind. This harmony is varied in the gray hair and the brown cloak of the third man on the right, who is seen in profile. The warmth of the brown is intensified first in the cloak, then in the tumbler full of wine in his hand, and finally in the reddish brown of his face. Obviously Velasquez was striving not only to recover the old Spanish surface tradition but to create a decorative surface texture woven of chromatic values rather than built up of solid forms. Moreover, he was already studying each color with a fine regard for what changes it suffered under the influence of the atmosphere. Unlike the realists with whom he had studied, he came to realize that colors are not unalterable attributes of the things about us, but depend on the atmospheric conditions in which they are perceived.

For all the progress it shows, *The Topers* falls short, as a visual impression in retinal terms, of the attainment that Velasquez was to demand of himself a decade later; there were still too many carry-overs from the school of the *tenebrosi*. Ponderously modeled as they are, the bodies, hands, heads, and draperies appeal more than they should to the beholder's sense of touch. The impressionistic system needed a further reduction of what is touchable to what is seeable. A great step forward in that direction is embodied in *The Surrender of Breda* of 1635 (*Las Lanzas,* Prado, Fig. 69); compare, in particular, the portraits of the Spanish generals, on the right side, with the heads of the grape-harvesters in *The Topers*. The portraits of the generals are painted as flats with next to no dark modeling, quite unlike the bulky, almost chiseled-looking, heads of the grape-harvesters.

Our language possesses no terms precise enough to define the phenomenon fully, nor wide enough to suggest the relativity of my judgment. *The Surrender of Breda* has been praised so often and so highly for the surprising sensation of depth which it conveys that it is actually embarrassing to comment on its planarity.

It all depends on the angle from which one approaches this stupendous work of art. If we are concerned with the place of the painting in the international development of the pictorial representation of space, and the painting is therefore contrasted with fifteenth- and sixteenth-century works in which similar bilateral masses of figures usually consolidate in wall-like planes, then of course we must agree with the eminent critic of style, Heinrich Wölfflin, that in the painting of Velasquez "the groups are *not* extended in a plane" and that "the recessional relations speak at all points."*

It is true that Velasquez threw open the gates of space in the age of the Baroque in quite another fashion than any painter of the High Renaissance could have done. On the other hand, it cannot be denied that within the much wider range of the European illusionistic painting of the seventeenth century *The Surrender of Breda* stands out as one of the most marked examples of Spanish planarity. If this is not easily credible, compare with it the painting of Rubens that inspired the Velasquez composi-

* Heinrich Wölfflin, *Principles of Art History* (New York, 1923), 82.

tion, *The Meeting of the King of Hungary and the Cardinal Infant at Nördlingen* (Fig. 70). All the tricks by which Rubens underscored the effects of spatial recession have been assiduously avoided by Velasquez. Whereas Rubens put oversized allegorical figures in the foreground of his painting as an optical device by which to push the main characters as far as possible into the background, Velasquez lined up his figures along the footlights, accompanying that front plane by a landscape which, instead of rapidly vanishing into depth, was tilted upward until it almost touched the top molding of the canvas (a typical Spanish habit, it will be remembered). Even the foreshortened horse in the right-hand foreground of *The Surrender of Breda* is considerably flattened out in contrast to the horse employed by Rubens in the right corner of his painting. Velasquez disliked the depthward line; it impaired the plane which he considered the constant of his composition. Therefore, too, he made his heroes meet in the center of the foreground instead of in the distance at the extreme corner of the canvas.

Velasquez reached his goal during the last five years of his career. His idea of retinal planarity was consummated in *The Maids of Honor*, painted in 1656 (Prado, Fig. 71). Once again I seem to hear the protest of those who have heard other critics comment on the masterful painterly representation of the depth of space in this very picture. But the protest is beside the point. I am not speaking of the illusion evoked by Velasquez of an expanding room in which the painter, the little princess, the ladies-in-waiting, and other persons are seen moving so freely to and fro. I am pointing out the undeniable fact that all the forms in this picture are expressed by colored flats and that each of these functions as an important factor in the *decorative* plan of the whole.

Quite apart from its illusionistic functions, the entire color fabric constitutes a decorative pattern; for this reason Velasquez deemed it permissible to alienate each color from the things and forms to which it belongs. In reality, the unwieldy skirt worn by the little infanta resembled a cone, and in his early career Velasquez would no doubt have made it look like one. But in this late period he distinguished between the form that *is* and the image that *appears,* and depicted what was a conical object in colorful flats—silver gray in the shade, and warm yellow in the light—

as he depicted the little crimson bows on the sleeves and bodice without any reference to their actual roundness. Most of this astounding transformation of bodies into planes can be seen only in the original canvas. Yet even a photograph of the court lady kneeling toward the left reveals Velasquez's ability to suggest bulk by planar brush strokes; note her face, her hair, and her hands, one of which is partly in the lighted region while the other is submerged in the transparent shade.

As a final illustration let me use the large likeness of *The Infanta Margarita* of about 1660 (Prado, Fig. 72). Without a turn of the body, the figure is as flat as a plank. The rounding shadows have been either omitted entirely or executed as surfaces of color which function as structural articulations rather than as modelings. The pictorial pattern resembles that of a wall ornamented with tiles of brick-red and silver.

The realistic approach of Velasquez goes a long way toward explaining this development, but it does not go all the way. One cannot discount the decorative approach. "It is a dilettantist notion that an artist could ever take up his stand before nature without any preconceived ideas. But what he has taken over as concept of representation, and how this concept goes on working in him, is much more important than anything he takes from direct observation (at least as long as art is creative and decorative and not scientifically analytic). The observation of nature is an empty notion as long as we do not know in what forms the observation took place. The whole progress of the 'imitation of nature' is anchored in decorative feeling. Ability plays only a secondary part."* There is no doubt in my mind that the eyes of Velasquez, as he discovered the new approach to the visible world of things, were constantly guided by that decorative instinct for planarity which we have considered. Indeed, I am convinced that his development would never have taken the direction it did had he been an Italian or Fleming rather than a Spaniard. For the impressionism of Velasquez was the temporary culmination of a trend that had been reinforced by every advance his artistic forebears had made since the fifteenth century. Such a culmination of experience was not to be repeated for a century and a half after his death. It was Francisco Goya in the early nineteenth century who spoke the last word in the matter of planarity.

* Heinrich Wölfflin, *op. cit.,* 230.

PLANARITY IN ARCHITECTURAL SCULPTURE The native preoccupation with planarity is no less conspicuous in the sculptures than in the paintings of Spain. To be sure, as an art, sculpture differs from painting in that its surfaces are not flat but protuberant. The tridimensionality of sculpture is palpable and real, not merely represented as in painting. The very tools of the sculptor are intended for the excavation of depressions and projections from solid bodies of stone or clay. A wall, a panel, a canvas, or a sheet of drawing paper stays flat to one's sense of touch regardless of the expanse of space depicted thereon. On the other hand, a bas-relief, however slight its elevation, remains a raised surface to one's touch even if the carving represents nothing spacious at all. This material difference between the flatness of pictorial art and the extendedness of sculptural art need not concern us here. What does concern us is the decorative manipulation of convex and concave surfaces by the Spanish carvers; more particularly, the relative planarity of Spanish sculpture as compared with the non-planar sculpture of other Western countries. A few typical examples of architectural sculpture in the Gothic, the Renaissance, and the Baroque periods may serve as an introduction to our problem.

In the entire Late Gothic period of Western art I know of nothing quite so emphatically planar as the garden and street façades of the Silk Exchange (la Lonja de la Seda) of Valencia, which were erected between 1483 and 1498 (Fig. 22). Manifestly, it was the intention of the architectural sculptors not to impair, but rather to emphasize, the planarity of the walls assigned to them for decoration. Otherwise it would be difficult to account for the extreme restraint in their use of decorative means. In the plan of the whole the undecorated surface predominates; the decoration is enjoined not to overstep the functions of a tactful accompaniment. Thus the rather expansive decoration around the main doorway and the two adjoining windows was confined to these places, and was not repeated on the wall of the corresponding wing to the left of the central tower. There the decoration was relegated to a single row of eight windows high up under the eaves; that half of the façade has no other decoration than the delicately spaced fenestration. The half to the right of the tower, with the doorway, looks the smoother for the geometrical framework of thinly molded ridges which, like a trellis, encompasses the door, the windows, and two pictorial reliefs. The fact that these do not jut forth, but have the same elevation as the enframing ridges, helps to make them an inseparable part of the entire surface of the façade. Because of the vast undecorated surfaces that surround them, the narrow stripes of storied relief work that are set in the moldings of the Garden Gate suggest so many embroidered borders on a chasuble.

The plateresque decoration of the southeast façade of the City Hall of Seville, begun in 1527 (El Ayuntamiento, Fig. 23), illustrates that no fundamental change in Spanish taste occurred in the era of Charles V. With its vigorously projecting central wing, this masterpiece of Diego Riaño is bulkier than the delicate Silk Exchange at Valencia, and its decoration differs from the latter in that it occupies the whole wall space, but it has the same planarity. At any rate, the timid elevation of the pilasters and engaged columns from the walls is strikingly dissimilar to the voluminosity of such architectural members in the cinquecento architecture of Italy; and so is the elaborateness of the ornamentation as compared with the puristic restraint of the latter. The Italians of the High Renaissance admitted a moderate amount of decoration upon those parts of the architecture that were of no significance structurally; that is, in between the pilasters and columns, but never, as here, upon them. Riaño's manner of decoration aimed to satisfy the Spanish taste. Lest the high

Fig. 22.—La Lonja de la Seda in Valencia

Fig. 23.—El Ayuntamiento in Seville

relief of the pilasters, engaged columns, and arches emancipate these men-
bers from the wall, he tied them down, as it were, with a web of graceful
surface decoration which envelops them from head to foot and continues
on the flat interstices.

The Baroque era of the seventeenth and eighteenth centuries was not
content with the gentle sculptural decoration of the plateresque style.
Only a sculpture more agitated, more vigorous, and rich with stronger
contrasts appealed to that age with its unrestrained, exuberant, and im-
patient state of mind and spirit. All the sculptures of the entire Western
Baroque were animated by the dramatic struggle between brilliant light
and deep dark, an effect that can be achieved only by churning the surface
until it becomes an incessant sequence of projections and hollows. The
Baroque sculpture of Spain, in so far as it was a part of the general
European development, also depended for its effects more than it had in
earlier periods on the recession of the forms into depth. But more than
elsewhere these novel effects were produced with a conservative regard
for the basic significance of the planar view. The sculptural work of
Pedro de Mena, Ignacio Vergara, and Narciso Tome has little of the spatial amplitude of the work of Bernini, Algardi, and the other Baroque
sculptors of Italy, not to mention the South Germans of the Rococo.

Relatively speaking, even the *estilo churrigueresco* of the mid-eight-
eenth century persisted in safeguarding the Spanish tradition of planarity.

When Ignacio Vergara decorated the gigantic alabaster doorway of the palace of the Marques de Dos Aguas (Fig. 24) with an allegory of the owner's name (Two Waters), he was anxious not to injure the surface character of the façade by forms that were too bulky. An Italian of the same period, as shown by Nicolo Salvi's Fontana Trevi at Rome, would

Fig. 24.—Portal of the Dos Aguas Palace in Valencia

most certainly have disenthralled from the surface all those twisted and heavily foreshortened figures. But where the Italian, by the bold forward projection of both the figures and the cascades, practically annihilates the effect of the wall from which they depart, Vergara keeps his figures imprisoned in the flat façade. His carving also suggests tumbling waters, but not gushing rapids, as does the Fontana Trevi. Rather, his composition reminds one of fan-like sprays trickling round the portal, never departing from the wall.

In the light of eighteenth-century German sculpture the relative planarity of the Spanish sculpture stands out even more boldly. The contrast is exemplified by nearly contemporary works: *Lo Trasparente* (Fig. 25), the retable carved of alabaster by Narciso Tome and set up behind the chancel of the cathedral of Toledo; and the altar of the Abbey of Weltenburg, on the Danube near Regensburg, which was erected at the same time as the present church, between 1717 and 1721, by Cosmas Damian Asam (Fig. 26).

Both works are the picturesque medleys of architecture, sculpture, and painting of which the eighteenth century was so fond. In both the effect depends on illumination which evokes the illusion of depth by deceiving the eye. The Toledo retable seems to become transparent, hence deriving its name, as it reflects the flood of light that pours in from an aperture concealed in the opposite vaults of the ambulatory. The Weltenburg altar and the adjoining interior of the church submit to an even more complicated illumination, coming from windows shielded in various intricate ways and modulating the spatial effect of the nave and the chancel exactly as the chromatic values modulate the effect of space in the paintings of

Fig. 25.—*Lo Trasparente* in the Cathedral of Toledo   Fig. 26.—Altar of the Abbey Church in Weltenburg, Germany

that time. Apparently both artists were influenced by the stagecraft of their epoch, particularly by its deceptive lighting and perspective, which made the depth of a stage setting seem much deeper than it actually was. It should be added that these two works, each in its own way, marked the most extreme outposts toward which the Spanish and the German art of the eighteenth century dared to advance in quest of effects of depth and recession. My comparison will bring the relative results of that quest to mind.

The *Trasparente* of Toledo resembles an extravagantly fanciful stage setting quite as much as does the Weltenburg altar. The swaying cornices of the concave walls that chamber the altar table with the statue of the Madonna, and the borders of the bas-reliefs of the flanking walls, converge rapidly toward the vanishing point. So, too, the niche around *The Last Supper* (in the upper zone) tapers funnel-wise into depth. A bewildering cluster of intersecting rays and angels (above the Madonna, in the middle zone) functions as a *repoussoir* by which *The Last Supper* is still further removed, optically, from the beholder. In view of this extravagant perspective make-believe, the reader may doubt whether the *Trasparente* is an apposite paradigm of Spanish planarity.

But if one has such a doubt, it is silenced by the contrast of the German Rococo. In Weltenburg many additional devices were brought into play to make the depth of space a more thrilling experience. It is veritably breath-taking to enter the interior after having passed through the door of an entirely unpromising facade. The entire church is calculated to conjure up, at the opposite end, the magic vision of an incandescent altar at what seems to be a vast distance—though actually it is only a few paces away. The plan of the nave is an oval elongated toward the chancel. Its depthward thrust is enhanced by gradations of daylight which seem to be quite inexplicable. The nave is filled with a mysterious dimness which is shaded to dusk and complete darkness (an unlighted section being interpolated between the semidark nave and the brilliantly lighted chapel in back of the altar). Thus the brightness that ultimately bursts forth from the extreme depth is overwhelming in its suddenness. It is the more exciting in that one's gaze into the depth is not arrested by any screen upon the altar. For instead of the traditional closing surface, there are floods of light pouring out of an aperture. In the center of that aperture a small silver-and-gold statue of St. George is set up in a boldly foreshortened view, as if he were riding forth from the unknown on billowing waves of luminosity. Surely the theme of depth could not have been treated more sensationally.

The Spaniards would undoubtedly have considered the work of Cosmas Damian Asam as in the worst of taste. Indeed, if after this breath-taking plunge into space we glance back at the *Trasparente* of Toledo, we must admit that even the most daring attempts of the Spanish sculptors of the eighteenth century resulted in little more than modifications of the native ideal of planarity.

PLANARITY IN FREE SCULPTURE Fundamentally, there is no difference between the sculptural decoration of the façade of a building and the façade of a retable; both belong to the field of wall decoration. A statue that is a part of a wall of stone, wood, or metal foregoes its tridimensionality; however well rounded it may be, it cannot be viewed from all sides, but only from one. Many of the statues used for the decoration of the Late Gothic façades of San Gregorio and San Pablo of Valladolid would give a striking three-dimensional effect if they were set up individually in a museum of sculpture, but set up as they are in the compartments of the façades, they are subject to the predominant planar effect of the whole. This is equally true of the carved decorations of the retable with *The Root of Jesse* in the St. Anne's Chapel of the cathedral of Burgos by Diego de la Cruz, who was Spanish-born; those of the screen of St. Anne's altar in the near-by Chapel of the Constable by Gil de Siloe, whose Spanish origin is uncertain; and those of the retables of the Seville and Toledo cathedrals, which exemplify the Spanish taste though they were executed by immigrants from Flanders and Germany: Dancart, Rodrigo Aleman, Felipe de Vigarni, and others.

Most Spanish statues were intended for large ensembles. Isolated figures were rare in the Spanish ecclesiastical art as compared with the sculptural decoration of the choir stalls, pulpits, lecterns, retables, and other smaller "façades" for which there was so great a demand. Almost without exception, the Madonnas, Saviors, and Saints which today are housed in various museums were executed to stand before an altar screen or to become so submerged in its recesses that, for all their individual rotundity, their effect was nevertheless planar.

For example, Alonso Berruguete's great retable, completed in 1532 for San Benito at Valladolid, was dismantled sometime during the nineteenth century and its statues and bas-reliefs were moved to the provincial museum. There, stripped from their original setting, the statues of the apostles and saints (Fig. 11) remind one more of Michelangelo's *Prigioneri* of the tomb of Pope Julius than of anything in the Spanish tradition. They seem to embody the sculptural ideal of the great Italian that a compact mass of stone should be pierced with the largest possible number of contrasting spatial axes. But if by some trick of magic Berruguete's carvings could be put back into the "façade" of the original retable, their projections and recessions would at once flatten out into a surface pattern. Moreover, if they were submerged in the wall, the agitation and convolution of their limbs would instantly be stilled. Had Karl Justi borne in mind that these sculptures have been torn from the unity of the flat screen for which they were made, he probably would not have condemned them for "being cut out of a madman's dream."

The greater the freedom that was granted to the separate carved figures to expand and move in space, the more emphatically the Spanish sculptors stressed the background as the surface to which the figures were optically related. This was necessary if the tradition of decorative planarity was to survive in the face of the increasing plasticity of the sculptures. In this connection, note what happened to the backgrounds of the sculptures during the latter part of the sixteenth century; by that time the carvers, having become quite proficient in representing the mobility of the human body, took an understandable delight in making the figures they modeled extend their arms from the body, incline their heads, move their shoulders in opposite directions, bend their knees, stoop or revolve around their perpendicular axis. This newly gained mastery of the naturalistic imperiled the tradition of decorative planarity. But as soon as the sculptors became aware of the danger, they introduced the practice of painting the background—not only the figures themselves as had been done throughout the Middle Ages—so that even a well-rounded carving acquired much of the appearance of a planar painting. By the close of the cinquecento period it was an established Spanish custom to add painted landscapes or interiors as backgrounds not only to bas-reliefs but even to statues and carved groups. The main altar of Las Angustias in Valladolid, carved in 1605 by Cristobal Velazquez, was transformed into a near-painting by Tomas de Prado. In 1614 Pacheco added polychromy to *El Cristo de la Luz,* the renowned carving by Gregorio Hernandez in the museum of Valladolid

(Frontispiece). Valdes Leal eventually painted and gilded both the figures and the background of Pedro Roldan's retable in La Caridad at Seville.

The bold realism which evolved toward the end of the sixteenth century, particularly in the workshops of Valladolid and Seville, might have given the sculptors an opportunity to break away from the traditional planar style and to develop in its place those effects of depthward foreshortening which Giovanni da Bologna, Bernini, and the other Italian sculptors of the Baroque period exploited so eagerly. But none of the leading Spanish masters capitalized on the given opportunity. Gregorio Hernandez and his followers emphasized the flatness of the background in their bas-reliefs and even had surfaces set up behind their round sculptures, a practice for which there was no justification but the esthetic one that every piece of carving should be optically related to a plane.

How deeply this principle was ingrained in the Spanish decorative taste may be gathered from the fact that almost every Spanish ecclesiastical sculpture was related to a diaphanous plane set up in front of it, namely the reja—the tall flat grating that shuts off the nave from the chapels in which the altars and their decorations stand. Since the Middle Ages the reja had been the most common optical filter through which the Spanish works of sculpture were, so to speak, strained to make them even more plane-like. Under normal circumstances no Spanish chapel or altar can be viewed in any other way than through the enclosing railing. In what measure the reja tends to planarize the bulky forms behind it is illustrated by Fig. 15, which shows the tombs of the Catholic Kings behind their enormous railings in the Chapel Royal at Granada. The picturesque patio of a typical Spanish residence is transformed for the optical enjoyment of the passer-by in much the same fashion by the reja, which closes off the main entrance (Fig. 24), as is also the view of the blue sky outside by the reja-like openwork of the alabaster shutters that occupy the apertures in the wall of a room (Fig. 3).

The reja is one of the oldest of Spanish fixtures. From time immemorial the Spanish suitor conversed with his lady through the reja, with which every front window of a Spanish house is provided, or on the street saw her face veiled by a reja-like lace mantilla. Not even landscape and vegetation were free from such veiling. The countless lithe rays of water rising from fifty-five converging fountains in the court of the Generalife, above Granada, weave an ever-shifting reja and only through this may the façade at the other end be beheld. In every instance these trellises, whether of metal, stone, lace, or water, work as planar filters. And if there is no actual reja to prevent a more direct inspection, of individual paintings, for instance, the unending ornamental pattern of the lines is, more often than not, so spun across the canvas that the bulk of the picture is flattened by it (Figs. 6, 16). Juan de las Roelas strained the glistening landscape in the distance of his *Crucifixion of St. Andrew* (Seville Museum) through

Fig. 27.—Gregorio Hernandez: *Pieta,* Valladolid,
Provincial Museum

the lattice-like arrangement of the figures that occupy the foreground, and Velasquez, in *The Surrender of Breda,* produced a similar effect by constructing a veritable reja of lances in the middle distance (Fig. 69).

But let us return to the question of planarity. The conclusive evidence that planarity was an ideal that must be enforced at any cost, in sculpture as well as in painting, is the fact that the increasing facility in the representation of the third dimension did not lessen the use of optical planes, as one might expect, but strengthened it. The decorative construction of the *Meninas* (Fig. 71) was more consciously planar than any sixteenth-century painting by Juan de Juanes—*St. Stephen and the Jewish Doctors,* for instance (Fig. 55)—just as the sculptures by Gregorio Hernandez were done in a more plane-conscious style than the earlier ones now on exhibit in the museum at Valladolid, such as the lifesized carvings that Juan de Juni made for the retable in the convent of St. Francis after he came from France, in 1540 or thereabouts. Granted that these must have looked less bulky and convulsed so long as they were incorporated with their original screen, the greater surface character of Hernandez's figures is apparent; they have retained it even after the original background to which they were visually related has been removed, as it has been from the *Pieta* which he carved for La Penitencia de las Angustias sometime in the 1620's (Fig. 27).

A comparison of that work with the group of the *Pieta* that Bernini made in 1628 for St. John of the Lateran in Rome (Fig. 28) will demonstrate the persistence of a planar style in the Baroque of Spain in contrast to the Italian which, in painting as well as in sculpture, demanded effects of depth at any cost. In Bernini's group the body of Christ zigzags away in the direction of depth. The head and the right arm droop forward. The abdomen recedes and the advancing lower limbs overlap one another. In the group by Hernandez, on the other hand, the dead body does not twist around its axis, but is viewed strictly from in front. The plane formed by it is no less conspicuous than it was in the sculptures

Fig. 28.—G. L. Bernini: *Pieta*, Rome, Church of St. John of the Lateran

of the late Middle Ages—in the *Pieta* by Pedro Millan, for example (Fig. 10). But Hernandez, in contrast to the Primitives, gained his planar effect more deliberately—more in defiance of his highly realistic approach, which might have lured him onto the path pursued by Bernini. The head of Christ is thrust abruptly into the profile view. The right arm, the trunk, the two legs, and the shroud are forcibly stretched out into so many straight, parallel planes. Moreover, the treatment of the drapery by the Italian and the Spanish sculptors was different. Hernandez uses rigid flats animated only by slight ruffles, the same manner of depicting drapery as Zurbaran and Velasquez employed in their paintings. Bernini, on the other hand, anxiously avoided such even surfaces. He preferred an arrangement which was at once more theatrical and produced a stronger sensation of touch. He gathered a bulky pucker of folds upon the one thigh and draped the whole shroud rearward from under the legs of the nude.

The style of Hernandez must not be confused with the plane-*boundedness* of the Primitives; it is an expression of the plane-*consciousness* of the Baroque period. Note how he exploited the dominant planar view to the greatest advantage of the emotional expression. It is only for its sudden forward projection across the mute plane that the foreshortened hand of the Virgin assumes the eloquence of a passionate indictment.

Assuredly, there must have been a psychological reason for this retreat from the "style in depth" and the conscious insistence on a "style in planes." Depth and foreshortening are dramatic means of expression; it is not by accident that they have been the favorite media in stagecraft. Just as a playwright restrains the plot of his drama from expanding in breadth, curtails it, and leaps from suspense to suspense, so those painters, sculptors, and architects who strive for a dramatic effect foreshorten the path of the eye from the foreground to the distance. Foreshortening speeds up our vision; it suggests the greatest quantity of form by means of the most concentrated visible mass. An interior composed "in depth," like C. D. Asam's church at Weltenburg (Fig. 26), drives the eye through space with breathtaking rapidity. An extensive representation in planes, on the other hand, is unexciting. The plane is a vehicle ideally suited to lyrical and epical expression; it gives the communication freedom to spread out broadly, whether it be in words, in musical phrases, or in pictorial forms. In that respect the tradition of planarity gives the lie to the conventional saying that Spanish art was uncommonly dramatic. In subject matter it was dramatic; in its decorative pattern it was not. It was more lyrical than the art of any other Western country. The Spaniard, reticent and stoical by nature, could not respond to the effects of that foreshortening which the volatile Italian temper so keenly enjoyed.

The very selection and interpretation of subject matter by the sculptors and painters of Spain show this to be true. Unlike the Italians, they preferred the lyrical, languishing moods to the dramatic. Their favorite themes, culled from the lore of the Virgin Mary, were *la Purísima* and *la Virgen de las Angústias*—the rapturous Mother and the stoically suffering Mother of Sorrows (Figs. 27, 51–53, 98). Their favorite theme from the Lord's Passion was the patient Man of Sorrows (Fig. 64), not the valiant conqueror. And even the most sanguinary image of the Crucified Christ was a lyrical outpouring intended for impassive religious contemplation (Frontispiece).

Throughout Europe the Baroque movement was bent on representing moments and motifs of religious ecstasy, the theme that implies the utmost in emotional excitement. But how differently did Italians and Spaniards of the seventeenth century go about it. Bernini, in *The Ecstasy of St. Theresa* (Rome, St. Maria della Vittoria), mobilized every imaginable device of the theater. He depicted a woman delirious and convulsed—a veritable feminine Laocoön. De Mena, on the other hand, expressed *The Ecstasy of St. Francis* (Toledo cathedral) by a figure motionless and flat as a plank.

In these first chapters I have endeavored only occasionally, notably in the last few paragraphs, to examine the usefulness of the Spanish patterns of ideation as vehicles of emotional communication. Nor have I attempted to trace their possible relationship to the basic propensities of the Spanish psyche. The answers to these questions should, I think, be found not by the historian of art but by the psychologist. It is within his province rather than mine to trace the principles of Spanish art back to their source in the soul of the Spanish people.

I may therefore proceed along the path marked out for the historian. Leaving the examination of the Spanish style behind, let us now turn to the examination of the Spanish period styles.

HISTORICAL PHASES
OF SPANISH PAINTING

BOOK TWO

The Middle Ages in Catalonia

CHAPTER FIVE

RELATIONSHIP OF THE PERIOD STYLES We now approach the history of
Spanish art from the second of the two points of view mentioned in the
opening paragraphs of this book. Our object now is to view chronologically
the acts and scenes that constitute the drama of Spanish art. We shall be
concerned less with the unchanging mirror which reflects the images of
the phenomenal world than with the different forms which the artists of
each epoch detected in the reflected images. More particularly we are concerned with the vital questions of why the reflected images were so differently interpreted by succeeding generations of artists and why the style
of one century was superseded by that of another.

From this point of view the history of Spanish art is to a large extent
the history of the evolving Spanish *Weltanschauung*. The transformations
of the epochal art styles reflect the transformations of the epochal mind.
The distinctive manners of perception and representation, valid first with
the Primitives, next with the classical school, and ultimately with the
masters of the Baroque, were expressions of a changing attitude toward
the world. The case of Renaissance versus Primitive art and the case of
Baroque versus Renaissance were adjudicated to only a very limited extent
on grounds of technical perfection or imperfection. Under normal circumstances every period mastered the presentation of that which it craved
spiritually. Always the artist's eye perceived exactly what the mind of
his epoch told him to perceive. What it did not crave remained artistically
undeveloped until a later day.

This is corroborated by the fact that on its evolutionary road the new art style usually relinquished about as much as it gained. Every artistic advance was made at the cost of a perhaps equally great loss. As measured by its fidelity to reality, the art of the seventeenth century was far in advance of that of the fifteenth and sixteenth centuries, just as the art of these centuries, in its depiction of nature in tridimensional forms, had been in advance of the abstract symbolism of the Romanesque and Gothic epochs. On the other hand, the religious solemnity and transcendental grandeur of the medieval styles was lost in the bourgeois styles of the fourteenth and fifteenth centuries. As to the seventeenth, how little of the sincerity of Zurbaran and Velasquez was left in the showy and sentimental art of Murillo and Claudio Coello, all their inimitable craftsmanship notwithstanding.

Entering the competitive race of the art-producing nations at a relatively late date, the Spaniards lagged behind on many international issues. For that reason I shall deal only briefly with the early phases of their art. Although significant signposts will, I trust, receive enough emphasis to mark the path along which the evolution traveled, our attention will be directed chiefly toward those periods in which the art of Spain participated in the international contest on a par with that of other countries; that is, from the late sixteenth century through the early nineteenth.

THE TWELFTH AND THIRTEENTH CENTURIES Medieval Spanish art begins in Catalonia. At an earlier date than the rest of the country this province on the northeastern seaboard, once a part of the Spanish Mark of Charlemagne's Frankish empire, was in steady communication with the culturally advanced Mediterranean countries. It served as a gateway for all those innovations in civilization and art that originated in the Byzantine East, in Sicily, and in France. After the union of Catalonia with Aragon in 1137 the new kingdom soon rose to great political power, ruling over Provence for thirty years, from 1166 to 1196, and expanding during the first half of the thirteenth century southward to Valencia, Jativa, and Murcia. Moreover, after the Moorish invaders had been swiftly expelled, Catalonia became a haven for many Christian refugees from the South; the province

was renowned for her independent spirit even after Aragon joined with
Castile, in 1492, to form the Spanish kingdom of Ferdinand and Isabella.

The earliest Catalan art works are the murals and altar frontals created
by native craftsmen during the eleventh and twelfth centuries. These were
executed for certain small churches perched upon the slopes in the wilds of
the northeastern Pyrenees, at places removed from the highways of com-
merce. A significant region is that which embraces the ancient bishopric of
Urgel, the valleys of Cardos, Noguera-Palaresa and Andorra, and, above
all, the Bohi valley with the churches of St. Climent and St. Maria at
Tahull.

To the historian of art the preservation of alfresco paintings in the early
Romanesque churches of this region is of inestimable interest. They throw
light not only on the history of art in Spain, but on the art of all Western
Europe. For they were painted at the momentous time when the pictorial
decoration of churches—which from the beginning of Byzantine art had
been entrusted exclusively to the painters—passed to the sculptors. In that
transition the Aragonese murals form the most important link.

At the time they were being painted, the churches being built across
the border in France were, for the first time since the decline of the
Roman Empire, decorated not with paintings but with monumental stone
reliefs. A renascence of sculpture was marked by the doorways embel-
lished with large storied carvings of the basilicas in Burgundy and
Languedoc—at Autun, Vezelay, Moissac, Souillac, and Toulouse in the
extreme south of France. All of them date from approximately 1120 to
1135. In 1168 another grand example of the new French school was
executed on Spanish soil: Master Mateo's Portico de la Gloria at Santiago
de Campostela, the great international pilgrim shrine, which had been
under construction since 1075 and was patterned on St. Sernin of Toulouse. Its style was a synthesis of the Burgundian, Provencal, and Languedoc varieties of Romanesque sculpture.

No sculptural repertory of forms or compositional patterns being available at the time, the French stonemasons turned for inspiration to the
only other source there was, the Byzantine paintings. The tympanum
reliefs of *The Last Judgment* over the doorway of St. Lazare at Autun,

The Pentecost over the entrance to La Madelaine at Vezelay, and *The Second Coming of the Lord* over the portal of St. Pierre at Moissac are translations of painted archetypes into stone reliefs.

What was the character and style of the paintings that inspired the sculptors? For obvious reasons it is likely that, having their minds set on the solution of monumental problems, the sculptors turned to the monumental rather than to the applied pictorial arts. In this general situation lies the significance of the Catalan wall paintings, which were unquestionably conceived in a monumental style. Prior to their discovery almost the only sources of pictorial influence known to the historians of the Romanesque sculpture were small ivory carvings and illuminations in missals. Since the discovery of the murals, however, historians have a much clearer conception of the sources of pictorial influence at the time of the second birth of sculpture. The materials used in the weaving of the early Catalan art fabric were imported from Byzantine art centers abroad. But its pictorial patterns were refashioned by that Spanish imagination which previously had been nurtured by the Roman, Visigothic, Mozarabic, and Arabian works of art in Spain.

In recent years the larger part of the Catalan murals and altars have been removed from their original sites to the shelter of the museums at Barcelona and Vich. Only the frescoes of San Miguel de Mur have been transported across the sea to the Museum of Fine Arts in Boston. Even in their present civilized environment there remains discernible in all these Hispano-Byzantine paintings a tinge of the rustic atmosphere that surrounded them as they were being executed by unpretentious virile painters. Whoever these artisans may have been, they were without doubt quite unfamiliar with the original splendor of the Byzantine art of the East or the Moorish luxuriance of the Cordovese. The rural and impecunious conditions under which early Spanish art grew to manhood are among the most important factors influencing it.

Al Makkari, an Arabian chronicler of the tenth century, draws a vivid picture of the simple standards of life to which even Spanish royalty was accustomed in those early days. He relates, for instance, that King Ordoño IV, on his first visit to the caliph's court at Medina Azhara, near Cordova, was so dazzled by its riches that speech failed him and he had to be taken home "in order that he might recover from the violent emotional concussions which he had suffered."*

The proverbial practical sense of the Catalans is not enough to explain the remarkably terse character of their earliest art. The provincial rusticity of their lives further accounts for their stringent economy in selecting

Fig. 29.—*Pantokrator*. Detail of the mural in St. Climent de Tahull, Barcelona, Museum of Catalan Art

Fig. 30.—*Pantokrator*. Detail of the mural in Esterri de Cardos, Barcelona, Museum of Catalan Art

only what they wanted from the motley trends and extravagant models imported to their region from the four corners of the world. An illustration of this is *The Last Coming of Christ*, which decorates the apse of St.

* This rustic Spaniard seems to have controlled his feelings better than the ambassador of Constantine VII *Porphyrogenetos*, who was so completely overwhelmed by the splendor surrounding Sultan Abderrahman III that, according to the same author, "he dropped to the floor unconscious" in the middle of the reception ceremonies. See Pedro de Madrazo, *Córdoba* (Barcelona, 1884), 527 ff.

Climent de Tahull (Figs. 29, 31, 32). In this astonishing masterwork the Spanish version of the Byzantine style has fully evolved from the less end-conscious and somewhat vague Byzantinism of certain earlier murals—those in St. Eulalia de Estahon and in the church of Esterri de Cardos (Fig. 30), for example. While these are impressive manifestations of the mystery-loving and awe-stricken medieval mind, they are still reminiscent

—the last-named eleventh-century frescoes especially—of that "international" Byzantine manner which was more or less the same in Europe as in the Orient. But the austere grandeur effected in St. Climent by means of a concise and keen manner of abstract expression is to be found nowhere except in the Spain of the early twelfth century.*

To begin with, let us consider only the decorative qualities of the composition (Fig. 31). Strictly divided into separate areas, the whole apse yields an impression of tectonic clearness, an articulateness that is absent in the earlier wall paintings. The semidome as a whole is set off from the semicylinder of the apse in a more determined manner. The inscribed transversal band and the frieze into which the four disks with the Evangelical

Fig. 31.—The Apse of St. Climent de Ta-hull, Barcelona, Museum of Catalan Art

symbols coalesce produce for the first time in Catalan art a horizontal strong enough to counterbalance the vertical masses above and below it. Articulation by means of interlocking contrasts is the decorative principle

* Although the problem of dating the Catalan murals cannot be unraveled here, the author must state where he stands at least with regard to the examples from which he has endeavored to trace the stylistic evolution of the Romanesque style in Catalonia.

The chronological order of succession of the Catalan frescoes pivots on the date of

underlying the Spanish Byzantine style in its mature phase. The opposition of the white halos and arches to the darker tones of the background sounds the keynote.

The scheme of coloration reveals the same feeling for impressive contrasts. In *The Last Coming of Christ,* from the apse of Esterri de Cardos, the Pantokrator and his angels were set off from the conventional three transversal background stripes (blue at the top, gray in the middle, and yellow at the bottom) much less sharply than in St. Climent, where the

those in the Bohi valley, more particularly on that of the apse decoration of St. Climent de Tahull. This church was consecrated by the bishop of Barbastro on December 10, 1123, as stated on an elaborate polychrome inscription upon one of the columns of the church (now in the Museum of Barcelona). In spite of this most valuable document, and on no other ground than "the high stylistic perfection" of the frescoes, Dr. Gertrud Richert (*Mittelalterliche Malerei in Spanien,* Berlin, 1925) contends that they cannot have been executed before the end of the twelfth century. But the fact that the commemorative inscription was *painted,* and that its colors as well as its lettering coincide with those used in the murals, suggests that the inscription was synchronous with the murals and that these, therefore, were actually completed in 1123. I agree with Chandler R. Post (*A History of Spanish Painting,* Cambridge, Massachusetts, 1930, I, 91), that "the laws of probability favor a dating of the frescoes in 1123 until exclusive proof is forthcoming to the contrary." And there seems to be very little likelihood that such proof will be forthcoming. The style of Catalan painting about 1150 and thereafter invalidates the later date suggested by Dr. Richert. Moreover, what little can be discovered concerning the probable period of the other Romanesque frescoes of Catalonia corroborates rather than contradicts the validity of the earlier date.

The style of the murals in the Bohi valley evolved from the more primitive style of the frescoes in St. Eulalia de Estahón and Ginestarre as well as Esterri de Cardós. "The latter should be dated, if anything, somewhat earlier than the cycles of Bohi" (Post, *op. cit.,* I, 111). Stylistic evidence even points to the probability that the frescoes in the apse of St. Eulalia de Estahón were among the earliest manifestations of the Romanesque style in Catalonia. In agreement with J. Folch y Torres (*Museo de la Ciudadela, Catálogo de la sección de arte románico,* Barcelona, 1926, 96 f.), who attributes them to the period when the church first appears in records, I am inclined to date them around 1062-1100. It is pertinent that here the Apocalyptic *Last Coming of Christ* is still rendered entirely in the Byzantine fashion and more exhaustively so than in any other Catalan church of the period, proving that the painter, unlike his successors, was not yet concerned either with stricter selection of what seems significant to the Western feeling, or with the reduction of the imported compositional pattern to one simpler and more highly stylized. The iconography of the Baptism was subjected to a certain simplification, but the subject as such was not yet completely eliminated from the assemblage of the Saints. Such an attitude reveals that the style was still in the making. For this there is further evidence. The painter did not take umbrage at the presence of the two

Lord, clad in a pike-gray tunic and a cloak of emerald green and ensconced in the black-edged *mandorla,* contrasts with three stripes of deep sapphire (top), warm ochre (middle), and bright azure (bottom). Moreover, the interlace of bright bands expanding over the darker ground lends to the whole an effect of close-knit unity and well-marked rhythm, making this painting of 1123 once more stand out as "classic" from the less articulate "archaic" ones of the preceding phase.

This more clear-cut pattern of decoration is in keeping with the apparent desire for a depiction of characters keener and more spirited than those with which the earlier painters had been satisfied. The Pantokrator in the semidome of Esterri (Fig. 30) seems morose by comparison. His face and frame are delineated in lifeless, unanimated outlines. In the conch of St. Climent, he appears as a wide-awake and capable judge, for the lines that define his face and drapery have precision and dynamic vitality (Figs. 29, 32). Of course, the ornamental line work upon which this non-naturalistic style of design depended as its logical vehicle of expression is free of any obligation to the actual human forms. This is seen to best advantage in the black lines from which little triangular knobs project at various points as they describe the eyebrows and sockets, the nose, the

windows which pierce the apse asymmetrically on only one side. He placed his pictures where there happened to be room for them—an all too well-known characteristic of all "immature" phases in the history of styles. The whole composition is wanting in stylistic consciousness. The figures of the Saints still convey a certain feeling of naturalistic actuality, yet lack that consummate stylization in the abstract which distinguishes the Romanesque manner in its more developed phase. Apart from the Latin robes worn by the Saints, the only non-Byzantine feature to be found in St. Eulalia is the representation of certain objects of local significance—for instance, the luminous cup of the Holy Grail in the hand of the Virgin Mary. The superimposition of local attributes upon imported figures without a refashioning of the whole picture pattern is likewise a typical sign of the inception of a style, not of its maturity.

Since, among other things, the drapery worn by the Pantokrator in St. Eulalia is practically identical with that of the Pantokrator in Esterri de Cardós (Fig. 30), the two frescoes must be approximately contemporaneous. Still there are, in Esterri, signs of a stricter selection from the current Byzantine iconography and a more pronounced sense of symmetry and tectonic order. Therefore I am inclined to date the Esterri murals a little, though certainly not much, later than those of St. Eulalia. Both antedate the frescoes of St. Climent. Esterri was under the administration of the bishop of Urgel between 1095 and 1122. Tentatively, the church and its decoration may be dated within that period.

Fig. 32.—*Pantokrator*. Detail of the mural from St. Climent de Tahull.
Barcelona, Museum of Catalan Art

lips, the curls, and the beard. Even the shadows depicting the angular structure of the facial surfaces resolve into linear patterns of great beauty. It seems to have been the artist's ultimate intention to redeem all the color surfaces from the clumsy deadliness of the preceding manner by breaking them up into separate linear ornaments (Fig. 32). The result of such efforts was an expression of vitality which is sensed even through the abstract medium of this art. Stoically indifferent though this Judge is toward man, this vitalist among the early Catalonian anonymi has ideated Him as a highly dynamic person. The Lord seems to raise his right arm and hand in the act of benediction under the spell of a sudden impulse. His garment-folds seem electric, and the rays emitted by the symbolical letters alpha and omega suggest smoke spirals wafted from an altar.

A glance at the Saints in the lower region of the apse shows that the dynamic conception prevails throughout. The Disciples are as different from the Saints of Esterri de Cardos as energy is from apathy. How energetically St. John the Evangelist extends his left hand! How proudly St. James carries his head on a neck that springs from swelling shoulders!

The panel paintings and stucco reliefs of the twelfth century reveal a similar stylistic development. They are limited to frontals; that is, panels by which the altar table was screened from the floor to its top, both in front and laterally. It should be remembered that in the early Christian churches, until about the middle of the twelfth century, no reredos was allowed to stand upon the altar because the priest, officiating behind it, confronted the congregation from there. The retable* rising from the top was not used until, with a radical alteration of liturgical custom, the priest assumed his place in front of the altar.

Although frontals were in use everywhere in medieval Christendom, comparatively few have survived outside of Spain. In the late twelfth and thirteenth centuries, when they were superseded by retables, they were either remodeled for use as altar screens or dismembered because of their intrinsic value; jewels and gems were sold and gold and silver was turned over to the mint unless some special historical significance warranted their preservation.† In Spain, however, a larger number of frontals have been

---

* The word is a derivation from *retro tabula*, a panel standing in back of the altar.
† Among the few precious antependia that have escaped destruction are the silver-

preserved than elsewhere, because of the fact that they had no intrinsic value. Catalan frontals were inexpensive substitutes for metal or enamel work, roughly carpentered of wood coated with gypsum, canvas, or parchment, and painted in imitation either of *champlévé* enamel or executed in stucco relief in imitation of metal work, perhaps in obeisance to the Arabic tradition.

The iconography and the composition of both the wall paintings and the frontals were at first borrowed from foreign sources. But it is remarkable that the paintings of the apse were generally duplicated on a reduced scale on the painted frontals. The Pantokrator, ensconced by the *mandorla* with the Evangelical symbols in the four corners, and assisted by the Disciples or other Saints, recurs in identical form upon the frontals. The artistic unity of a Byzantine Catalan choir, including the apse and the altar, was effected by applying the same principle which we discovered to be at the root of early Spanish music and literature, and which eventually controlled the system of order in the Romanesque and Gothic retables: the Spanish "variational form."

A number of painted frontals in the museums of Barcelona and Vich represent the further development of Catalan art. We cannot stop to consider all of them, but even a few will suffice to indicate the trend. Two rather similar frontals from Seo d'Urgel prove that the Catalonian peculiarities of the Byzantine style were not confined to the murals. The frontal with the Disciples grouped around the central Pantokrator in four separate compartments might be by the same hand that produced the Saints in the lower zone of the apse of St. Miguel de la Seo, the original cathedral of Urgel. This identity of manner establishes the date of the frontals as the second or third decade of the twelfth century.*

and-gold reliefs made by Master Vuolvinus, in 835 A.D., for the altar of St. Ambrogio in Milan; the *Pala d'Oro* of St. Mark's in Venice, a magnificent series of sacred images in *émail cloisonnée* framed in jewel-studded gold, ordered from Constantinople in 976 by the Doge Pietro Orseolo; and the gold-embossed frontal made in Ratisbon between 1000 and 1024 for the Emperor Henry II, who presented it to the minster in Basel (now in the Cluny Museum in Paris).

* The murals cannot be of later date because the masonry of the apse is of the late eleventh century. I disagree with the contention of Chandler Post (*op. cit.,* I, 222) that "the special similarity that J. Folch y Torres endeavors to trace in the draperies does not hold."

At about that time the first *narrative* frontals began to appear in Catalonia. The earliest known example, the St. Martin antependium in the museum at Vich, reminds one of the Romanesque art of France. A later example of about 1150 representing *The Passion of St. Yolita,* from her hermitage in the parish of Durro (Barcelona Museum, Fig. 33), reveals another, more recent, source of influence, the art of the British Isles. Four oblong pictures which, according to the Apocryphal Acts, relate how the Saint was successively sawed, blinded, boiled, and decapitated, are grouped around her effigy in the center. Holding her son, St. Quiricus,

Fig. 33.—Frontal of St. Yolita, from Durro. Barcelona,
Museum of Catalan Art

on her lap, St. Yolita is enthroned within a *mandorla* after the fashion of the Byzantine *Madonna with the Infant Jesus* in the semidome of the apse of St. Maria de Tahull.

But the four lateral panels represent a striking reversion from the monumental Byzantine tradition, as well as from the French Romanesque design, to an infantile kind of "expressionism" reminiscent, I believe, of certain typical Anglo-Saxon illuminations of that period. Nobody seems to have noticed the similarity between the style of the Yolita frontal and that of the miniatures produced in the scriptorium of Bury St. Edmunds during the fifth decade of the twelfth century. The thirty-two illuminated pages of the *Passio Sancti Edmundi* (New York, J. P. Morgan Library) made for Abbot Anselm, who died in 1148, reveal an undeniable stylistic parallelism. Here one encounters the same puppet-like figures disporting their attenuated bodies with a similar jerkiness, and usually exhibiting their profiles; the same peculiar design of the draperies, particularly the empty areas bordered and crisscrossed by a few stiff and unexplanatory hatchings. Whether the "expressionistic" manner came to Catalonia directly from England or was transmitted through the Burgundian cathedral sculpture of Autun and Vezelay still remains to be decided. The conspicuous differences between the frontal and the book illuminations might have resulted from the fact that the illuminators of Bury St. Edmunds were skilled masters, whereas the maker of the Yolita frontal was a rustic craftsman who probably found it difficult to comprehend the aims of the British designers.

This frontal is significant for two reasons. First, it is the earliest evidence of an opposition to the ruling Byzantine style (which does not mean that the Byzantine influence ceased; quite the contrary, it continued in other Catalan art works for nearly another century). Second, the Yolita frontal is the first example of a practice that became almost the rule for four centuries to come; namely, that Spanish art, being too weak to create new styles of its own, resorted to an imitation, full of miscomprehensions, of whatever happened to be most fashionable in the art of other European countries.

If the Catalan painters had permitted their Byzantine tradition to unfold organically as a flower does from its root, instead of experimenting time and again with novelties from England, Germany, France, and Italy, Spanish varieties of the Romanesque and Gothic styles might have ensued which would have become quite as expressive of the national character as was the Spanish variety of the Byzantine style in the early twelfth century. But the indiscriminate surrender to alien fashions prevented such a development.

Two other frontals, of the early thirteenth century, in the museum of Barcelona, demonstrate the germination of the Romanesque style in Catalonia at a time when France had already created the Gothic style and Germany was entering the latest phase of the Romanesque. These are the

frontal from Vila de Encamp, of which all three sides are extant, and the
frontal from Feneras (Fig. 34), the lateral panels of which have perished.
The former has all the characteristics of the dying Byzantine manner; the
latter leaves no doubt that its author was acquainted with the Late
Romanesque, obviously its German variety. The coincidence of a waning
and a budding style is especially evident in this instance because the two
frontals apparently originated in the same workshop, and probably at

Fig. 34.—Frontal from Feneras. Barcelona, Museum of
Catalan Art

about the same time. The subjects are identical. In each the Pantokrator,
enthroned within the *mandorla* and surrounded by the four Evangelical
signs, occupies the center and the Apostles the sides, except that the Encamp master ranged only eight Disciples in the four fields on the front
(three more, double the size of those in front, being added on one of the
lateral panels), whereas the Feneras master placed all twelve in the sections
to the right and the left of the Pantokrator, each standing under an arcade
of Late Romanesque design. The similarities of the two frontals extend to
such details as the coloration of brick-red, green, blue, and yellow; the
composition of the Pantokrator, including his drapery and the pattern of
the cushion under his feet; and the decorative *rinceau* of the moldings
on the sides of the Encamp altar and on the front of the Feneras altar.

But there are significant differences, as well as common features, and these can best be explained on the theory that the maker of the Encamp frontal was an older man pledged to the conventions in which he had been reared, whereas the Feneras master, very likely his pupil, was an impetuous youth animated by the revolutionary spirit of the rising generation.

With a little study it may be discerned that the Feneras master was endeavoring to disentangle himself, so far as his convention-bound period permitted, from the Byzantinisms of his teacher. Unprecedented stress is placed upon the delineation of the heads of the Disciples. These have about them a feeling of portraiture; the mouths, noses, and eyes have a more penetrating expression of vitality and animation than the conventionalized facial forms of the Encamp master. It is no joyful vitality, to be sure, but a weary expression which betrays the psychical pressure that burdened mankind at the outset of the twelfth century.

Nonetheless, the tongue of nature has been unloosed. No one would feel inclined to call the Disciples of the Encamp altar fanatical confessors as one must the Disciples of the Feneras frontal. Those of the Encamp frontal resemble the saints of the Byzantine murals; each is an anonymous effigy. The Disciples of the Feneras master, on the other hand, are individualized characters. Each participates in the spiritual conversation which is in progress and is the real theme of the frontal. And it is no dramatic dialogue. Rather it is a learned disputation, the kind of didactic dialogue which had just been introduced in the monastic schools as the only proper method by which to ferret out the truth: *Disputatio est rationis inductio ad aliquid propagandum vel contradicendum* (The disputation is the application of reason to the proving or disproving of anything). In the upper zone, one on each side, two Disciples turn to each other: St. Andrew questions St. Philip, who responds by pointing from his distant arcade to the Pantokrator in the center. On the opposite side St. Matthew challenges St. James. The two cardinal Apostles, occupying their traditional place of honor on either side of the Lord, carry on their dispute across the throne of the Judge, St. Paul querying from the right, St. Peter lifting his left hand in reply.

If the relationship between the two frontals is properly understood, the Feneras master emerges as an artist filled with an ardent desire for a new spiritual truth, a desire common to the rising generations of the early thirteenth century, but one that could not be satisfied until the individuals had wrested themselves free of the manacles of the Byzantine conventions. In this respect the Spanish frontal joins hands with that contemporaneous German work of sculpture from which, I believe, the Catalan painter received his inspiration, however indirectly: the Late Romanesque choir screens of St. George's Chapel in the cathedral of Bamberg (1225–35), a work of more pretentious dimensions and of far greater artistic

Fig. 35.—Frontal of the Virgin, from Avia. Barcelona,
Museum of Catalan Art

importance. The similarities are not confined to those features peculiar to the period style: the arcades with foliate capitals and leaf bases and the calligraphic undulations of the draperies, particularly at the seams. The fundamental similarities extend to the spirit, to the craving for personal freedom, for realism; in short, for delivery from the obsolete world view of Byzantium. The master of the Bamberg screens made the disputation between strong personalities the central motif of his twelve groups of Apostles and Prophets. His theme also was a fanatical avowal of faith, the expression of which burst forth from heroic, expressive faces. The Feneras frontal might well have become a significant signpost in the history of Catalan art. If it failed to leave any traces, it was probably for the reason that creative geniuses are ever rare on earth.

Yet another influence, known as "Italo-Byzantine," appeared in the mid-thirteenth century, exemplified by the beautiful frontal from Avia depict-

ing the Madonna enthroned and episodes of her life (about 1250, Barcelona, Museum of Catalan Art, Fig. 35). A new architectural order was
established by the finely trilobed Early Gothic arch in the central section,
under which Our Lady with the Child is silhouetted against what was
once a limpid golden surface; today, with the gold peeled off, the white
gypsum ground produces a background too glaring in effect. The monumental composition also reminds one of certain pictures on the stained-
glass windows of French churches of the period, such as Notre Dame de la
Belle Verrière in the cathedral of Chartres, though it is more likely that the
models were culled from less monumental examples—probably from illuminated manuscripts of the early thirteenth century. In a number of these
are groups reminiscent of this very *Annunciation* and *Visitation,* enlivened by the same affectionate gestures and undulating draperies.

The influence of Latin lucidity is felt equally in the design and in the
narration. On the lateral paintings the characters are linked with one
another in a more intimate fashion than are the characters of the Feneras
frontal. Even where two or more figures occupy the stage in the earlier
Byzantine narrative pictures, each gives the impression of speaking his
lines without regard for the other. The actors never unite in a duo or trio,
either spiritually or optically, as do the Virgin and the Angel in the
Annunciation of the Avia frontal, or Mary and Elizabeth in the *Visitation,*
by virtue of their corresponding lines and gestures.

Moreover, by the middle of the thirteenth century the entire spirit of
Catalan art was utterly different from that which had ruled the Byzantine
art of the early twelfth. The rigid, superhuman formalism of the Byzantine style was superseded by a spirit of humanity when the gentle Mother
of the Avia frontal superseded the stern, unapproachable majesty of the
Madonna in the apse mural of St. Maria of Tahull and a new voice appeal-
ing to the human emotions of every Christian presaged the still more
intensely human spirit of the religious art of the fourteenth and fifteenth
centuries.

THE TRECENTO For the next three centuries art in Spain continued to
resemble a colonial art. Exposed to the erratic changes of fashion that

were blown in from abroad with every shifting wind, it could not evolve steadily toward a sharply defined ultimate goal. In the meandering course, moreover, the artists relied more upon the exploitation of foreign manners than upon their own creative talents: The twelfth and thirteenth centuries were ruled by the Byzantine, French, English, German, and Italo-Byzantine traditions; those of the fourteenth by the Florentine and Sienese; those of the fifteenth by the Flemish schools; those of the sixteenth by the Italian Renaissance. Thus it was only natural that the development lacked those normal, logical transitions that took place in the other European countries, above all in Italy.

In Florence the pre-Renaissance style of Giotto evolved almost imperceptibly from that of his master Cimabue, even as Cimabue's *maniera nuova* departed gradually and organically from the *maniera greca* of his Byzantine forerunners. No better evidence that this evolution was gradual can be given than the uncertainty of modern critics as to exactly when the new Italian art began, and to which of the two masters its birth should be credited. In Spain the advent of the *manera nueva* invaded the medievalism of the ducento like a thunderbolt from a clear sky. A chasm separates Ferrer Bassa from all his predecessors.

Nevertheless the revolution was not led by a single individual. It was brought about by an underlying change of sentiment after 1300, which was felt in Spain no less than in the other European countries. The artistic change is only the more striking in Spain, where her conservative Church was dictator in all artistic matters.

The change of sentiment was marked by a more earthly conception of the Divine. Christ and the Madonna, supernatural and exalted godheads in the past, were now humanized. The Byzantine *Theotokos* (the God-Bearer) gave way either to the tearful Mother of Sorrows—*La Virgen de las Angústias*—or to the humble young woman nursing her babe—*La Virgen de la Leche*. Similarly, the impassive majesty of the Pantokrator was superseded either by the Man of Sorrows or by the Son of Man dying on the cross—a subject wholly unknown in earlier Spanish art but common in most of the altars of the late fourteenth and fifteenth centuries. The saints, formerly no less deified, were now represented as ordinary men and women, distinguished from other mortals only by the attributes of their martyrdom.

The changes in form which attended the change of sentiment were precipitated by the universal shift from the Romanesque to the Gothic style of building. An example is the cessation—better, the recession—of mural painting in favor of panel painting and stained-glass work. Gothic edifices, such as the cathedral of Barcelona, begun in 1298, having far less wall space than windows, did not encourage mural painting but called for pictures made of colored glass. The numerous chapels, on the other hand, so prevalent in the Gothic edifices of Spain, invited the erection of those expansive retables decorated with paintings and carvings which played the most important role in the Spanish ecclesiastical art after the beginning of the fourteenth century. Within a short time they assumed enormous proportions. Pedro Serra's retable of *The Pentecost* in Manresa, for instance, completed in 1394, is composed of a large central panel representing *The Descent of the Holy Ghost on the Virgin Mary and the Apostles,* thirteen smaller panels representing the Divine Plan of Human Salvation from *The Creation of the Universe* down to *The Pentecostal Sermon of St. Peter,* and numerous effigies of saints and angels on the frame and its pinnacles (the predella is a fifteenth-century addition).

The style of the fourteenth century came from Italy, through uncertain channels, and was disseminated, chiefly from Barcelona and Valencia, throughout the country. Italian artists visiting Spain may have helped to propagate the novel doctrines, and Spaniards in turn may have gone to Italy for study. Eventually Avignon became an intermediary. A colony of painters from Siena gathered at the papal residence, particularly under Clement VI. Here Simone Martini spent the last years of his life, from 1339 to 1344. Before that time Ferrer Bassa of Barcelona (about 1285–1348) must have studied in Padua, Florence, and Siena.

According to the archival records, this first identifiable personality in the history of Spanish trecento painting who reveals an acquaintance with Italian art had some of the same traits of temper and character as the latest exponent of Spanish art, Francisco Goya. In a sense Ferrer Bassa and Goya may be called the two cornerstones of the more recent art of Spain.

If extant records may be trusted, the life of Master Ferrer was a tempest of uncontrolled passions. In 1315 he was sentenced to death for three cases of criminal assault, and only five years later he was exiled for some other grave crime. In each instance he was pardoned by James II of Aragon, who revered Ferrer Bassa as the greatest painter of his day.

Nothing has been preserved either of the numerous altars that Bassa painted or of his illuminations for a Book of Hours and another entitled *Usatges de Barcelona y costums de Catalunya* (Usages and Customs of Barcelona). Those of his works which survive are a series of murals painted shortly before his death in the chapel of St. Michael adjoining the cloisters in the convent at Pedralbes, a suburb of Barcelona: seven episodes from the Lord's Passion, eight from the life of the Virgin, and twelve effigies of saints. These unusually well-preserved wall painting of 1345–46 are the earliest existing examples of the style of Giotto in Spain.

Besides Giotto's Florentine manner they betray also the influence of the Sienese painters Duccio di Buoninsegna and Simone Martini. Yet Bassa's art is basically more Giottesque than Sienese. It is true that *The Virgin with Angels* (Fig. 36) resembles Duccio's and Simone's *Majestas* pictures (in the cathedral and the Palazzo Publico of Siena) and that *The Annunciation*—with the Angel flying in and the Virgin reeling back as though frightened by the unexpected visitor—resembles Duccio's temperamental interpretation (London, National Gallery) more than Giotto's statuesque restraint (Padua, Scrovegni Chapel). On the other hand, Bassa followed Giotto's bulky style. He liked ponderous, solid, and angular forms emerging from an unexplained dark. He preferred the inherent strength in simple, straight outlines to the winsome Gothic undulations of the Sienese, who made the cantilena of a silhouette rise from a background of polished gold.

As an artist, it must be admitted, Ferrer Bassa did not rank on an absolute par with any of his distinguished models abroad. He lacked the creative genius of Giotto, the draughtsmanship of Duccio, and the color imagination of Martini. Viewed in the light of coeval European accomplishments, Bassa was merely a satellite reflecting the bright rays of foreign suns. Occasionally, however, his mystic emotional fervor makes one forget his technical shortcomings.

Giotto's art taught Bassa much, above all the value of economy in monumental painting, the value of restraint. He accepted neither the

complicated poses of Duccio's or Martini's figures nor their lavishly undulating draperies. A figure posed and robed in the fashion of the angel
on the edge of the empty sepulcher in Duccio's picture of *The Three
Marys* (altarpiece of the cathedral of Siena) occurs in no painting of
Ferrer. He preferred the planimetric simplicity of Giotto. In the mural of
The Three Marys (Pedralbes) the angel's garment is thrown into puckered
folds only where the heavy material touches the ground—distinctly reminiscent of the drapery of Giotto's kneeling Magdalen in the *Noli me
tangere* at Padua.

The strength of Ferrer Bassa's art lies in his conscious economy. He
selects the indispensable at the expense of the detail. *The Entombment*
(Pedralbes*) probably derives from a small diptych of Simone Martini,
painted in Avignon and now scattered all over Europe (the shutter with
The Entombment is in Berlin; another is in the Louvre; the remaining
four are in the Antwerp Museum). The Pedralbes picture translates the
exuberant Sienese presentation into a speech more raucous, but also more
concise. The model and its imitation compare as the guttural Spanish
compares with the sonorous Italian. Where Simone employed a chorus of
two dozen lamenters, Bassa was content with eight. But he knew how to
build a clear triangle out of three heads on the left, and to join the five
figures on the right into a mass of parallel diagonals. The lamenters are
swept by the intensity of their emotion, like a forest by a gale.

Bassa's art, like Giotto's, was essentially an art of figures. He ignored
the elaborate landscapes of the Sienese. His stage settings are scanty. From
the world around him he gleaned only what he required to articulate the
dark background and to clarify its recession. He paid astonishingly little
attention to ornament. His faces are drawn without the slightest regard
for an attractive flow of lines, but with the strongest emphasis on the cubic
structure of the head. In the three-quarter profiles, which he preferred to
any other view, the noses protrude heavily. They are modeled by sharp
contrasts of light and shade and designed as though hewn from stone. The
recessional effect that such a nose lends to the head as a whole is remarkably strong, and the illusion of tridimensional space produced by the
succession of three such heads into depth—note the kneelers in *The Ascen-*

* Gertrud Richert, *Mittelalterliche Malerei in Spanien* (Berlin, 1925), Plate 29.

Fig. 36.—Ferrer Bassa: *The Virgin with Angels,* Convent of Pedralbes

Fig. 37.—Pedro Serra: *The Pentecost,* Barcelona, Santa Ana

sion*—must have been a startling revelation to the Spaniards who were accustomed to a more ornamental display.

The trend inaugurated by Ferrer Bassa did not outlive the middle of the fourteenth century. Its forcefulness, reflecting something of the violent character of this unusual man, was superseded by the more elegant, conservative manner of the school of Siena and the so-called "international style." It is significant that Spain, whenever she had to choose between progressive and conservative influences, in the end always decided on the latter.

The artistic trend of the latter half of the fourteenth century is most clearly represented by the school of the three brothers Serra of Barcelona. Only two of them are known by their work: Jaime Serra (active 1361–95) and his younger and more advanced brother Pedro (active until 1400). The stylistic differences between Simone Martini's *Annunciation* of 1333 (Uffizi) and Giotto's mural of the same subject (Padua, Scrovegni Chapel)

* *Ibid.,* Plate 31.

distinguished Bassa's *Virgin with Angels* of 1345 at Pedralbes (Fig. 36) from Pedro Serra's *Pentecost* of about 1390–95 (Barcelona, St. Ana, Fig. 37). Bassa's composition did not record what is pretty or pleasing to the eye; it was concerned with forceful modeling rather than with graceful decoration. Emerging from the dark and fashioned out of ponderous, square-cut, bulky masses, its form reminds one of a solid wall of ashlars. Pedro Serra's picture, however, glitters like a flowerbed in the sunshine. Its mood is sweet and mystic, its forms ethereal. In other words, the whole

is a reincarnation of the spirit of the school of Siena—a delightful interlace of undulating curves springs from the golden ground, a triumph of graceful design, a melodious song in praise of an enchanting damsel.

Emulating as it does this conservative, pleasing manner, Jaime Serra's *Resurrection* (Fig. 38, from the Alpartil altar of 1367 in the museum of Saragossa) strikes one as really less "progressive" than, for instance, Ferrer Bassa's *Ascension* of 1345, in Pedralbes. The stiff, frontalized figure of the Lord and the scalloped, ornamental clouds with angels, timidly drawn in front of the golden ground, lack the volume of Ferrer's art. C. R. Post remarks that while Jaime Serra draws better than

Fig. 38.—Jaime Serra: *The Resurrection*, Saragossa Museum

Ferrer Bassa, his forms are nevertheless less well realized in three dimensions.*

Still the Serras must be given credit for certain new and promising contributions to Catalan painting. Novel ideas inspired their narratives with a cheerful worldliness. The stout face of the donor Friar Martin de Alpartil, who ordered the retable for his own tomb, shines like a full March moon from *The Resurrection* and *The Last Judgment*. In the

* C. R. Post, *op. cit.*, II, 222.

Limbo picture of the same altar* the little horned devils that corner the doomed and watch the exit of the saved souls from the mouth of Hell add a touch of eerie humor that was completely absent in the earlier art.

Never before had Spanish painting included so many entertaining anecdotal details. This is surprising in the light of the Byzantine artists' fondness for them. In *The Nativity* from the same altar† the scanty setting with which Bassa was satisfied when he painted *The Adoration of the Magi* (Pedralbes) appears amplified. Even the star shining from within the gable of the elaborate shed has been given a human face. The dramatis personae are augmented. Another woman kneels behind the adoring Mother. It is Salome, one of Mary's midwives, atoning for her sin of skepticism by serving as a nurse to the Child. The Byzantine iconography occasionally included, in the story of the Nativity, the episode from the Apocryphal Gospels describing the withering of Salome's hand as punishment for her skepticism of Mary's virginity. In the more ancient art, however, this reminder of virgin birth was not allowed to vie with the main character; in Serra's painting the minor character has usurped a leading role.

Thus the Serras, by this direct genre approach, laid the foundations for a more flexible and expansive narrative style, which may be illustrated by the retable of St. Stephen, painted for a church at Gualter, near La Seo (now in the Plandiura Collection at Barcelona). The panels representing the protomartyr's ordination, disputation, stoning, and burial are early forerunners of the famous altar of St. Stephen by Juan de Juanes, in the Prado, which in a later chapter will be discussed as an example of Spanish sixteenth-century art.

One wonders why similar fictional amplifications did not appear in Spanish painting, as they did in early Spanish literature, before the second half of the fourteenth century. The *General Estoria* of Alphonse the Wise, written at the close of the thirteenth century and drawn largely from Arabian sources, illustrates how the Oriental imagination was given free play, for instance, in the histories of the Old Testament. In the story of Joseph, King Alphonse gives to the wife of Potiphar the name of Zulaime

* Gertrud Richert, *op. cit.*, Plate 32b.
† *Ibid.*, Plate 32a.

and introduces a number of her friends to make it more entertaining. In his version of Judith the heroine has for her partner not only Holofernes but also his master of ceremonies, the eunuch Vagoo. The description of the beheading of the Assyrian general abounds in imaginative details which supplement the scriptural account. The reader learns that Judith hit Holofernes twice before she succeeded in severing the head from the body, and that she tore down the canopy from over the bed and wrapped the dead man's body in it. Why such embroidery should for so long have been confined to literature is difficult to explain, except on the theory that nothing new was admitted to Spanish medieval painting until it had been internationally accepted and sanctified.

The Catalan painters may have received their inspiration for the popular anecdotal amplifications from the numerous international ateliers that sprang up after Avignon in Italy, France, and Bohemia. If so, it is all the more noteworthy that the genre conception was soon colored by regional features—the direct portrayal of Spanish life, including local costumes and settings—and enriched by a more carefully thought-out action. All of this made the religious paintings more complete, more natural, and warmer than they had been in the past. A wider range of imagination than was apparent in his early altar for Fray Martin Alpartil is evident in Jaime Serra's late work, the retable from Sijena in the Barcelona Museum. Here the sepulcher of the Resurrection is laid within a walled courtyard in the corners of which trees are growing. Christ climbs from his grave with shaking, emaciated limbs, and the Virgin Mary kneels at His side in prayer (though, according to the Scriptures, she did not witness the Resurrection). At the Last Supper the Apostles are Spaniards, and the table is set with Spanish earthenware on a Spanish homespun cloth. The stage business of certain minor actors is quaintly elaborated, probably on the inspiration of the *autos sacramentales*. One of the doctors in the temple is so enraged by the precocious wisdom of the young Jesus that he tears his books to shreds.

With the immediate followers of the Serras the picturesque genre narrative became even more expansive. On a retable by the elder Jaime Ferrer, in the museum at Solsona, *The Last Supper* is enlivened by a cat romping with a dog over the crumbs that have fallen under the table. On his retable in Manresa, Jaime Cabrera spins out the legends of St. Nicolas as if he were illustrating a folk ballad. From *The Destruction of Diana's Tree* we learn how Catalan lumberjacks felled trees in 1404. Every person, of course, wears the dress of the period. In *The Miracle of St. Nicolas* the butcher making sausage of the three youths who have begged for shelter goes about his awful job wearing the cap and apron of his trade. What with the butcher's wife standing in the doorway, with a lamp that casts eerie glints across the coffered ceiling, that whole nocturnal scene may have reminded the good Manresans of some sinister local crime. The idyllic and mirthful note was perhaps less relished in the depiction of the Christian legends. Still the simple folk may have chuckled over a St. Joseph who stirs the Christ Child's porridge with a wooden spoon that his inexperienced hand holds upside down (*Nativity* on Gerardo Gener's retable of Saints Isabel and Bartholomew, of 1401), or over an infant Jesus whom an angel is teaching to use his little legs by the aid of a "walker" on three wheels (on the retable of the Virgin Mary; likewise in the Catalan Museum, painted somewhat later by an unknown artist*).

In many respects the advance over the Serras was naïve and timid. But from such an intimate observation of the world there ultimately sprang that coherent and brilliant pictorial narrative style which is the chief feature of the Spanish quattrocento.

THE QUATTROCENTO In Spain the evolution of the quattrocento art from that of the trecento was marked by no such decided break as in Italy. How magnificent was the advent of Masaccio's art in Florence! After his murals in the Brancacci Chapel the reign of the trecento was definitely over. His rise brought more than a few novel expressions to Florentine art; it brought an entirely new pictorial grammar and syntax as well. But in Spain an artistic sentiment and a pictorial style comparable to those of the Italian Renaissance made their appearance only very reluctantly. Here no new art sprang full-born and in full panoply, like Minerva from Jove's head.

* J. Gudiol, F. Soldevilla, and C. Zervos, *Die Kunst Kataloniens* (Vienna, 1937), CLXXVIII, CLXXIX.

In fact, no one naturalistic school stood out in Catalonia as it did in
Florence. The leading studios, if they can be compared with any Florentine studios at all, resembled the old-fashioned ones of Lorenzo Monaco
and Gentile da Fabriano more than the studios of the "modernists,"
Masaccio, Uccello, and Castagno. Throughout the century the gilt background continued to be used; plain at first, it was eventually diapered and
lavishly ornamented with multiplied Gothic patterns of gilded stucco.
Now and then some one dared to voice his disapproval—Lluis Dalmau,
for instance, who represented *The Virgin with the Councillors* (Fig. 42)
in a Gothic interior, thus violating his contract, which called for a background of gold. But such occasional outbursts did not destroy the age-old
conventionalism. Under Jaime Huguet the gilded background and other
mannerisms which were obsolete in other countries still persisted. Hence
one does not receive the impression that the fifteenth century produced a
marked change in Spain, as it did in Italy. Even so spirited a painting as
Ramon de Mur's retable of *The Creation,* from Giumera, was less a beginning than a consummation of the mystic trend initiated by the Serras.
Moreover, in contrast to the Italian quattrocentists, the primitive Spanish
schools continued to exploit foreign models. It is indeed strange that,
despite the incessant influx of painters and paintings from abroad, the
local artists of Barcelona continued to be, for the most part, technically
inferior to the foreign schools. This is especially true of the weaker imitators of the Serras, such as the Master of Albatarrec and the Master of the
Cardona Pentecost. But in a sense it is equally true of Pedro Serra's more
important successor, Lluis Borrassa (active about 1380–1424).

Spanish painters who really bore comparison with the great early
Flemings and Italians were still rare. Some might have progressed faster
had they thrown off the brakes of conservatism. Lluis Borrassa, whose
work extended into the second decade of the fifteenth century, illustrates
by at least one of his documented paintings the tenacity of certain traditions. His *Retable of the Savior,* which passed from the church at Guardiola into the Soler y March Collection at Barcelona, has for a central panel
the Pantokrator in the archaic frontalized pose, ensconced by the *mandorla*
and the four Evangelical symbols, quite as if it had been planned in the
twelfth century and not, as it actually was, in 1405. True, the surround-

ing narrative panels are more animated by emotional expression than were Jaime and Pedro Serra's pictures. Yet, as a whole, the Guardiola retable was conceived in the spirit of the Serras and their Sienese ancestry.

Moreover, those few masters whose exceptional craftsmanship enabled them to hold their own beside the genius abroad towered like solitary cliffs above the rank and file of their contemporary countrymen. As a result, the modern critics tend to overrate them. At the turn of the last century it was Borrassa who was overrated; at present Bernardo Martorell is in similar danger. Such distorted evaluations are natural in view of the fact that the average Catalan accomplishments were not on the high artistic level of those in Italy. As yet Spain had only scattered provincial schools, and these were not, like the schools of Venice, Emilia, Umbria, and Tuscany, nurtured with novel ideas springing from the competitive spirit which made progress in Italy ubiquitously steady and consistent and lifted even the lesser artists' level of craftsmanship.

Amid the mediocrities of the Barcelona school of the early fifteenth century, Bernardo Martorell tends to stand out as a greater genius than he would amidst the early quattrocentists of Florence or Venice. But the fact remains that he was a finer craftsman than any of his predecessors. Moreover, because he passed through an artistic development conditioned by changing convictions he is a more fascinating object of study than either Ferrer Bassa or the Serra brothers.

Martorell's work has only recently been identified. Not very long ago only his name was known, his great reputation as a book illuminator, panel painter, and designer of stained glass, and the fact that his activity extended from 1427 to 1452. His resurrection would be interesting even if his personal development had not reflected the general development of Catalan art in the first half of the fifteenth century, when the older tradition of the Serra atelier was giving way to the new tradition of Jaime Huguet and Bartolome Bermejo.

Martorell's first mature work betrays the conception of the book illuminator even when his assignment was not the calligraphic decoration of a vellum page, but a retable. Eventually he retained the Gothic calligraphy only when he was illuminating books, and aspired to more monumental forms when he was painting altarpieces and murals. An example of his early manner is the retable of St. George, of which the central panel with *The Dragon Fight* (Fig. 39) has entered the Art Institute of Chicago, and the wings, depicting various episodes of the Saint's martyrdom, the Louvre at Paris. The delicate execution of this retable, which I should date about 1430, points toward the influence of two distinct schools: first, the Burgundian school of illuminators which centered around Paul de Limbourg and the brothers van Eyck; and, second, Pisanello, the Veronese muralist and medalist.*

For the first time in Spanish painting the conventional gold ground is conspicuously absent in the Chicago picture. Instead, the yarn of the narrative is spun out in a most elaborate little

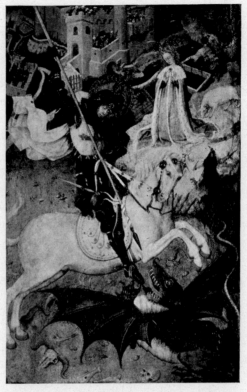

Fig. 39.—Bernardo Martorell: *St. George and the Dragon*. Courtesy of the Art Institute of Chicago

landscape. The parents of the imprisoned princess are watching the fight of the saintly caballero from the carpet-hung balcony of a turreted castle around which sweeps a moat, enlivened by ducks and swans and surrounded by neatly hedged-in vineyards and orchards.

* An illuminated Book of Offices in the Mestres Collection at Barcelona, which has been identified as Martorell's work of 1444, and an illuminated page in the *Commentaries on the Usages of Barcelona* (in the municipal archives of that city), for which Martorell received payment in 1448, leave little doubt that he was acquainted with manuscripts like the Book of Hours of the Duke of Berry. A comparison of the page in the *Commentaries*, showing the scene of the dedication of the book to the councillors

By 1437, when he painted the retable of St. Peter at Pubol (the contract has recently been found by Sanpere*), Martorell had abandoned the involved calligraphy and the dainty elaboration of detail in favor of a style of almost puritanical simplicity. Gothic unrest gave way to poise and solemnity. In the main picture, with *The Consignment of the Keys to St. Peter,* the figures stand very quietly side by side, each draped in the long perpendicular folds of his robe. There are no wavy curls and whimsical headgears. Judging by *The Liberation of St. Peter* and the *Quo Vadis*

of Barcelona, and the page with the Madonna enthroned and the Holy Virgins worshipping the Lamb, attributed to Van Eyck, in *Les très riches heures du Duc de Berry,* discloses striking similarities in regard to the distribution of the pictures over the page, the illuminated initial, the lines of the script, and the ornamental border with its various *drôleries,* birds, and music-making angels.

Inasmuch as Pisanello's influence on Martorell has never been noticed, I must go a little more into detail. It has been pointed out that Martorell may have visited Italy before 1433 (see C. R. Post, *op. cit.,* VII, 755, 826, and Georg Gronau's article in *Rivista d'Arte,* XIV, 385 ff.). Pisanello, on the other hand, worked for several distinguished Spanish patrons. He struck at least three medals of Alfonso V at Naples and one of Don Iñigo d'Avalos. It should be borne in mind that he was famous for his interpretation of the legend of St. George, in the well-known mural in Santa Anastasia at Verona, for instance. This, and his *Miracle of St. Eustach* (London National Gallery), reveal a feature of Pisanello's style that is also characteristic of Martorell's retable of St. George: the integration of the figures with the expansive landscape, an integration that permits the respective paintings to be defined as narratives in terms of open landscapes. The *St. Eustach* was the first picture of its kind in Italy, the *St. George* the first of its kind in Spain. Pisanello's landscape also shares with Martorell's the striking disregard for correct perspective space construction and the attendant lack of an effect of distance. Both artists liked to raise the horizon line to the topmost molding of the frame. Of course Pisanello was himself not free from the influence of the Burgundian school of book illumination. He had, however, from the start that mastery of the larger forms which Martorell acquired only in the course of time. The closest kinship between Pisanello and young Martorell is revealed by their Late Gothic decorative proclivities— the distaste for lines that are quiet or simple: their lines swirl, jerk, or bend into quaint clusters and knots of curlicues. Note, in the Chicago panel, the twitching design of the horse's trappings, its curly mane with three of its locks plaited above the forehead, and the crown of the princess composed of a filigree of lilies (see Gudiol, Soldevilla, Zervos, *op. cit.,* CXC). A similarly imaginative and involved headgear is worn by Pisanello's *Luxuria* on a pen drawing acquired in 1923 for the Albertina Collection of Vienna (Invent. No. 24018). The wavy curls of Martorell's princess, which reflect the same decorative intent, are likewise similar to the hair of St. George on Pisanello's mural in Verona.

* See C. R. Post, *op. cit.,* VII, 908.

episode, which are united on another panel, Martorell turned his back on his whole early manner, as sometimes happens when a sterling artist is carried away by some reform ideal. No longer does he allow the setting to distract the beholder's attention from the narrative of the figures. The stage is stripped except for one indispensable stage property—the keep from which St. Peter is delivered by the angel. The gold ground has come back, but it is employed in a novel manner to clarify the silhouettes of the actors. Only the beautifully drawn contour of one of the angel's wings sounds an echo of Martorell's early calligraphic manner.

About eight years later, when he painted the retable of *The Transfiguration* (now in the Barcelona Museum of Catalan Art), Martorell had entered another phase of his stylistic development. The theme of the retable—which was probably executed in 1445, following the death of the bishop who had ordered it as a memorial—is *The Transfiguration of the Lord* (Matt., xvii), adjoined by four other spiritual "transformations": the transformation of well water into that mystic water which will never let one thirst, in the story of *Jesus and the Woman of Samaria* (John, iv); *The Transformation of Five Loaves and Two Fishes* into food for five thousand men, besides women and children (Matt., xiv); and the transformation of the unclean—the miracles of *Christ Delivering the Possessed of the Legion of Devils and Healing the Woman of the Bloody Issue* (Mark, v).

The style of this altarpiece is best described as a synthesis of Martorell's manner in his early and middle periods: a fusion of the succinct, monumental, but generalized style of the retable of St. Peter with the effusive, but playful, decorative style of the retable of St. George. The predominance of impressive figures and the *desornamentado* design, characteristics of the middle period, were retained; but the puritanical abstention from elaborate landscapes was abandoned. Detailed scenery was again admitted (except in *The Transfiguration* panel, which, with its ornamented gold ground, sets off the supreme mystery from the four other, more earthy, Gospel selections). But the landscapes employed in these were significantly different from the landscape in *St. George and the Dragon*. The difference is well illustrated by *Jesus and the Woman of Samaria* (Fig. 40). The new settings, however specific they are, are less for the entertainment of the eye; their function is to intensify and clarify the story as enacted by

Fig. 40.—Bernardo Martorell: *Jesus and the Woman of Samaria,* Barcelona, Museum of Catalan Art

the figures. Evidently the painter sought the most lucid manner of narration possible. Every brick of the walls, every tile of the roofs, is scrutinized for surface texture and color, as are the flowers growing in the hedges along the roadside, the human figures, and the animals. In addition, the perspective vistas guide the eye instead of distracting it. They lead the beholder securely from event to event into the most remote distance of space. The figures themselves also have a degree of clarity which was lacking in the earlier pictures. This is true of the draperies, which are better rounded by light and shadow, as well as of the bodies proper, which are bulkier and stand more firmly upon their feet, and of the faces and gestures, which are more eloquent.

As I see it, it is not difficult to understand the inner necessity motivating Martorell in this ultimate development of his style, which I have called a synthesis. At the time he produced the retable of St. Peter, he was so preoccupied with the form problems of the *estilo desornamentado,* which was to supersede his early ornamental and garrulous manner, that he probably deemed the indifferent faces and the scanty scenery an asset rather than a loss. But as the novelty of the plain monumentality began to wear off, the artist became critical of its merely formal purism. The uncommunicative faces, gestures, and settings of his middle period no longer satisfied him. And so, realizing that he had sacrificed values he had possessed in his early manhood, he set out to retrieve the loss. The result was the style of the retable of *The Transfiguration.* How Martorell intensified the communicative elements of the narrative is revealed by a comparison of the face of St. Peter emerging from the dungeon on the retable of Pubol with the face of *The Man Possessed of the Legion of Devils* in the left-hand corner of that panel of *The Transfiguration* altar. The former is a well-drawn but otherwise empty face. The latter is the unforgettable face of a pitiful man; haunted by demons throughout his life, he cannot, now that he is cured, grasp the peace that has been restored to his mind.* Another striking example of the psychological depth of Martorell's late manner is *The Woman of Samaria*. In all the art of Spain prior to *The Transfiguration* retable there is no more veracious and poignant psychological study than the one of this depraved Spanish woman of the street, whose whole bewildered attitude and facial expression reflect dumbfounded surprise at what she is suddenly told to her face by the Lord: "Thou hast had five husbands and the one thou hast now is not thy husband." Like a whipped dog she will crawl away and tell the people in the city: "Come and see a man which told me all things that I ever did."

For all its monumentality, Martorell's mature art was realistic to the least detail; not by a hair's breadth did it depart from the homely milieu of the Catalan peasantry. His genre approach was far more comprehensive than that of the Serras and their immediate followers. Martorell used the most minute detail if it promised to clarify or animate the characteristic mood of his story. He did not forget the long rope the Woman of Samaria carried on her arm with which to lower the jug into the well, or the meat the Disciples went to purchase in the city and which made their haversacks bulge (Fig. 40). The most striking example of his keen realism is the servant girl in *The Wedding of Cana* who is emptying the water out of a wooden pail into one of the big jars that crowd the foreground.† It is a brilliant bit of drawing: the stooping girl watching that no water is spilled, the bent forearm and the well-foreshortened hand that holds the handle of the pail. But what makes the movement of that arm look so cramped? It is the fact that, with both hands occupied, the girl must keep her arm tightly pressed to her bosom to hold in place the circular pad with which women in the Mediterranean countries alleviate the pressure of the heavy jugs on their heads. By such a seemingly insignificant detail Martorell explains how the water was brought in besides showing how it was poured into the jar.

* Gudiol, Soldevilla, and Zervos, *op. cit.,* CLXXXVIII, CLXXXV.
† *Ibid.,* CLXXXVII.

Fig. 41.—Bernardo Martorell: *The Miracle of the Loaves and Fishes,* Barcelona, Museum of Catalan Art

During his early period Martorell may have catered to the fastidious taste of the Spanish aristocracy. Toward the end of his career he would have no more of that. Now his art was for the consumption of simple folk. His every nuance was snatched from the life of the lowly. The multitude of *The Miracle of the Loaves and Fishes* (Fig. 41) munch their food with that completely blank facial expression which only hungry people have who just eat and eat when they are fed.

The close observation and conscientious representation of the homely milieu which is typical of Martorell's later manner reflect a general trend of the mid-fifteenth century: the rejection of the aristocratic ideal of what is pretty and pleasant to behold, which had governed art throughout the second half of the fourteenth century, and the return of the plebeian ideals of the first half. In that respect Martorell ultimately saw eye to eye with Ferrer Bassa rather than with the Serras. A kindred change was apparent at this time in the outlook of Jan van Eyck in Flanders, as he turned from book illumination to panel painting. An influence of his novel outlook is also evident in van Eyck's Catalan pupil, Lluis Dalmau, who was perhaps also a student of Martorell.

It seems that Dalmau became acquainted with Jan van Eyck toward the end of the 1420's, when the latter visited Valencia. We may further assume that Alphonse V of Aragon sent his young sergeant painter to Bruges, in 1431, not only for diplomatic reasons but with the understanding that he should for a few years enjoy the benefit of studying under the great Flemish naturalist.* In Bruges Dalmau witnessed the completion of the

* Few original paintings of van Eyck were in Spain at that time. *The Fountain of Life* was in the cathedral of Valencia (an ancient copy is now in the Prado). Two years after van Eyck's death, King Alphonse acquired *St. George Fighting the Dragon.* Pedro

famous polyptychs of the cathedral of
Ghent and saw other masterpieces issue
from van Eyck's shop, among them
*The Madonna with the Canon van
der Paele* (Bruges, Fig. 43). The profu-
sion of detail, reminiscent of these
paintings, that is assembled in Dalmau's *Virgin with the Councillors*
(1445, Fig. 42) has won for it the odium
of being "one of the most servile examples of the dependence upon the
style of the van Eyck brothers that may
be found anywhere in Europe."* It
should be noted, however, that adap-
tations, or even appropriations of

Fig. 42.—Lluis Dalmau: *The Virgin with
the Councillors,* Barcelona, Museum of
Catalan Art

whole sections from the work of some other artist, were not considered
plagiarisms in the Middle Ages. Rather they were taken for signs of a
painter's education. At any rate, they were common practices.

Even a greater amount of borrowing from van Eyck's work could not
lessen the impressive effect of Dalmau's retable in the museum of Barcelona, where it has been completely preserved, with Francisco Gomar's
original frame, except for the predella, which has perished. Moreover, the
style of the retable of *The Councillors* shows that the artist was in perfect
accord with Martorell's consistent realism. Dalmau was the first to relinquish the traditional pattern of a multipartite retable for the novel
conception of a single scene unified by a naturalistic stage setting, a Gothic
hall with a central niche for the Virgin, and lateral windows through
which one catches glimpses of landscape outside.

Shortly after Dalmau had completed his retable, the bright star of Jan
van Eyck, whose uncompromising *verismo* was perhaps too forthright and
direct for the aristocratic taste of the period, was eclipsed by the brilliance

Nisart's picture of the same subject in the archeological museum at Palma de Mallorca,
painted between 1468 and 1470, is believed to be an adaptation of van Eyck's (non-
extant) painting.

* C. R. Post, *op. cit.,* VII, 10.

of the younger Frenchified Flemings of the school of Tournai—Roger van der Weyden and Dirk Bouts. Proof of Roger's popularity in Spain lies in the fact that Pope Martin V, eager to ingratiate himself with King John II of Castile for political reasons, presented him with a triptych painted by the Flemish artist rather than with an Italian work.* Undoubtedly the

Fig. 43.—Jan van Eyck: *The Madonna with the Canon van der Paele,* Bruges, Communal Museum

pope had asked his envoys abroad to advise him what would best please the discriminating Castilian ruler.

The probable reason for the sudden appreciation of Roger's art was that it was less subjective than van Eyck's and possessed other values which were bound to endear it to the conservative Spaniards. They valued his masterful blend of spirituality and mundanity, of fidelity to nature and schematization of design. His coloration was at once fastidious and reticent. His line work was as precise as sculpture, yet as fanciful as medieval embroidery. His noble portraits depicted character without a touch of

* The triptych of St. John in the Kaiser Friedrich Museum at Berlin. See Antonio Ponz, *Viaje en España* (Madrid, 1793), XII, 57. Roger van der Weyden was, on the whole, more popular in Spain than van Eyck. His *Descent from the Cross* and his *Pieta* were the most widely imitated Flemish paintings of the last half of the fifteenth century. One of the numerous Spanish replicas of the last-named picture is the *Pieta with the Donors* by Fernando Gallego, in the Weibel Collection at Madrid. The original of

that impoliteness which was characteristic of the irreverent likenesses of
Jan van Eyck. The imitation of Roger van der Weyden and Dirk Bouts
instead of van Eyck was, I believe, more than an accident. Similar reasons,
I repeat, accounted for the change
from the virile manner of Giotto to
the more polished taste of the school
of Siena in the latter half of the fourteenth century, when the Serras superseded Ferrer Bassa. History repeated itself. Once more the Catalans
coveted the dainty and the winsome.

The painter who gave them what
they wanted was Jaime Huguet, a disciple of Roger van der Weyden and
the head and absolute leader of the
Barcelona school from the sixties
throughout the eighties. Huguet was
the last of the great Gothic painters
of Catalonia and perhaps the most
refined of them all. In his *Episcopal
Investiture of St. Augustine*, painted
about 1486 (Fig. 44), he realized the
monumental grandeur to which Martorell had aspired. On the other

Fig. 44.—Jaime Huguet: *The Episcopal Investiture of St. Augustine*, Barcelona, Museum of Catalan Art

hand, Huguet substituted for Martorell's incisive realism an august formality and an awe-inspiring gilded magnificence. This departure is the
more interesting for the fact that Huguet's early path crossed Dalmau's.
The great retable for the church of the Augustinians, of which Huguet
painted only *The Episcopal Investiture* of the titular Saint (the other panels fell to Rafael Vergos), was originally ordered from Dalmau. After Dalmau's death, in 1463, Huguet assumed the contract, but kept the tanner's
guild waiting nearly a quarter of a century for the painting.

Roger's *Descent from the Cross* did not enter the Escorial until the second half of the
sixteenth century, when Mary of Hungary, then governor of the Low Countries, presented it to her brother Charles V.

Jaime Huguet, like his great master, dressed his actors in the Burgundian fashion, attenuating their bodies and even employing Roger's facial types. Occasionally he adapted one of Roger's compositions; for *The Epiphany* of the retable of the Constable of Portugal (1464, Barcelona Museum) it was probably transmitted to him through Martin Schongauer's engraving *B. 6.* Huguet's style is distinguished from that of both Roger and Dirk Bouts by his Spanish predilection for strict bilateral symmetry and decorative planarity. The rigid and tapestry-like composition of *The Episcopal Investiture of St. Augustine* was obsolete in Flanders and Italy by 1486.

The inspiration of Roger van der Weyden's delicate art is also apparent in the spirited portrait-like heads which enliven Huguet's sacred narratives, and which remained unrivaled in Spain until the very end of the sixteenth century. The sensitive head and hands of the reader in the left-hand corner of *The Episcopal Investiture* anticipate those of the celebrant who occupies the corresponding place in El Greco's *Interment of Count Orgaz* (Fig. 6). Huguet's earlier pictures include many other exquisite faces. Dalmau's *Councillors* look clumsy beside Huguet's fragile effigies of the Persian martyrs, *Abdon and Sennen,* on their retable of 1461 in Santa Maria at Tarrasa. Other examples are the *St. Bernardino of Siena* on a retable of 1463, recently discovered in the cathedral of Barcelona, and *The Magi* of the retable of the Constable, of 1464.* Rafael Vergos caught something of Huguet's method of using the facial expression of the protagonists as a psychological clue to the dramatic plot embodied in a picture. In his *Disputation of St. Augustine,* one of the panels of the retable of the Augustinians,† one senses at once that the heretic is about to surrender to the Saint. Who could resist the gentle persuasion of such eloquent eyes?

Certain other traits link Jaime Huguet to Dirk Bouts. It seems remarkable that a Spaniard should so deliberately eschew the sanguinary horrors of execution pictures as Huguet does on the retable of the *Saints Abdon and Sennen.* The surgical nicety with which the decapitations of the two

---

* Gudiol, Soldevilla, and Zervos, *op. cit.,* CXCIII, CCXII, CCVIII, CCX.
† Gertrud Richert, *op. cit.,* Plate 88 (where the picture is ascribed to Huguet).

princes and of the Saints Cosmas and Damian are performed* is second
only to that in Dirk Bouts' *Ordeal of St. Erasmus* (Louvain, St. Peter's), in
which all trace of blood is likewise absent, and *The Beheading of the
Innocent Nobleman* in the museum at Brussels, where the blood that one
expects to see streaming from the truncated body turns into a dainty bed
of flowers.

Decisive departure from the aureate Gothic formality and finesse of
Huguet, toward an emotional style foreshadowing the Renaissance of the
sixteenth century in Catalan painting, was brought about chiefly by two
artists: Bartolome Bermejo and Master Alfonso. Both were probably An-
dalusians. Their fascinating art has aroused among historians an insatiable
curiosity about their personal histories, but unfortunately the available
records are meager. Every attempt to write their biographies has therefore
resulted in guesswork. If one tabulates some of the guesses and conclusions
arrived at by inference, one is left with a number of perplexing questions:
Was Bermejo an Italian named Bartolommeo Brasoni Rosso? Or perchance
a Frenchman by the name of Berthelemy Roux? Did he study in Naples?
Did he paint the great *Pieta* of Villeneuve-les-Avignons, which is now in
the Louvre? Was he a German residing in Cordova? Was he a Portuguese?
Or was he really an Andalusian from Cordova? Was he a converted Jew?
Did he have relations with Guatemala? Was his real name Bartolomeo de
Cardenas, and Bermejo (which means "red") only his nickname? And if
so, was it given to him because of his ruddy complexion or his red hair?
So far as I know, it has never been suggested that the name might have
something to do with that Flemish red which was his favorite color; a
similar predilection for a particular shade of green gave to the German
artist Hans Baldung the nickname "Grien."

Yet we have several documented paintings and a number of others that
can be safely attributed to Bermejo. In the light of archival evidence he
can be traced, in the 1470's, to Saragossa; in the eighties and early nineties
to Barcelona, where he collaborated with Huguet, polychromed a statue,

---

* Gudiol, Soldevilla, and Zervos, *op. cit.,* CCXI, shows the whole retable. *The
Decapitation of Abdon and Sennen* is in the upper register of the right wing; *The Decapitation of Cosmas and Damian* is in the extreme left of the predella.

and designed stained glass windows for the cathedral; and in the late nineties to Vich.

But of Master Alfonso we have only two fragments of a retable that once adorned the apse of the monastic church of San Cugat de Valles, for which he was paid nine hundred florins in 1473. One of these two panels (acquired in 1907 for the Museo de la Ciudadela) portrays the martyrdom either of St. Medin (Emeterius, who was put to death on the site of the church depicted in the background) or, as other critics believe, of St. Cugat himself. The other panel, a shutter with the effigy of St. George, patron saint of Catalonia, passed from the monastery of San Cugat de Valles into the Muntadas Collection at Barcelona.*

A profound emotionalism, an eye extremely susceptible to luminous atmospheric effects, and a vivid color imagination, these are the chief characteristics of Bartolome Bermejo. He was not the conservative that Huguet was. His extremely individualistic outlook made him depart further than any earlier Catalan from the traditional iconography of certain dogmatic or Biblical stories. This is well illustrated by an early panel of a

---

* It is still a moot question whether the painter of the two extant panels may be identified with one or several homonyms that can be traced in Italian and Spanish documents from about the middle of the fifteenth century until 1476. A Spaniard named Alfonso was active about 1450 at the court of the Este in Ferrara. A miniaturist, Alfonso de Cordoba, was employed before 1458 by Alfonso V at Naples. An alfresco painter of the same name, in 1465, decorated the vaults of the chapel of the Constable at Barcelona and was recorded as living near Santa Maria del Mar. In the 1936 edition of this book I inferred from *The Martyrdom of St. Medin* that the painter was of youthful age: "It bears all the signs of storm and stress. Presumably the painter was not older than twenty-three or twenty-five." If Master Alfonso was identical with the Alfonso de Cordoba, who was a citizen of Barcelona, my assumption is borne out by the marriage contract of December, 1474, according to which Alfonso married the widow of a Neopolitan (see C. R. Post, *op. cit.*, V, 102). Inasmuch as only the bride is mentioned as widowed, I assume that it was Alfonso's first marriage; in other words, that he was a young man. If that was the same man who received payment, in 1465, for the decorations in the Royal Palace at Barcelona, then he must have been a decade or so older than I first believed. Incidentally, there was nothing remarkable in the marriage of a younger man to a widow in the fifteenth century. Michael Wolgemuth, Dürer's teacher, married the widow of his former employer, Wilhelm Pleydenwurf, thus making himself the head of the shop. In 1618 Juan de Ribalta, aged twenty, married the widow of a physician and obtained the patronage of his bride's high-ranking relatives: the bishops, archdeans, and patriarchs of the dioceses of Valencia, Segorbe, and so forth.

retable said to have been in Guatemala
in the sixteenth century, whence it was
eventually returned to Barcelona. This
panel was one of four, of which two,
The Resurrection and *The Descent
into Hell,* are now in the Museum of
Catalan Art; the other two, somewhat
smaller, panels, which portray *The Ascension* and *The Entry into Paradise,**
are now in the Amattler Collection.

On the last-named panel Bermejo
depicts Jesus leading to heaven the
souls he has saved from the Limbo.
His portrayal of the walls of paradise
as Spanish walls sealed with azulejos
and the crucifix exalted between the

Fig. 45.—Bartolome Bermejo: *Pieta with
St. Jerome and the Donor, Lluis Despla,*
Barcelona, Museum of Catalan Art

branches of the Tree of Knowledge is original with him. These are obviously the ideas of a mystic poet. But the full range of his spontaneous
poetical imagination is revealed in the Adam who is kneeling in the front
row of the Saved. Tradition had it that the Blessed have their hands folded
in prayer. But Adam's hands are no longer folded. Recognizing the symbol of salvation upon the tree from which once he plucked the fruit of
sin, he clasps his right hand over his mouth—the naïve gesture of the child
who suddenly realizes that he has unknowingly done wrong.

Bermejo's early manner, best represented in his *San Domingo de Silos*
(1474–77, Prado), was still under the thrall of Huguet and his Tournai
ancestry. His advance over Huguet, beginning about 1480 and culminating
in the Barcelona *Pieta with St. Jerome and the Donor, Archdeacon Lluis
Despla,* of 1490 (Barcelona, Museum of Catalan Art, Fig. 45), is best
explained on the theory that he was younger than Huguet; exactly how
much younger is difficult to say, since the years of his birth and death are
unknown.† However that may be, after 1480 Bermejo's manner is less comparable to that of Jan van Eyck and Roger van der Weyden than to that of

* Gertrud Richert, *op. cit.,* Plate 104.
† Obviousy Bermejo was older than Master Alfonso, whose *Martyrdom of St. Medin,*

van Eyck's younger Flemish disciples, Hugo van der Goes and Geertgen tot Sint Jans. It is true that his *Virgen de la Leche* in the Prado resembles Dirk Bouts' well-known *Madonna with the Child* in the National Gallery of London as regards the general arrangement; but the mood of sadness that lingers on the face of Bermejo's Madonna brings to mind the more advanced spiritual note that rings from similar paintings of van der Goes —for instance, his *Madonna with the Child* in the gallery of Budapest. More than any of his older contemporaries Bermejo reflects the mystic emotionalism which entered Spanish literature at the end of the fifteenth century. At that, he seems not to have found it easy to relinquish the older, more rigid, and statuesque conception of the school of Tournai and adopt the more modern painterly atmospheric illusionism of van der Goes. Indeed it seems as if Bermejo, in about 1480, had started all over, almost as a beginner.*

The origin of Bermejo's art is quite as uncertain as the story of his life. Whether he actually studied in the Low Countries or derived his technical

though painted at least a year earlier than Bermejo's *San Domingo,* was already quite free of the solemn medievalism of Huguet's style.

* The influence of the school of Tournai is still noticeable in paintings done after the *San Domingo:* the *St. Engracia* (Fenway Court, Boston) and the *St. Michael with the Donor* (Lady Ludlow's Collection, London). The influence of van der Goes, so obvious in *The Epiphany* at Granada (recently attributed by Post) and *The Madonna with the Donor* (cathedral of Acqui, Italy), becomes evident for the first time in *The Dormition of the Virgin* (Kaiser Friedrich Museum, Berlin). I cannot agree with Post's hypothetical construction of an early period of Bermejo in the 1460's and, least of all, with his contention that the Berlin *Dormition* is Bermejo's earliest known painting. If art historians may be certain of one criterion, it is the period style of any fifteenth-century painting, regardless of who painted it. Long before anyone thought of attributing it to Bermejo the Berlin *Dormition* was dated "about 1480" on the indubitable evidence that its period style is written all over the panel. The same period was also accepted by D. Elías Tormo, who first recognized Bermejo's hand in the painting (*Archivo español de Arte y Arqueologia,* II, 48, 1926). Inasmuch as it is impossible to date the Berlin picture in the sixties, Bermejo cannot conceivably have painted it prior to the *San Domingo* retable of the mid-seventies. Post's hypothetical early period of Bermejo is founded "on the assumption that the earlier the work, the stronger is the Flemish influence." More comprehensible would be the dictum that the earlier the work, the stronger is the influence of the school of Tournai; the later the work the more the manner of van der Goes and the younger van Eyck followers supersedes the tradition of Roger van der Weyden and Dirk Bouts. Post frequently mentions old van Eyck, who probably died before Bermejo was born, but does not anywhere in 131 pages so much

knowledge from migrant Flemings in Spain is not for us to decide here. After 1490 his manner was so large and his chiaroscuro so grand and noble in a free combination of figure and landscape painting that his biographers have concluded he must have fallen under the influence of Giorgione before he painted the great *Pieta with St. Jerome and the Donor* in 1490 (Barcelona, Museum of Catalan Art, Fig. 45). But which one of Giorgione's paintings could conceivably have exercised any influence upon Bermejo as early as 1490? And why should not such a talent as his have developed quite independently? More significant than the coincidence of Bermejo's depiction of a thunderstorm in his *Pieta* and Giorgione's use of the same motif in his *Tempesta* is the individuality of that late work of Bermejo, its dissimilarity to any other painting of its time anywhere in the world.

Bermejo's mature art is quite unlike that of other Spanish Primitives, which was based on accurate observation of externalities, so much so that the men and women depicted on the early retables often seem devoid of a soul. It foreshadows the art of the sixteenth century in that it is saturated with emotionalism. The *Pieta* is one of the few Spanish paintings of the fifteenth century whose profound lyrical expression the student never forgets. It is a dirge sung jointly by the figures and the landscape. The entire coloration is tuned in a dark minor key. There is no landscape like it in any of the earlier Spanish paintings, not even in Bermejo's own *Madonna with the Donor* in the cathedral at Acqui, which he painted shortly before the *Pieta*. The landscape of the *Pieta* is lashed by a rainstorm and is filled

as mention van der Goes. So, likewise, he rejects A. L. Mayer's suggestion of Geertgen's influence on the ground that this would put him into a desperate dilemma with his chronology. It does indeed create a dilemma. And the only way out is to surrender to the fact that the Berlin painting is not of the sixties but of the eighties, when influences from both van der Goes and Geertgen come within the pale of possibility. Bermejo's *Dormition of the Virgin* is unthinkable without the premise of van der Goes. I repeat what I have said before: "It must be dated after 1480 because of its derivation from a picture of the same subject in Bruges, one of the latest and most mature works of Hugo van der Goes—not one of the earliest, as Sir Martin Conway proposed on page 180 of *The van Eycks and Their Followers* (London, 1921). . . . The poor proportions of the figures and certain other signs in Bermejo's picture leave little doubt, if any, that the Spanish painter was a beginner in 1480." To make myself clear, I would add: a beginner in a new manner with which he was not yet as familiar as he was at an earlier time with the manner of the school of Tournai.

with the gloomy illumination of a sun setting behind dark clouds. The artist portrayed far more than the external image of a mother caressing her dead son; Mary's grief is expressed in every brush stroke. And for the first time in Spanish art the donor's attitude and facial expression participate in the tragedy. The face of the archdeacon, like that of the Virgin— distorted in agony, helpless and without hope—sounds a note of *tristeza* that one would not have expected to hear until the days of Luis de Morales, El Greco, and Ribalta.

Beside Huguet with his noble restraint and Bermejo with his gloomy lyricism, Master Alfonso emerges as the ebullient dramatist of the late fifteenth century. He was the most original and technically perhaps the best equipped of all Spanish quattrocentists. One cannot tell what surprises are in store for us should any later work of the master be suddenly discovered.

Within the provincial framework of Spanish primitive art, 1473 seems an incredibly early date for *The Martyrdom of St. Medin,* a masterwork

Fig. 46.—Master Alfonso: *The Martyrdom of St. Medin,* Barcelona, Museum of Catalan Art

that transcends the borders of the epochal style in more than one respect (Fig. 46). It anticipates the vigor, the directness, and the vehement temper of Goya. The execution of the Martyr is depicted with unprecedented veracity. Indeed, the efforts of the executioner to sever the Saint's head are analyzed with so much scientific detachment that the beholder often forgets to notice other features of the picture which are no less significant: the psychological revelation in the expression of the dying Saint; physical suffering, psychical self-control, and religious fanaticism (Fig. 47); the admirable, keenly modeled portraits of the bystanders; the exquisite study of the sleeping dog and the still life of

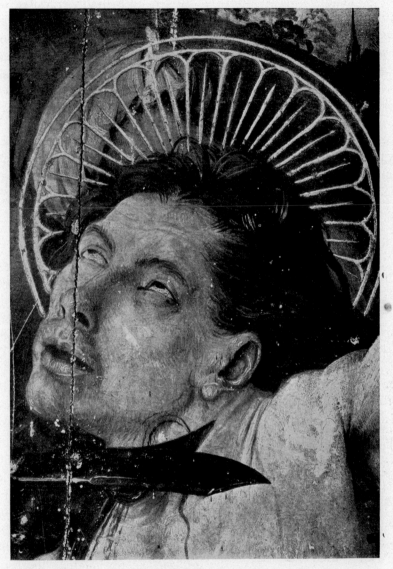

Fig. 47.—Master Alfonso: *The Martyrdom of St. Medin* (detail), Barcelona,
Museum of Catalan Art

the basket with the hangman's tools; the mellow harmony of the bright illumination.

The types of humanity and, more especially, the treatment of the nude betray Alfonso's acquaintance with the Flemish tradition. All the more surprising, then, is his unsparing directness, so utterly unlike the polite and unsanguinary executions depicted by the school of Roger van der Weyden and Dirk Bouts. The sunny brilliance of the illumination, however, could not, I believe, have been acquired elsewhere than in Italy. The *St. George* in the Muntadas Collection, on account of the Chiaroscuro treatment, points to Venice or Mantua. The cool, limpid luminosity of *The Martyrdom,* on the other hand, reminds one rather of the *plein air* of Piero dei Franceschi. It is curious that the group of three onlookers in the right-hand foreground, which has proved an iconographical puzzle to many writers, has reminded none of them of the similar (and similarly puzzling) group of men in the right-hand foreground of Piero's *Scourging of Christ* in the cathedral of Urbino. To me it seems revealing that the Italian picture, like the Spaniard's, derives its startling effect from the same cruel contrast: the physical suffering inflicted on an innocent victim and the callous indifference of three witnesses. Compositionally the two pictures are, of course, as different as the Italian and the Spanish quattrocento. Considered as a whole, Alfonso's manner of expression was a highly personal creation, the creation, indeed, of a solitary personality, a leader without followers. Yet the influence of Italy is appreciable. It signals the inception of another era for Catalan art; one, in fact, in which the Italian Renaissance effaced every vestige of the preceding Flemish trend.

The Cinquecento

CHAPTER SIX

At the dawn of the sixteenth century the artistic horizon of Spain was a much wider one than it had ever been before. Until the latter part of the quattrocento the view embraced only the eastern littoral. The other provincial schools of the peninsula were relatively negligible. Painting and sculpture, to be sure, had been practiced during the fourteenth and fifteenth centuries in every important city of the kingdoms of Leon, Castile, and the South, but the art works produced there were of that "Hispano-Flemish" manner which may be studied to better advantage and from finer examples in Aragon, Barcelona, and Valencia.

Now, beginning with the cinquecento, the schools of central Spain, the Northwest, and the South began to contest the supremacy of the schools of the eastern seaboard, where, incidentally, Barcelona was fast ceding her leadership to Valencia. Now began the rise of the schools of Cordova and Seville. By the close of the century Seville had outstripped all other Spanish schools, stimulated as it was by the commercial boom that followed the discovery of the Americas and the beginning of American colonization. Castile, too, began to prepare herself for her eventual role as a rival of the school of Seville.

Yet, all this fresh activity notwithstanding, the wider horizon does not yet afford a unified view. Rather, one beholds a multitude of unrelated provincial schools. Spanish art did not suddenly become an organic whole when the Catholic Kings created a united Spanish Kingdom. The birth of an integrated Spanish art was still remote, and even more remote was its rise to the rank of a leading world art.

This may seem strange in view of the imperialistic expansion of Spain during the sixteenth century, under Charles V. When the whole world was going Spanish, when everyone of consequence in Europe and the Americas was speaking Spanish and wearing Spanish dress, why did Spanish art fail to attain international significance? Why was the springtime of Spanish art delayed until the late autumn of Spanish imperialism?

There are several good reasons. One is that Spanish imperialism was such a mushroom growth that Spanish culture could not keep up with it. So long as Spain had been a discordant group of petty states, controlled partly by Christian and partly by Mohammedan rulers, the motley assemblage of local schools had probably satisfied her cultural needs. Not so when the kingdom of Ferdinand and Isabella suddenly expanded into an empire on which the sun never set. The provincial thing that Spanish painting still was in the early sixteenth century was ill-prepared to compete in regions where Italian art ruled unconditionally. Unlike Italy, Spain of the Renaissance had no Leonardo da Vinci, no Michelangelo, no Giorgione. Indeed, artistic enterprise on a scale comparable to the Renaissance in Italy was impossible in Spain in an era devoted almost exclusively to conquest and military action.

In any case, the art of a country can surge to international significance only if it is organically national to begin with. And the sad fact was that the Spanish mode of artistic expression was less Spanish in the early part of the sixteenth century than it had been in the fifteenth. An art of painting strong enough to vie with that of Italy or that of the North might have been attained sooner had the Spaniards systematically elaborated the native elements latent in their primitive realistic art. Instead, they continued to believe that salvation lay outside.

So, since Italian art and literature ruled the rest of the world, Spain, too, throughout the era of Charles V and Philip II, absorbed them both as a dry sponge absorbs water. And since the Flemings, the French, and the Germans had also succumbed to the southern enchantress and were imitating the alien patterns instead of developing their native conventions, the rampant Romanism of Spanish art was deprived of any wholesome antidote.

In many ways the Italian influence was destructive of wholesome trends.

After all, the van Eycks, the Roger van der Weydens, and the Dirk Boutses had been companions in the spirit of direct realism. What the Florentines and the Romans of the sixteenth century propagated was something wholly un-Spanish—a formalistic "ideal" art that ignored the simple realities of everyday life. Yet both the literature and the plastic arts of Spain were, for a time, flooded with Italianism. In the preceding century there had been no Italian influence to speak of for at least seventy years; few Italian painters established themselves on the peninsula, as did Dello Delli of Florence from about 1455 to 1470 (his work is in Salamanca and Valencia). At the time of his death, however, Italian artists were for the first time being encouraged to go to Spain, either by certain munificent patrons of the arts in Naples (which fell to Aragon in 1442) or by the Renaissance pontiffs of Spanish blood—Alfonso Borja, who became Pope Calixtus III in 1455, and his nephew Rodrigo Borja, who became Pope Alexander VI in 1492.

The obliteration of the Gothic in the grandiose style of the Renaissance began shortly before the turn of the century in the towns of the eastern seaboard and thereafter proceeded everywhere in Spain. Master Alfonso's and Bermejo's exceptional ventures in Catalonia were continued during the last decade of the quattrocento in Aragon and Valencia by Bermejo's pupils Martin Bernat, Miguel Jimenez, and Rodrigo Osana. The Castilian disciples of the early Renaissance, notably in Avila and Toledo, were the painters Pedro Berruguete (died 1503) and Juan de Borgoña (active 1495–1533), the brother of the equally famous sculptor Felipe Vigarni, whose name is forever associated with the great retables of the cathedral of Toledo and the Chapel Royal at Granada. Several foreigners were attracted by the sudden prosperity of southern Spain. The inaugurator of the Renaissance in Andalusia, Alejo Fernandez (about 1470–1543), was a Low German who came to Cordova and married there in 1498. Ten years later he and his equally distinguished sculptor brother, Jorge Fernandez Aleman, moved to Seville, where they acquired great wealth and reputation. In 1537 two younger artists came to Seville from the Low Countries: Ferdinand Sturm, born in Zinkzee, Holland, and Pieter Kempener (Pedro de Campaña, 1503–80). The latter, a man of wide learning—in fact, an architect, sculptor, mathematician, and astronomer as well as a painter—

was a scion of a family of tapestry-weavers long established in Brussels. After spending twenty-five years in Seville (1537–62) he returned to his native city to become the head of the famous tapestry looms there. Both Pedro de Campaña and Alejo Fernandez were also experts in a craft highly characteristic of the festival-loving Renaissance—let us call it incidental decorative painting on a large scale. In 1526, on the occasion of the state visit of Charles V to Seville, Alejo Fernandez was put in charge of all the decoration of the city. In 1529 Pedro de Campaña, who happened to be in Italy at the time, decorated with his paintings one of the great gates of the Via Triumphalis for the visit of the same monarch to Bologna.

The Spanish cinquecentists who went to Italy for more or less prolonged sojourns of study are too numerous to be listed in this chapter. Some of the quattrocentists never came back at all. Such a one was a certain Jacopo de Valenza, who established himself in Venice after studying there, presumably under Bartolommeo Vivarini; another was Lo Spagna (Juan de Pedro, about 1450–1528), who belonged to the group of Umbrian painters around Pietro Perugino. Among the native Spaniards of the early sixteenth century who did return to their homeland are the Castilians Berruguete and Borgoña, already mentioned, and the Valencians Ferrando de los Llanos (active until 1525) and Ferrando Yañez de l'Almedina (active until about 1536). Among the leaders of the Andalusian schools of Cordova and Seville in the latter half of the sixteenth century may be mentioned Luis de Vargas (1502?–68), who spent no less than twenty-eight years in Rome, and Pablo de Cespedes (1538–1608), who went to Rome twice, once in 1565 for seven years and again in 1583 for two years.

As the Spanish taste became more and more Italianized, increasing numbers of Italian artists sought employment in Spain. The unknown master of the retable of St. Narcissus in the cathedral of Valencia was, it is believed, a Ferrarese painter trained under Lorenzo Costa. In 1471 the chapter of the cathedral of Valencia invited Paolo de San Leocadio, a Lombard from Reggio-Emilia (Paolo Aregio), and Francesco Pagano of Naples, to execute (non-extant) alfresco decorations in the choir of the cathedral. Andrea Fiorentino collaborated with Juan de Borgoña. Undoubtedly many more Italians visited Spain than can be identified today; the origin of some of them remains hidden under their adopted Spanish names exactly as that of the Spaniards in Italy was hidden for a long time under their Italian names—Pietro Spagnuolo (Pedro Berruguete), Fernando Spagnuolo (Ferrando de los Llanos), and others. The Italian tide reached its peak in Castile at the time of the erection and decoration of the Royal Monastery of the Escorial. It was a tragedy that the first really big task of architectural decoration which Spain could offer was assigned almost entirely to mediocre foreigners. El Greco had come to Castile for the job, but King Philip II was blind to his genius. El Greco's masterpiece, *The Martyrdom of St. Maurice and the Theban Legion,* was rejected, and a shallow painting of the same subject by Romulo Cincinnato took its place. Other Italians were called upon to decorate the Escorial during a quarter century beginning in 1567 or thereabouts: Giovanni Battista Castello, better known as El Bergamasco; his two sons, Niccolo and Fabrizio; the Genoese muralist Luca Cambiaso and the Roman Federigo Zuccaro. The latter's work was eventually replaced by the even flimsier productions of Pellegrino Tibaldi, a student of Giorgio Vasari. The painters Bartolommeo Carducci, Patricio Caxes, and Bernardino de Aqua and the sculptors Pompeo and Leone Leoni complete the roster of the "school of the Escorial," which was little more than a disconcerting repetition of the "school of Fontainebleau" of Francis I.

Likewise too varied and motley for a complete enumeration are the Italian trends that were transplanted to Spain by both the Italianate Spaniards and the visiting Italians. Pietro Perugino's manner and the influence of Melozzo da Forli were transported to Castile with Pedro Berruguete, who had worked with Melozzo and Josse van Ghent at the court of the Duke of Urbino. The manner of Domenico Ghirlandajo and of other Florentine quattrocentists was imported with Juan de Borgoña, who completed the work on the high altar of the cathedral of Avila, which Pedro Berruguete and his successor, Santos Cruz, had left unfinished when they died. Ferrando de los Llanos, who in 1504 and 1505 assisted Leonardo da Vinci in the execution of the mural of *The Battle of Anghiari* in the Great Hall of the Palazzo Vecchio at Florence, returned to Valencia a full-fledged *Leonardesco*. The mannerism of the upper Italian followers of Leonardo and Correggio was a decisive factor in the formation of the style of Luis de Morales, a native of Badajoz, Estremadura, and one of the most refined of the Spanish eclectics (about 1509–86); at any rate, it was a factor more decisive than the Flemish and German influences which have been emphasized, unduly I think, by the more recent critics of Morales. In addition to Leonardo, Fra Bartolommeo of Florence became the model for Ferrando Yañez de l'Almedina, who eventually handed the influence on to his pupil Juan Vicente Macip (about 1475 to 1545 or 1550) and so also to Macip's son and successor, Juan de Juanes (about 1500–79). Juan de Juanes, however, also studied Italian painting at its source, bringing back to Valencia not only the compositional patterns and the design but also the coloration of certain Florentine masters whose work had not yet been seen in Spain: Andrea del Sarto, Francesco Salviati, and Angelo Bronzino. Michelangelo's influence is plainly evident in the work of Alonso Berruguete, Pedro's son (1486–1561), the chief exponent of the *estilo plateresco* of the mid-sixteenth century. Alonso went to Florence when he was still in his teens and did not return to Spain until he was forty-six. Both Vasari and Michelangelo mention him, the former several times in his *Lives,* the latter in letters written while he was working on *The Bathers*—the painting that was to be placed opposite Leonardo's *Battle of Anghiari* in the Palazzo Vecchio. Alonso Berruguete's version of Michelangelo's style was, it is true, a manneristic version. Generally speaking, all the Spanish imitations of Michelangelo and Raphael were conditioned by the manneristic Florentine followers of these masters rather than by their own more direct styles. The Sevillians who admired Pedro de Campaña for his intimate knowledge of both Michelangelo and Raphael visualized those artists, as Campaña himself did, through the medium of Giulio Romano's distortions. The Florentine-Roman mannerism reached its height with Luis de Vargas in Seville. Its culmination—that intolerable, boring phase characterized by a deliberate disregard of nature and the consciously artificial construction of heads, gestures, and draperies—is encountered in Cordova with Pablo de Cespedes. This artist, while living in Rome under the name of Paolo Cedaspe, collaborated with Federigo Zuccaro, the arch-mannerist, on alfresco paintings in Maria in Aracoeli and in Santa Trinita al Monte.

The influence of the Renaissance and its manneristic aftermath did not always travel to Spain by so direct a route. To Alejo Fernandez, for instance, it seems to have come through the medium of Albrecht Dürer and Quentin Massys of Flanders.

Incidentally, this abandonment of the honest realism of the Spanish Primitives for the artificial doctrines of the Italian Late Renaissance was matched in the field of literature by such writers as Juan Boscan, Garcilaso de la Vega, and Gutierre de Cetina, who substituted for the native poetical forms of the *Romancero* and the *Cancionero* the Italian forms of Dante, Petrarch, Sannazaro, and others: the *terza rime (terceto),* the *ottava rime,* and the sonnet.

The national tradition, it is true, never really died. Luis de Morales made it survive in painting perhaps as much as Cristobal de Castillejo and Antonio Villegas did in poetry. But the fact that Philip II dismissed Morales, because his work was "too old-fashioned" as compared with that of the manneristic Italians, indicates how far the Spanish taste had altered by the second half of the century. Morales was perhaps too honest to surrender to the official change in taste for the sake of remunerative employment. His contemporary, the poet Gregorio Silvestre, was more willing to compromise. When the new fashion had been officially indorsed, he extolled to the skies the same Italianates upon whom he had showered his contempt when he was young.

But though Roman formalism triumphed, the Spanish spirit was never completely submerged in the foreign tide. The religious fervor of the Spaniards could not, and would not in the long run, have anything in common with an art which was fundamentally irreligious. Since rank paganism was invading the Roman Catholic Church in Italy, turning divine services into esthetic functions, the devout Spaniards would have preferred the Reformation rather than see such heresy go on; provided, of course, that it could be brought about without infringing on the authority of the pope. Among the literary spokesmen of such a move were the twin brothers Alfonso and Juan de Valdes. The latter was chamberlain to Pope Hadrian VI in 1522, and later, with his brother, was prominent at the imperial court of Charles V. These authors of exquisitely written "Dialogues" were openly sponsoring a religious reformation. In describing the sack of Rome in 1527, Alfonso declared it God's just punishment of an entirely corrupt Church* and described how the Church should be reformed.† It is not commonly known that during the siege of Rome in 1527 a number of distinguished Spanish clerics, headed by the Great Inquisitor and archbishop of Toledo, were actually planning such a reformation, with a view toward the intensification of individual faith, the reading of the Scriptures in the Spanish language, and their critical revision. Cardinal Cisneros was about to invite Erasmus to Toledo when the whole movement collapsed. The people at large, whipped into resistance by the mendicant friars, did not want to see such plans carried out.

In view of the strong opposition to the irreligious art of the Italian cinquecento it does not seem at all curious that many Spanish artists turned to the art of Albrecht Dürer, never noticing the tacit protestantism that is inherent in his engravings and woodcuts. These were eagerly copied and exploited up until the seventeenth century by Fernando Gallego, Alejo Fernandez, Juan de Juanes, Alonso Berruguete, El Greco, Alonso Cano, and Ribera. From the point of view of creed it is ironical indeed that Francisco Pacheco, the official censor of ecclesiastical art, should have considered Dürer "the model Catholic artist." But from the point of view of a desirable revival of religious enthusiasm his judgment was reasonable enough. Dürer was played off against the Italians. Unaware of the famous passage in his diary in which he summons Erasmus to ride forth as a crusader and save Martin Luther from the persecution of the Roman Catholic Church, the Spaniards admired Dürer for his human interpretation of the Lord's Passion. Precisely that was his "catholicism," according to the Spanish opinion; in that he differed from the "paganism" of the Italians, who did not shrink from dealing even with scriptural events in terms of esthetic formalism.

JUAN DE JUANES AND LUIS DE MORALES Religious faith and, in a measure, the police force of the Spanish Church—the Holy Office of the In-

---

* *Diálogo en que particularmente se tratan las cosas acaecidas en Roma el año de 1527.*
† *Diálogo de Mercurio y Carón.*

quisition—saved Spanish art from an utterly slavish imitation of the Italian. This may be illustrated by one characteristic Spanish adaptation of a famous work of the Italian Renaissance.

Leonardo da Vinci's *Last Supper* was "translated" into almost every European language of the sixteenth century; its most notable Spanish translator was Juan de Juanes of Valencia. True, his *Last Supper* on the

Fig. 48.—Juan de Juanes: *The Last Supper,* Prado

predella of the altar of St. Stephen (after 1564, Prado, Fig. 48) is twice removed from Leonardo's wall painting in the refectory of St. Maria delle Grazie at Milan, being an adaptation of Titian's much mutilated canvas of 1564 in the refectory of the Escorial, which was itself a translation of Leonardo's composition into the more spacious and mundane manner of the Venetian Late Renaissance.* But for that very reason Master Juan's work reveals all the more clearly his radically different approach to the heart of the story: an almost medieval enthusiasm of faith instead of the "pagan" humanism of the Italians. He retained the Italian compositional idea—agitated groups rising to an emotional crescendo on either side of an imperturbable center. But the passionate action does not tell us of a tragedy among friends. It is not treated as an outburst of human, essentially irreligious, feelings on the part of twelve participants at a supper to whom their master unexpectedly announces the imminent treason. Unlike

* See Crowe and Cavalcaselle, *Tizian* (Leipzig, 1877), 641.

Leonardo and Titian, Juan de Juanes was not preoccupied with *la pensée humaine*. He did not make the Disciples express their disdain, assert their innocence, or offer their protection. The "unshakable rock amidst a roaring sea of passion"—this pictorial metaphor, invented by Leonardo and retained by Titian, was translated by Juan de Juanes into an expression of purely religious ecstasy. The passion of faith is stirred in the hearts of the Disciples as the Savior exalts the Holy Host. The table at which some of them kneel is an altar table rather than a supper table. The platter on it does not contain the Easter lamb. There are the symbolical loaves and a decanter of wine, but otherwise it is occupied only by the *Santo Cáliz*—the Holy Grail, which is guarded as a sacred relic in the cathedral of Valencia. The Disciples reveal no feelings other than religious faith. Their hands are raised and clasped in the transport of worship. One is reminded of what the chroniclers tell of this God-fearing artist, that he never painted any sacred subject without first going to confession and Holy Communion.*

The art of Luis de Morales,† known as El Divino, represented an advance over Juan de Juanes toward the further emancipation of Spanish religiosity from the purely esthetic outlook of the Italians. Morales was influenced quite as much as Juan de Juanes by the art of Italy—not, however, through the Florentine following of Michelangelo and Raphael, as I have pointed out earlier, but through the upper-Italian following of Leonardo and Correggio. Yet the influence registered differently as it passed through the devout mind of Morales. Juanes adopted and intensified the more external features of the Italian style: the grand compositional pattern and, as part of it, the involved contraposto—what the Italian theoreticians called *la figura serpentinata* (the sinuous figure), explaining that it signified *la furia della figura* (the figure's fiery enthusiasm). Morales did not imitate

---

* Ceán Bermúdez, *Diccionario*, II, 318.

† The life of Luis de Morales and especially the beginnings of his development as an artist are something of a mystery. Unfortunately, guesswork tends to increase the enigma. In an article entitled "Luis de Morales El Divino" (*The Connoisseur*, XCVI, London, 1935, 333–389), Werner Goldschmidt suggests that there may possibly have been two artists of the same name and that the younger of the two—born, it is assumed, in 1554—was El Divino. This suggestion is out of joint with the available records. Our earliest sources say that El Divino died in 1586 at the age of *seventy-seven*. Moreover,

that at all. His saints are outwardly calm; they do not remind one of expressionistic dancers. Rather, he selected and emphasized those inner feelings that produce the most incisive emotional expression, particularly of sorrow and mental suffering. His *Mother of Sorrows* (Fig. 52) and his *Pieta* (Fig. 12) illustrate the basic difference between his approach and that of Juan de Juanes. In the paintings of Morales the facial features of the protagonists are mournfully distorted and the attenuation of their bodies, added to the unearthly chiaroscuro in which they float, lends to them a mysterious semblance of creatures not of this world.

If the style of Morales is classified as mannerism, as it usually is, one must bear in mind that classifications based on outward criteria alone are generally misleading. The distorted design of Morales and his excessive use of chiaroscuro differ essentially from similar means of expression used by his Italian contemporaries. The difference lies in the ends which are served in each instance. It is not by accident that the religious paintings of Morales remind one more of the holy icons of the Eastern Church than of the easel pictures which the Italian Mannerists produced for the esthetic delectation of their connoisseur patrons. El Divino's devotional panels bear no relation to the *art pour l'art* ideal that guided Parmigianino in painting *The Virgin with the Long Neck* (Dresden) or Angelo Bronzino in painting *The Descent into Hell* (Uffizi). Morales groped for that profoundly mystical expression which evokes religious contemplation. Like a prophet's visions, his pictures of the youth, the life, and the suffering of the Lord sink away from brilliant light into a fathomless abyss of blackness. The mood of *tristeza* created by this most reticent artist haunts one more than the calculated excitement of his forerunner, Juan de Juanes, or even the ecstatic frenzy of his follower, El Greco.

according to Ceán Bermúdez, King Philip II commented on the artist's advanced age in 1564, making the insulting remark, *"muy viejo estais, Morales!"* Of this Goldschmidt makes no mention. Instead, the artist's son Cristóbal Pérez, who died in 1554, is explained away as having been the artist's elder brother. The truth being as shrouded as it is, one should be doubly careful lest the scantly documented facts be further obscured by fancies like these which would make of the great early Spanish mannerist of the generation of Juan de Juanes a man fifteen years younger than El Greco, the last of the mannerists, and, indeed a member of the generation of Francisco Ribalta, which fought mannerism tooth and nail.

EL GRECO   Domenikos Theotokopoulos, known as El Greco (1541–1614*), was the last of the Spanish mannerists (by classification). Apart from any classification, however, he was the first painter of international magnitude in the history of Spanish art. Naturally, therefore, he surpassed not only Juan de Juanes and Morales by his brilliant coloration and intensely expressionistic design, but all other forerunners by the incomparable versatility of his creative genius.

He carried the distortion of nature's true forms further than had even the boldest of the Italian mannerists. The latter's departure from nature was confined to far-fetched postures, abnormal proportions of the human figure, and other esthetic whims; in other respects they were more bent than even Michelangelo and Titian on producing an illusion of realness in regard to dress, hair, and still life. Upon El Greco, however, mysticism took so powerful a grip that he ultimately rejected nature altogether as a criterion of his art.

At the beginning of his Spanish career El Greco adhered faithfully to the Italian tradition. For a time he did not depart from the reality of nature. *The Assumption of Mary*† (Chicago, Art Institute), painted in 1577 as the central panel for the main altar of St. Domingo Antiguo in Toledo, was in a sense merely another grandiose Tintoretto,‡ transformed only by El Greco's color imagination, with its peculiar fondness for white light and cool tints, and his more "modern" brushwork. Even when he painted *The Martyrdom of St. Maurice and the Theban Legion*§ (about 1581, Escorial), he was not completely emancipated from the Venetian manner of his day. True, there are in the design some suggestions of the artist's later tendency toward attentuation, and the color chord is quite unique. Its "glacial, moonlit effulgence" is based on the consonance of ultramarine with a brilliant yellow, and a very lustrous cold green with

---

* El Greco's birth in 1541 has been established by D. Francisco de B. San Román; see *De la vida del Greco* in *Archivo español de Arte y Arqueologia* (Madrid, 1927), p. 141.

† *El Greco,* Phaidon Press (Oxford University Press, New York), 22.

‡ See Tintoretto's color sketch for an *Assumption,* reproduced by Josef Meder in *Albertina Facsimiles, Handzeichnungen der Italienischen Meister* (Vienna, 1923), Plate 34.

§ *El Greco,* Phaidon Press, 51–53.

carmine and pink. Moreover, the spacing of the figures and the landscape through atmospheric color gradations marks an advance toward Velasquez which no Venetian of the time could have made. Only as time went on did El Greco revert more deliberately to those ideas and manners of execution which had guided the more mystical art of centuries before. For his own day did not furnish the repertory of forms that was necessary to express the strange otherwoldly images that his genius envisaged. This alone goes a long way toward explaining the growing influence that the Late Gothic exercised on him.

The Dream of Philip II, a sketch for a proposed larger canvas, was a translation of Albrecht Dürer's *Allerheiligenbild* (Vienna, 1511) into the more recessional and vaporous manner of Tintoretto. *The Holy Trinity in the Clouds* (Prado), another panel of the retable of St. Domingo Antiguo in Toledo, was patterned on Dürer's woodcut *Der Gnadenstuhl in Wolken.* This early evidence may suffice to show that even while El Greco was fully conversant with the more advanced sixteenth-century painting of Venice, he was nonetheless preoccupied with the expressionism of the German Late Gothic. Its influence persisted in his later work—in his *Christ in the House of Simon,** for example (owned by Mr. Joseph Winterbotham of Burlington, Vermont). Here the general arrangement follows rather closely a drawing of Tintoretto,† but the exciting glitter of the faceted folds, the lights of triangular shape, and the zigzagging outlines stem from Late Gothic carved-wood altar screens whose rectilinear schematization of the drapery and the other ornamental surface work was devised to break into a thousand prismatic flares the reflected light of the altar tapers. The disposition of today's Greco experts to explain exclusively on the basis of Byzantine models what seems inexplicable in the light of Renaissance conventions or Baroque propensities is open to question. There can be no doubt that the Gothic played an appreciable part in shaping Greco's style.

On the other hand, there is no question that the strongest and most enduring influence came to El Greco from the Byzantine East, his home-

---

* *Ibid.,* 49, 20, 232.

† Chalk-and-pen drawing, Inv. No. 24477, in the Albertina Collection of Vienna, reproduced in *Beschreibender Katalog der Handzeichnungen in der Albertina* (Vienna, 1926), Vol. I, Fig. 92.

land. Almost every pamphlet on Greco is concerned with his Byzantine ancestry. The story has been told in detail,* but a few points which perhaps have not been sufficiently stressed may be repeated here.

Icons and frescoes of the Cretan-Byzantine school of the mid-sixteenth century were the works of art that El Greco knew in his youth. This accounts for the lasting impression that their iconography, proportions, coloration, and even the display of Greek inscriptions near the figures left on him. Moreover, if the whole evolution of El Greco's art in Spain was impelled, perhaps unconsciously, by the desire to synthesize the ancient Eastern mysticism with the more recent Western realism, it was probably fostered by the school in which he grew up. For, as Oskar Wulff first pointed out,† in the days of El Greco's youth his native island was the center of a school of artists who aimed at precisely the same thing: to infuse the sacred iconography of middle Byzantine painting with the color technique of Titian, and with a certain modified Western naturalism.

Common sense compels one to assume that El Greco's early instructors must be sought among the Cretan reformers. If our fragmentary knowledge of the history of sixteenth-century Cretan art did not prohibit so rash a conclusion, one might even venture to name his probable master: Friar Anthony, the creator of the murals of 1544 in Xenophantes (Mount Athos), whose *Agony in the Garden* bears striking resemblance to several of El Greco's compositions of the same subject. The assumption that he was trained in Crete is also borne out by his sojourn in Venice for further training; the fact that Crete was a part of the Venetian Republic does not in itself explain why a young Cretan painter should be studying with Titian. Panselinos, the founder of the Cretan school, and his younger followers, Theophanes and Zorzi of Crete, had their eyes fixed on everything that was going on in the Venetian studios, particularly in Titian's.‡

* Robert Byron, "El Greco," in the *Burlington Magazine,* October, 1929; Robert Byron and David T. Rice, *The Birth of Western Painting* (New York, 1931).

† *Altchristliche und Byzantinische Kunst* (Berlin-Neubabelsberg, 1914), II, 596 ff.

‡ Frank Rutter, *El Greco* (New York, E. Weyhe, 1930, p. 9), has endeavored to explode "the theory that El Greco was actually a pupil of Titian." But this was not a *theory;* it was an established *fact* known to everybody in Spain when Greco first arrived there. When Philip II expressed his dissatisfaction with the *St. Maurice,* everybody wondered why El Greco was abandoning the manner that had made him famous in

Oskar Wulff mentions the unmistakable Venetian coloration of the frescoes which Theophanes completed in 1536 in the Lavra of Mount Athos.
Those of Zorzi of Crete in the Katholikon of Dionysiou (Mount Athos), of

Toledo; and so, Ceán Bermúdez (*Diccionario* V, 5) says, "The courtiers surmised that
the painter changed his style because he *was tired of having his works mistaken for
Titian's.*" Even if this was mere talk, it proves the antiquity of the "theory." Furthermore, the letter from Giulio Clovio to the Cardinal Farnese, dated November 16, 1570
(reprinted in Manuel Cossío's *El Greco,* Madrid, 1908, p. 8) is neither an "unsupported
scrap of gossip" nor "the first documentary evidence." Its content is buttressed by another letter written almost three years earlier, on December 2, 1567, by Titian himself
to Philip II of Spain (reprinted on page 780 of Crowe and Cavalcaselle, *Tizian,* Leipzig,
1877). Although no name is mentioned, historians have been agreed for decades that the
"very talented young student of mine" (*Molto ualente giouine mio discepolo*) to whom
Titian refers can mean but one man—El Greco. In the eyes of the aged Venetian master,
then ninety-two, an assistant aged twenty-six was naturally "young"; Titian's own son
Orazio, then thirty-nine or forty, is mentioned in the same breath as *mio figliuolo.* Any
doubt as to the identity of El Greco is removed by Clovio's letter—provided that this
first-hand source is not brushed aside with the careless remark that it is "the tittle-tattle
of a gossiping correspondent," but read with due attention to all attendant circumstances. Clovio's letter was written when El Greco, just arrived in Rome, had not yet
found time to look for a room. Therefore Clovio asks that the young man, *"a student
of Titian* and, in my judgment, a painter of rare talent, be provided with some room
near the top of the Farnese Palace until he can find other accommodation." One wonders where Clovio found time in such a rush to form a *personal opinion* concerning the
artist's talents. He must have had reliable information. And that this was contained in
a letter from Titian himself is made probable by other considerations. If Titian wished
to recommend his pupil to the Farnesi, he could have selected no better agent than
Clovio, and if Clovio wished for prompt action in securing the protection of the Cardinal, he could not have acted more wisely than he did when he substituted his *own
judgment* for Titian's recommendation. In the Farnese circles Titian was no longer the
popular figure he had been ten or fifteen years before. In 1567, when Titian requested
Cardinal Farnese to put in a word or two in his favor with the Spanish legate, his urgent
letter received no answer. After waiting a whole year, Titian wrote again and tried to
persuade the cardinal by the present of another painting; but it took still more time
before the Farnese remembered him (see Crowe and Cavalcaselle, *op. cit.,* 661 ff.).
Giulio Clovio, on the other hand, whom Titian had known since 1560, was *persona
gratissima* in the Farnese Palace, where he resided until his death. The Macedonian
miniaturist had been on intimate terms with Alexander Farnese since 1545. He had
spent nine years on the illumination of a Book of Hours for him. He accompanied him
to Florence, in 1551, for a three years' stay, and again to Parma, in 1556. Moreover,
Clovio was considered one of the greatest artists of his day, and not only by the Farnesi.
Vasari's biography teems with praise. Incredible though it may seem to us, the name of
Giulio Clovio once had the power of magic. A recommendation from him carried more
weight than one from Titian.

1547, seem to have an even greater significance in relation to El Greco. One encounters in the paintings on the vaults not only what seem to be the twin brothers of El Greco's half-length *Apostles,* but many other iconographical and coloristic similarities, in short, the clue to his later style.

Fig. 49.—Titian: *The Pentecost,* Venice, St. Maria della Salute

I would not be misunderstood. The genius of El Greco cannot be *explained* from these or any other influences, however widely one may rationalize the causes of the evolution of his manner.* In the last analysis, the enigma of El Greco's art resolves into the fact, already mentioned in connection with Morales, that certain technical means, brought in from without, were put to quite another end than that for which they had been invented. The brushwork in *The Thunderstorm over Toledo†* (Metropolitan Museum) can very well be traced to Tintoretto's mannerisms—for instance, in his *Jesus Stilling the Storm* (New York, Mr. Arthur Sachs). But the mannerism ministers to a conception that never entered the mind of any Venetian; the mystic vision of a city seemingly engendered by lightning. In quest of the world of the spirit, El Greco finally relinquished the world of things and the esthetic rules derived from it. The verity of the senses no longer bound him when he created the *Purisima* of

* Frank Rutter, *op. cit.,* 23, accounts for El Greco's manner by its adventitious resemblance to the Romanesque Catalan murals. One wonders whether in the days of the Renaissance, when Medieval art was practically synonymous with "mediocre art," any artist bound from Venice for Toledo or Madrid would have spent day after day climbing the forbidding mountains and valleys of North Catalonia in quest of murals that nobody except the village communicants knew anything about. After all, those murals were not in the City Museum of Barcelona in Greco's days!

† *El Greco,* Phaidon Edition, 223.

1613 (Toledo, Museum of San Vicente), or the truly Apocalyptic *Opening of the Fifth Seal** (Ignacio Zuloaga Collection at Zumaya).

A comparison of his *Pentecost* (Prado, Fig. 50) with that of Titian (Venice, St. Maria della Salute, Fig. 49), which undoubtedly inspired the Spanish composition, makes it perfectly plain how El Greco, in applying the Creto-Byzantine conventions, transformed his teacher's Renaissance ideas into ideas more akin to the mysticism of the Spanish mind. Titian's statuesque body poses enacted by athletic men or women were translated into a self-expressive weft of abstract lines, bands, and other ornamental configurations of colored light. The actors in El  Greco's painting are said to be much more ecstatic than those in Titian's. As a matter of fact, El Greco's Disciples cannot be considered as real actors at all. They are simulacra, not persons. They are quite unreal. No normal physical being could, for instance, imitate the pose and action of the entranced Apostle in the right-hand foreground, whereas he could easily reproduce those of the figure occupying the same place in Titian's painting. El Greco's Disciple can be interpreted only by dint of a simile, and not even a human simile at that. He is fashioned like the undulating leaf of a tulip, curling the more languishingly as it droops backward, while the other stems and petals in this fragrant bouquet rise and unfold.

El Greco carried emotionalism to a crest that lesser talents could scarcely have achieved, even if the epoch of which his ecstatic art was an expression had not been rapidly nearing its end. With the dissolution of the fanatical Catholic Reformation of the Jesuits toward the close of the sixteenth century, and the widespread growth of a less romantic and more matter-of-fact attitude toward life, this fantastic mannerism was doomed.

Fig. 50.—El Greco: *The Pentecost*, Prado

* *Ibid.*, 226, 215, 217.

At this point it becomes apparent that, indirectly, the Italian tide did benefit the art of Spain. The doctrines imported from abroad proved to be so utterly alien that they could not have long endured. But the complete inadjustability of the foreign molds to Spanish self-expression aroused, first, ardent opposition and, ultimately, a radical esthetic reformation from which Spanish art emerged like a phoenix.

Moreover, the Italian tide swept the *entire* country. However destructive its effects upon native realism may have been for a time, the tide succeeded in fusing what had previously been an agglomeration of scattered provincial studios into something more like a single Spanish school.

This generalization should not, of course, be taken for more than it is worth. As has been said, Spain, the land of individualists and lone adventurers, never developed "schools" so well organized as did Italy, for instance. Still, as compared with the erratic conditions that prevailed in the fifteenth century, Spanish art of the late sixteenth century appears to have a common national trend in spite of its foreign inclinations. So when at the close of the century a number of forceful leaders rose in protest against this mystic formalism and fought for a renascence of the genuine Spanish directness of expression, their opposition no longer appealed to the art of this, that, or the other regional party, but to all Spanish artists. And since their efforts were successful, the whole of Spanish art reformed. The renascence which occurred in Spanish art as well as in Spanish literature shortly before the dawn of the seventeenth century was the first united movement toward a Spanish national art.

SPANISH ART
COMES OF AGE

BOOK THREE

The Age of Cervantes and Ribalta

CHAPTER SEVEN

NEW IDEALS AND NEW GOALS The trend in literature inaugurated at the turn of the century by Cervantes (1547–1616) was congenial to the trend in art inaugurated by painters born within fifteen to thirty years of the poet: Francisco Ribalta (1565–1628), reformer of the schools of Madrid and Valencia; Juan de las Roelas (about 1560–1625) and Francisco Herrera *el Viejo* (1576–1656), reformers of the school of Seville; and Francisco Pacheco (1564–1654), theoretician and historian of the whole movement. The community of their artistic tastes, particularly their aversion to the formalism of the art of the immediate past and their revolutionary aims, makes it appropriate to consider them together in this chapter.*

It is a comparatively recent theory, whose validity, however, has already been widely recognized in the field of *Geistesgeschichte,* that in each generation the exponents of art share certain ideals and aversions, and that the solidarity of their thinking is conditioned by the predominant spirit of the period of their birth and adolescence.†

The problem may be approached from two points of view: the common repertory of subject matter and the common repertory of forms. For this comparison of art and literature in the age of Cervantes the formal aspect alone is of significance; more precisely, the mode of expression devised by

* See Américo Castro, *El pensamiento de Cervantes* (Madrid, 1935), for the significance of the poet and novelist in the ideology of his epoch.

† See José Ortega y Gasset, *El tema de nuestro tiempo* (Madrid, 1923), published in English as *The Modern Theme* (New York, 1933); Wilhelm Pinder, *Das Problem der Generation in der Kunstgeschichte* (Berlin, 1928): Walter Scheidt, *Lebensgesetze der Kultur* (Berlin, 1929); Julius Petersen, *Die literarischen Generationen* (Berlin, 1930); and Eduard Wechsler, *Die Generationen als Jugendreihe* (Leipzig, 1930).

both writers and painters to drive home their messages with new force and precision. So far as this problem is concerned it is immaterial that, as in *Don Quixote,* the novel tells of a romantic mind upset by reading too many absurd novels or that, as in Ribalta's *Vow of St. Francis,* the picture tells of an ecstatic friar whom the Lord on the Cross rewards with His crown of thorns.

The artists of the Cervantes age, that is, those born in the second half of the sixteenth century, strove for an *estilo nacional** and for an *estilo desornamentado.* Underlying these ideals was the universal desire for a simple, captivating naturalism stripped of ornamental trimmings and free from affectation. They greatly disliked the otherworldly, flamboyant, and therefore obsolete, mannerism of El Greco.† Indeed, the true nature of the new trend could not be worse distorted than by likening El Greco to Cervantes, as has been done.‡ Artists of equal genius, whatever their generation, will always have certain traits in common, but Cervantes' and El Greco's disparities are manifestly more significant than their similarities. El Greco, born six years before Cervantes, was the last exponent of mannerism; Cervantes derided mannerism.

The revolutionary impulse of the age of Cervantes sprang from the conviction that the formalism of the older generation, which reached its crest in the early seventies, was basically un-Spanish. The nationalistic reaction was emphatically voiced in 1575 by Argote de Molina, who took an energetic stand for old Spanish folk poetry; again in 1599 by Lope de Vega, who (in the preface to *San Isidro de Madrid*) condemned every literary form that was not genuinely Spanish; and finally in 1605 by Cervantes, who laughed the whole manneristic show off the stage in his *Don Quixote.*

In the preface to his novel Cervantes draws a self-portrait: "Sitting once

* *"Fué el primero que sacudió en Andalucia la manera timida y se formó un nuevo estilo que manifiesta el genio nacional"* was the judgment of Palomino concerning Francisco Herrera *el Viejo.*

† See José Ortega y Gasset's remark on El Greco, in *El punto de vista en las artes* (*Revista de Occidente,* Madrid, 1933, p. 109); *"Yo creo que se ha exagerado su modernidad y su cercania a Velázquez."*

‡ Hans Rosenkranz, *El Greco and Cervantes in the Rhythm of Experience* (London, Peter Davies, 1932).

in a very studious posture, with my paper before me, my quill behind my ear, my elbow on the table, and my cheek on my hand, considering how I should begin; a certain friend of mine, a cheerful and bright fellow, entered unexpectedly. Finding me thus, he asked me what I was so very intent and thoughtful upon. 'What will the public think of me [exclaims the author], the old legislator, the vulgar? They will say, I have spent my youthful days very finely to have nothing to recommend my gray hairs to the world, but a dry, insipid story, wanting good language as well as invention, barren of conceits or pointed wit, and without either quotations on the margin, or annotations at the end, which other books, though never so fabulous and profane, have to set them off. Other authors can pass upon the public, by stuffing their books from Aristotle, Plato, and the whole company of ancient philosophers; thus amusing their readers into a great opinion of their prodigious reading. Plutarch and Cicero are slurred on the public for as orthodox doctors as St. Thomas, or any of the Fathers. And then the method of these moderns is so wonderfully agreeable and full of variety that they cannot fail to please. In one line, they will describe you a whining amorous coxcomb, and the next shall be some dry scrap of a homily, with such ingenious turns as cannot choose but ravish the reader. Now I want all these embellishments and graces: I have neither marginal notes nor critical remarks; I do not so much as know what authors I follow.' " Whereupon the friend gives this reassuring reply: "I always took you for a man of sense, but now I am sufficiently convinced to the contrary. Those fabulous extravagancies have nothing to do with the impartial punctuality of true history. *Nothing but pure nature is your business; her you must consult, and the closer you can imitate, your picture is the better.* Do but take care to express yourself in a plain, easy manner, in well-chosen, significant terms and to give an harmonious and pleasing turn to your periods; study to explain your thoughts, and set them in the truest light, laboring, as much as possible, not to leave them dark nor intricate, but clear and intelligible. . . . Mind this, and your business is done."*

It is common knowledge that *Don Quixote* was written with a special literary purpose. The author himself stated that repeatedly, not only in

* Paraphrased from the translation by Matteaux.

the preface. The necessity for a reformation was clear in his mind when he began to compose his novel. But even while composing it he matured personally throughout the many years of its production. Ideas and plans vaguely sketched to begin with materialized more and more. What at first had been merely a program became, as time went on, a vital experience. The nature of the poet's personal development casts valuable light upon his entire period.

As his novel grows, "Cervantes wishes instinctively to remove himself as far as he possibly can from the bad road along which he first started." Abandoning the style of a conventional comic writer, he becomes a psychological realist in the modern sense of the word and strives to make his characters profoundly real. In the second part of the novel Cervantes no longer writes as a satirist but almost as a tragic poet. Only on the assumption that a gradual inner evolution took place in the author can the death of his hero be explained—that death which so curiously reminds one of the Ajax tragedy of Sophocles: ". . . the hero is convinced that he will not . . . see Dulcinea in all the days of his life, and so he dies of sorrow—and sanity. He has recovered his reason, but lost the ideal in which he lives and breathes, so naught is left to him but to die." Cervantes' ultimate achievement thus consisted in "destroying the moulds in which the novel of chivalry was formed, taking its fictions from the world of Chimera and *bringing them to the world of reality.*"*

The advice of the "friend," quoted above, contains in a nutshell the plan of an esthetic reformation which applies quite as well to the art of Ribalta and Herrera the Elder. Similar theories were expressed in Pacheco's *Arte de la Pintura*. Significant truth was the goal. It was to take the place of hollow rhetoric. The revolution aimed to destroy the formalism of the past, of which there is no better illustration than the pompous prose of Antonio de Guevara, court chronicler of Charles V. No doubt such books as his *Menosprecio de Corte y Alabanza de Aldea* were oratory per se, oratory as an end in itself: the phraseology and verbal prestidigitation of Cicero wedded to the euphony and the sonorous sway of Isocrates. Like these ancients, Guevara commanded every imaginable trick of oratorical

* R. Menendez Pidal, "The Genesis," in *The Anatomy of Don Quixote* (Ithaca, New York, 1932), 21, 38, 40.

style. Thoughts were merely the excuse for sounding phrases. The sound outweighed the sense.

In precisely the same fashion Juan de Juanes, Luis de Vargas, Pablo de Cespedes, and other painters active after the middle of the sixteenth century trimmed their paintings with all sorts of mannerisms lifted from Roman antiquity; with pretentious gestures and contorted poses purloined from the schools of Leonardo da Vinci, Michelangelo, and Raphael; with lighting stunts borrowed from certain Dutch masters; with unusual foreshortenings derived from Correggio; and with a scheme of coloration taken from the Venetians. In the pictures of these mannerists simple gestures and natural attitudes are unknown. The uselessness of the action of the figures—the bulging muscles, extravagant drapery, complicated bends and turns—is absurd; there, too, the sound is more significant than the sense.

The new outlook manifests itself first in the artist's interpretation of his subject matter. In pictures of both religious and profane subjects the painters of the new age—Ribalta, Ribera, Zurbaran, and Velasquez— depict characters as characters. Ribalta's *Vow of St. Francis* (Fig. 62) conveys succinctly a notion of the Saint's personality, more tangibly real than any previous image and much more plausible as a psychological characterization. Here St. Francis is a person one understands and sympathizes with, a deeply moving character quite unlike the indifferent effigy one usually encounters in the paintings of the Renaissance.

Ribalta's purpose in developing each significant character and boldly communicating his concept to the beholder was much the same as Cervantes'. As characters, Don Quixote and Sancho were far removed from the type figures in the chivalrous novels of the sixteenth century, which followed one upon another like so many links in a chain. In its want of psychological depth Renaissance literature was on the same level as Renaissance painting. Indifference to the faithful characterization of the protagonist is found even where it is least expected—for instance, in the archetype of the picaresque novel *Lazarillo de Tormes* (first published in 1554, but written somewhat earlier). A critic judging this novel only in relation to the formalistic period in which it was born is quite justified in admiring its precocious realism, but when he compares it with novels composed half a century later, such as *El Buscón* (1626), Francisco de Quevedo's mordant satire on the social conditions of his period, or Vicente Martinez Espinel's *Marcos de Obregón* (1618), he must admit that these later authors stressed the psychological portrayal of character far more, and that it was they who first made the hero a dominant character. Certainly Lazarillo was not a character comparable to Don Quixote or to Sancho, but a comic generalization, and not a dominating one at that. He is constantly employed as a connecting link between the other type figures—the representatives of typical professions whom the picaro serves in succession. His masters are depicted with greater care than he, the hero, is. On the other hand, all these exponents of Spanish society are reduced to some common denominator. All have certain typical features: the blind man, the priest, the nobleman, the friar, the indulgence-vendor, the constable. The one is as avaricious as the other; each hands to his servant a flogging instead of food; Lazarillo picks the pockets of each, and then relishes his revenge time and again in exactly the same manner.

In much the same way the Spanish paintings of the Renaissance differ from those of the Baroque. The executions of saints were as popular in pictorial art as the adventures of knights and fools in contemporary literature. In the cinquecento the interpretations were less bloodthirsty than they had been in the quattrocento. Juan de Juanes, for instance, did not include in his *Death of St. Ines* (Prado) the appalling details that Master Alfonso portrayed in *The Martyrdom of St. Medin* (Figs. 46, 47). Master Juan was too much concerned with the Italian theory of composition to indulge in pathological sensationalism. The invention (or imitation) of startling plastic postures and their enclosure in circular or semicircular group outlines were almost all that mattered to the sixteenth-century idealists. But the cinquecentists and the quattrocentists had this in common: they did not single out any characters for a predominant role.

Ribalta, with his pupil Ribera, revived realism, although with less cruelty. The more mature sensitivity of these seventeenth-century artists accounts for their avoidance of the horrible. The more naïve quattrocentists had described atrocities with great gusto because they were not yet fully aware of their atrociousness. Despite its realism, the decapitation of St. Medin was perhaps little more than conventionalism to Master Alfonso; at any rate it was no fearful reality. In a sense these Primitives were like children who thrill over the report of some dreadful murder case, and even re-enact it with their playmates. The artists of the Baroque are like adults who are conscious of the horror of the real thing and shrink from it.

In his early work Ribera did sometimes analyze, say, *The Flaying of St. Bartholomew,* with an exasperating veracity that reminds one directly of the Primitives. Compare, for example, his etching of 1624 (*B. 6*) with Huguet's painting of the same subject on the retable which came from San Celoni into the Barcelona Museum. But the older he grew the less he stressed factual atrocities. In the period of the Baroque it became customary not to represent the ordeal proper but the tense moment preceding it. See *The Flaying of St. Bartholomew* (Madrid and Berlin) and *The Crucifixion of St. Andrew* (Budapest) by Ribera, and *Christ at the Column,* the moment preceding the scourging, by Zurbaran (at one time in the Johann Ahrens Collection at Hamburg) and by Velasquez (London, National Gallery).

This, however, is noteworthy above all else—the martyr pictures of the Cervantes age are psychological studies of the respective saints as personal characters. By comparison with Ribera all the earlier effigies of saints seem to be impersonal and anonymous. His executioners, judges, onlookers, and so on, are all treated merely as a setting, though individually they may be marvelous studies from life. Juan de Juanes, in the above-mentioned *Death of St. Ines,* had his stage crowded with actors none of whom—or, rather, each of whom—plays the leading part. The contrast with the Baroque is remarkable. Upon the stage that Ribera set for his *St. Ines* (1642, Dresden, Fig. 63), only the martyr is present. Yet even without the attendant details, the beholder seems to sense the presence of a hostile mob and the imminence of the ordeal. With one figure the artist re-creates the suspense of the moment when this pure maiden, exposed to the greedy eyes of the patrons of a house of ill fame, kneels and prays with great composure.

The dramatic "suspense" is symbolized in the very pattern of the (geometric) composition. The posture of St. Ines is of an almost archaic simplicity and "purity." Her body is strictly frontalized and rises from a limpid rectangle. Her lower limbs are horizontals and the rest of the body is a perpendicular coinciding with the central vertical axis of the picture. A trapdoor in the foreground to the right repeats the right angle. But this severe schema is abruptly thwarted by the blanket which the angel graps around the maiden—a harsh diagonal precipitated from the upper left-hand corner that threatens to overthrow the whole, carefully calculated equilibrium.

In other words, Ribera's painting is animated from within; the very composition is determined by something spiritual that is difficult to define. The significance of this achievement will become more apparent if we review the evolutionary course of character depiction from the time of the Primitives and cite some illustrative examples.

The complete and fully rounded characterization that Ribera strove for and achieved was quite beyond the range of primitive imagination, if for no other reason than that the Primitives did not conceive of "life" in terms of a harmonious union of mind and body. They were satisfied with a fairly exhaustive depiction of unanimated reality and accordingly confined their efforts to copying life's outer shell.

The spiritual element that the Primitives disregarded became the chief objective of the mystic painters of the sixteenth century. Morales and El Greco hated the materialistic realism of the past. Not only did they repudiate the old conception that life was synonymous with corporeality, but they adopted the opposite concept, that life was synonymous with the living soul. This explains why they so concerned themselves with spiritual expression that physical accuracy soon suffered. Morales and El Greco revealed the soul at the expense of the body. With their deliberate distortion of physical proportions, character depiction departed more and more from physical verity.

The rising generation of realists joined together what had thus been torn asunder by the Mannerists. Their attitude was distinguished from the Primitive as well as from the Manneristic. The representatives of the Cervantes-Ribalta generation acknowledged neither a body without a soul, nor a soul without a body—rather, the harmonious synthesis of both. If the Primitives had sought unanimated physical verity and the Mannerists fanciful animation at the expense of natural accuracy, the goal of Ribalta, Ribera, Zurbaran, and Velasquez was completely animated corporeality. Instead of studying the model detached from the mood, environment, and event, they considered the attendant conditions and the psychological effect they had upon the model's spirited expression. The interdependence of spirit and matter was realized for the first time.

Illustrations will be more convincing than abstract definitions. *The Mother of Sorrows* by an anonymous Castilian (Prado, Fig. 51) is as conscientious a study from the model as could be expected in the Spanish quattrocento. The face, the hands, and the costume have been scrutinized closely, but so strongly are the physical features stressed that no animation could be conveyed even if the artist had wished to do so. In contrast to the spirited *Mother of Sorrows* of Luis de Morales (Prado, Fig. 52), the primitive picture seems lifeless. The Mannerist, however, went to the other extreme. His picture is an expression of feeling, and feeling alone— an unprecedented sentimental outpouring; obviously physical accuracy comes off second best. The excessive animation comes from partial accentuation. The ghostly illumination emphasizes the convulsed fingers and

Fig. 51.—Fifteenth-Century School of Castile: *Mother of Sorrows*, Prado

Fig. 52.—Luis de Morales: *Mother of Sorrows*, Prado

Fig. 53.—Jose Ribera: *Mother of Sorrows*,
Kassel, Picture Gallery

the tearful eye, but at the same time obliterates a part of the face and leaves the beholder guessing what has become of the left arm. Such an obscure presentment was repulsive to the artists of Cervantes' generation. Ribera, as his *Mother of Sorrows* (Kassel Gallery, Fig. 53) shows, avoids such unclearness. One need only compare the two pairs of hands of the respective Virgins. Nothing could be simpler and more lucid than the ten interlocking fingers which Ribera presents in elementary coordination. Moreover, these hands form an inextricable unity; they are not two separate hands, but a pair of hands clenched in agonized prayer. Their simple union is the secret of the intense emotional effect. It will be noticed also that there is no overacting. The physical accuracy of the Primitives is harmoniously welded with the emotionalism of the Mannerists, but the whole seems the more perfect because now a living soul speaks eloquently through its physical vehicle, the living body.

THE NARRATION OF THE ESTILO DESORNAMENTADO The ascetic purism of Francisco Ribalta must have dismayed the admirers of manneristic art. An example is *St. Matthew and the Angel* (Fig. 54), one of the smaller panels of the retable from the Cartuja de Porta-Coeli (1626–27), now in the gallery of Valencia.

The Evangelist is writing at the dictation of the angel in a drab and utterly unattractive room. What little of it is visible lacks the customary decoration. There is no handsomely tiled floor, no *artesonado* ceiling, no Roman architecture. A plump man is seated at a table roughly carpentered of raw wood. His clothes of thick wool glower in the dark; where the scarlet cloak is spotted out by a ray of light it has a warm luster, but there its beauty ends. The upright bearing of the Evangelist, his right hand heavily poised on the book, his head thrust around at the angel in eager anticipation of his message—all this is entirely "unstudied." And that was the novelty. An innovation also was the fusion of the actors and the setting in the nocturnal dusk, from which only a few important areas are spotted out by the light. Because the details are thus obscured and the whole can be perceived only as an indivisible entity, it yields a surprising impression of reality.

The freshness of Ribalta's approach will be realized by comparing his painting with those by Juan de Juanes depicting similar situations. Let us select *The Dispute between St. Stephen and the Jewish Doctors in the Synagogue of Jerusalem*, one of the five panels of the retable of St. Stephen, of Valencia (Prado, Fig. 55).

Fig. 54.—Francisco Ribalta: *St. Matthew and the Angel*, Valencia, Picture Gallery

There is no denying that Juan de Juanes admitted a modicum of natural truthfulness. He planned his "history" of St. Stephen with the rational logic of a playwright. It was of no small importance to him that the dramatis personae be clearly distinguishable. They were apparently portrayed from life. Leonardo's *Tractate on Painting* may have convinced him that "the greatest defect in a painter is to repeat the same attitudes and the same expressions . . . in one. . . ."* Of course Renaissance portraiture was not portraiture as such. It was Leonardo's opinion that a painter should sketch faces from life whenever he had a chance, and carry those sketches in a booklet upon his person so that he might draw inspiration from them when in need of character heads. But when using them, he was to make a choice from among them of the perfect parts. The paintings were to be generalized and idealized.† Still it should be noted that Juan did not use mere type figures, and that he assigned definite roles to each of his actors.

* *The Notebooks of Leonardo da Vinci*, arranged, rendered into English, and introduced by Edward MacCurdy (New York, Reynal and Hitchcock, 1939), 914.
† *Ibid.*, 883–886.

Saul, for instance, "at whose feet the false witnesses laid down their clothes before the stoning," appears not only in the closing scene where his presence was required. The same short-whiskered, handsome young man—in all likelihood it is a self-portrait—appears in all five acts and always in the role of a compassionate onlooker (which is contrary to the Golden Legend). In *The Disputation with the Jewish Doctors* (Fig. 55)

his spirited profile is seen against the landscape; in *The Trial* it looms out of the darkness behind the judge's chair; next, in *St. Stephen Led to the Execution,* it emerges *en face* between the Saint and one of the false witnesses; it appears for the last time, somewhat aged, in the left-hand corner of *The Interment.* Only in the last-named scene does the Golden Legend call for Nicodemus and for Gamaliel, the teacher of Saul; but Juan puts both characters on the stage from the start. Likewise, the two false witnesses make their first appearance at the city gate, that is, before their required entry in *The Stoning.* In all this there is about as much "naturalism" as in the works of

Fig. 55.—Juan de Juanes: *St. Stephen and the Jewish Doctors,* Prado

any graduate of the school of Leonardo. The distinguishing mark is that the fundamentally rational conception is curiously at odds with the entirely unnatural attitudinizing of the actors.

None of the Jewish doctors foregathered in the rich Renaissance hall simply "sits" as Ribalta's St. Matthew does. Their postures are "heroic." Again Juan's painting reminds one of the standard rules of Leonardo's studio, such as this one*: "The compositions of painted histories shall induce the beholder to respond with emotions similar to those expressed

* Marie Herzfeld, *Leonardo da Vinci, Traktat von der Malerei* (Jena, 1909), 126, paragraph 246 (author's translation).

in the picture. . . . If the emotional agitation is not so communicated that it stirs the beholder's soul, causing him to move his own limbs as though he were himself participating in the event, all the trouble and genius of the artist has been spent in vain."

For the most part, Juan patterned his postures, probably indirectly, upon Michelangelo's *Prophets* and *Sibyls* of the Sistine ceiling. Except for slight variations, the pose of the man seated in the center (Gamaliel) resembles that of Michelangelo's *Prophet Isaiah,* with an added typical manneristic twist, familiar from certain paintings of Francesco Salviati. St. Stephen overacts the gesture of Michelangelo's *Prophet Ezekiel,* combining it with the swagger of Fra Bartolommeo's *Prophet Isaiah* (Uffizi). Rabbis deport themselves like ancient Prophets, for anything less ambitious would have seemed puerile to the Spanish taste of the mid-sixteenth century. Naturally, under such circumstances, the whole fails to yield an impression of "organic" unity, in spite of the skill with which the numerous figures and parts have been combined quite artificially by a pin-wheel composition, triangulation, and bilateral symmetry.

How then would such an assembly picture have been painted in the disornamented style? A little way up the main gallery the visitor to the Prado discovers an example. *The Initiation of St. Buenaventura to the Franciscan Order,* by Francisco Herrera *el Viejo* (1629, Fig. 56), depicts a Spanish hidalgo who renounces earthly riches for monastic vows. The narrative is one that would have offered an opportunity for histrionic display to any cinque-centist. Not so, however, to the early seventeenth-century foes of "ornamentalism." Herrera stilled the external action and replaced

Fig. 56.—Francisco Herrera the Elder: *The Initiation of St. Buenaventura,* Prado

the conventional color brilliance with color drabness. Instead of excessive
individual movement there is the sustained mass of the friars. The much-
indented group outline of Juan de Juanes' *Disputation* is replaced by a
near horizontal of heads. Gesticulation is reduced to a minimum. The story
is related in terms of faces rather than of bodies. Most of the friars have
their hands buried in their cassock sleeves. In contrast to the twelve lo-
quacious hands belonging to the eight individuals in Juan's painting,
Herrera's thirteen characters exhibit only seven hands, and of these only
four are eloquent. The scarcity of gesture is all the more forceful because it
is in keeping with the temper of these simple-minded descendants of
Andalusian peasants—friars stubbornly reticent by nature.

The art of Herrera cannot be explained by the artist's closer observation of life alone. It was a new *art*. All compositional resources were employed with the utmost economy. What an ado of heads, tilted backward,
forward, and sidewise, in Juan's *Disputation!* And yet, how slight the
effectiveness of that bag of tricks when compared with the singular
strength of the tilted head of the Prior amid a unison of verticals in the
painting of Herrera. It is startling because it marks the exception to the
rule and, further, because it is reinforced by the parallel movement of the
more isolated friar on the extreme right. And the image of that be-
spectacled simpleton! Leaning forward awkwardly, his hands in his sleeves,
he expresses an inner participation in the event, much more gripping
than the select histrionic pose of Juan's St. Stephen.

When, on the other hand, it came to the depiction of mystical or transcendental themes, the new realism was less well equipped than had been
the mannerism of Morales and El Greco. This is not surprising. Apoth-
eoses and celestial apparitions had been the domain of the cinquecento. To
the earth-bound views of the Cervantes age such phantasms were re-
fractory. For all its poignant portrait heads, Herrera's *St. Basil Dictating
His Doctrine* (Louvre) makes one long for Raphael's *Disputa,* in which
the communion of heaven with earth seemed to have come true. *The
Apotheosis of St. Thomas Aquinas* by Zurbaran (1631, Seville Museum),
despite its inimitable painterly qualities, also makes an entirely unvision-
ary impression in comparison with Raphael's *Transfiguration.* Unlike the
idealism of the cinquecento masters, the rationalism of Zurbaran chal-

Fig. 57.—El Greco: *The Interment of Count Orgaz* (detail), Toledo, Santo Tome

lenges the criticism of the intelligent beholder. It seems simply absurd that men as corporeal as these should disport themselves on clouds.

THE PORTRAITURE OF THE ESTILO DESORNAMENTADO The forte of the Spanish Early Baroque was portraiture—the one branch of art that refers the eye to the factual and puts the checkrein on subjective imagination. In the erratic evolution of Spanish painting, portraiture had always been the stabilizing element. The crude *verismo* of Master Alfonso's *Martyrdom of St. Medin* (Fig. 46) was mitigated by the placid portraits of the bystand-

Fig. 58.—Ferrando Yañez de l'Almedina: *Portrait of a Man,* Prado

ers. The soaring mysticism of El Greco's *Interment of Count Orgaz* (1586, Toledo, Santo Tome, Fig. 6) was counterbalanced by the pithy likenesses of the Toledan gentlemen in the lower half of the picture and the portraits of Saints Augustin and Stephen laying the body of the pious count to rest (Fig. 57).

On the whole, the Spanish Mannerists refrained in their portrait painting from the distortions and exaggerations employed in their religious pictures. In fact, they practiced more restraint than their forerunners, the straight imitators of the Italians. The noble likeness of *Don Luis de Castelvi* by Juan de Juanes (Prado) has nothing of the excessive lyricism of attitude, facial expression, and coloration of *The Gentleman with the Golden Box* by Ferrando Yañez de l'Almedina (Prado, about 1510, Fig. 58), whose head tilts languishingly to the left after the Italian fashion then in vogue.* The congenital Spanish sense of personal dignity probably

* Giampetrino's *St. Magdalen* (Milan, Brera) illustrates the exuberant intentions of such a contraposto pattern. Sodoma loved to lend that tilt to the heads of his protagonists. Sebastiano del Piombo's so-called *Fornarina* (Uffizi) is very similar to Ferrando's portrait in compositional arrangement. The keynote to the inherent mood is best found in the head of the Friar in Giorgione's famous *Concerto* (Pitti Palace).

Fig. 59.—Alonso Sanchez Coello: *Alexander Farnese* (?), Dublin, National Gallery

caused the sitters to protest against such sentimental exhibitionism.

It is remarkable how seldom any action was admitted in the portraits of the later Spanish realists. From Sanchez Coello (Fig. 59) to Velasquez (Fig. 72) the models were viewed squarely from in front, either standing or sitting with both arms loosely drooping or, if need be, with one hand resting on the arm of a chair, on a table, on the hip, or on the pommel of the sword. More, it seems, was contrary to Spanish *sosiego*. In this respect the Spanish portraits of the seventeenth century differ markedly from the Flemish ones by Rubens or van Dyck. The portraitists of the Cervantes period shunned the devices by which in earlier days the likenesses were rendered more attractive or flattering. The realists wanted nothing but the unadulterated record and permitted neither the addition nor the subtraction of the most minute characteristic.

This may be illustrated by a single detail. In other countries no contemporary painter would have dreamed of reproducing the eyeglasses of his model. Spaniards were the first to realize that eyeglasses lend an ineradicable stamp to the features. El Greco did not hesitate to portray the large goggles of *The Great In-*

Fig. 60.—Francisco Pacheco: *A Knight of Santiago*, Richmond, Collection of Sir Frederick Cook

quisitor (New York, Metropolitan Museum). The spontaneous effect of Pacheco's likeness of *A Knight of Santiago* (Richmond, Sir Frederick Cook Collection, Fig. 60) is in large measure owing to the horn-rimmed spectacles. For the sake of matter-of-fact verity Sanchez Coello went even farther. He portrayed *Princess Eboli* (Madrid, Duke of Infantado) wearing the square patch of ugly black bandage which covered her blind eye. But in Italy even such a quattrocento realist as Piero dei Franceschi painted *The Duke of Urbino* (Uffizi) in profile so that his missing eye would be concealed. Raphael, the cinquecento idealist, in his portrait of *Count Tommaso Inghirami* (Boston, Fenway Court) minimized the cast of his sitter's right eye by giving him a pensive heavenward look.

It has been said that the Mannerists often used portraits to enliven their religious "histories." But not only were the portraits "idealized"; they were also submerged in a mass of negligible appendages. Thus the Baroque may be distinguished from the Renaissance, for in religious paintings the former made more of the portraits. Pablo de Cespedes included a great number of authentic portraits in his *Last Supper* (Seville Museum, Fig. 17). But they cannot assert themselves against the turmoil of poses and gestures, the unrest of light and dark, the multifarious still life upon and around the table, and the countless appurtenances of the room. Compare with this manneristic concoction Ribalta's *Last Supper* on the high altar of Corpus Cristi Church in Valencia (1606). The intensity of its portraits results from the fact that all that might have obstructed their pure effect has been pruned away with unwavering determination. The hall is no longer broadly extended, nor is it lavish with niches, statues, vistas, draperies, and what not. The solemn surge of a simple apse is adumbrated in terms of a few vertical strips. Save for the *Santo Cáliz* in its center, the round table is bare. The Disciples are so grouped around it that, with the exception of the two kneeling in front, nothing becomes eloquent but a few hands and faces. Among these are the spirited portraits of Archbishop Juan de Ribera, Pedro Muñoz, and Ribalta's nagging shoemaker, who, if local gossip may be trusted, had to consent to being cast in the role of Judas Iscariot.

Ribalta's mature style did not come to him fortuitously. Only very gradually did he tear himself from the conventions of mannerism. The self-criticism that guided him ultimately toward greater simplicity is akin to that of Cervantes in aim as well as in method. The smaller *Last Supper* in the gallery of Valencia is, I think, an early milestone on his evolutionary path.* It marks the transition from mannerism to realism. Here Ribalta was already aiming at a more concentrated expression. Heads and hands alone should speak. There are only half-length figures and the picture space is cut down at the bottom as well as on either side. On the other hand, the histrionics of mannerism are still quite noticeable. The congestion of thirteen agitated figures upon so slight a canvas is in keeping with the boisterous deportment of the Disciple in the left-hand foreground, who turns to the spectator, summons him with his protruding right hand, and simultaneously points out Christ with the other, like a "barker" before a circus show. To be heard above the clatter, the Lord must lift the Sacred Host high above His head and point out the chalice with the index finger of the other hand. In the mature painting of 1606 such exclamation marks are dispensed with.

SIDELIGHTS FROM THE HISTORY OF MUSIC From what has been said it is apparent that the "disembellished" style implied not only a more direct and penetrating study of life but also a reshaping of the current principles of decoration. "Do not leave your thoughts and periods dark or intricate, but make them intelligible and clear"—Cervantes' demand for compositional clarification applies to pictorial art no less than to literature. In the paintings of Ribalta the expression became more pithy through the elimination of the negligible ornamental appendages. His reticence makes the preceding cinquecentists seem garrulous and somewhat confused.

I would not be misunderstood. I say the cinquecentists *seem* confused; I do not say they *were* confused. The esthetic departure around the year 1600 does not entitle us to criticize adversely the art of the past. No one

* Delphine Fitz Darby, in *Francisco Ribalta and His School* (Cambridge, Harvard University Press, 1938), attributes the painting to Vicente Castello.

would condemn the polyphonous music of Pierluigi Palestrina and Or-
lando di Lasso on the ground that the composers of the early seventeenth
century abandoned polyphony for the monody of Claudio Monteverdi.

My reference to music is not casual. For the *stilo rappresentativo* of the
Italian seicento music was related in more than one respect to the *estilo
desornamentado* of the Spanish painters, sculptors, and architects. At the
beginning of the seventeenth century all were aiming at expression in
lucid, well-chosen, and significant *natural* terms. Monteverdi relinquished
the figurate interlace of numerous voice parts, the ornamental coloratura,
and the merely fanciful lyrical melody of the past, and replaced them with
a recitation simulating the natural inflections of speech, similar to the
Sprachmelodie of Richard Wagner. "Nothing but pure nature is your
business; her you must consult, and the closer you can imitate, the better"
—that axiom of Cervantes might well be inscribed in large letters over
Monteverdi's *dramma per musica,* in which the monody, accompanied by
a few scanty chords, superseded the florid choral music of the sixteenth
century.

That the "disembellished" style of Spanish art and the "representative"
style of Italian music were really parallel expressions of *Zeitgeist* is evidenced by three significant dates. The first part of *Don Quixote* was published in 1605. A year later Ribalta's *Last Supper* was placed in the church
of Corpus Cristi at Valencia. In the following year, 1607, the epoch-making
first performance of Monteverdi's *Orfeo* occurred in Mantua. This con-
temporaneity warrants a closer investigation.

Polyphony developed to an unprecedented degree of contrapuntal re-
finement in sixteenth-century Spain. The people enjoyed it as much as
the clergy. Without the insistent pleading of the Spanish delegates, the
Council of Trent would have banished polyphonous singing from the
liturgy. And the Spaniards watched the ensuing reformation of ecclesiastical music in Rome with zealous attention. In fact, it was Fernando de las
Infantas who persuaded Pope Gregory XIII, about 1577, to refuse to give
official approval of further simplification of choral church music as
planned by Palestrina.

The Descent from the Cross by Pedro de Campaña (before 1547, Montpellier, Fig. 61) should be viewed as though it were a "polyphonous" com-

position, a madrigal or a *villancico,* in pictorial terms. If it is approached from the inapplicable viewpoint of "imitation of nature," its formulated action must seem stilted and affected. But if it is regarded as a decorative composition—in terms of a more or less abstract interlace of lines and color masses—its mood will be easily grasped.

Campaña's composition is arranged like two corresponding choirs: a male quartet above with motives gloomy, sustained, and rigid; and an exuberant quartet of female voices below. (I trust my readers will understand that I am

Fig. 61.—Pedro de Campaña: *The Descent from the Cross,* Montpellier, Musée Fabre

comparing the lines of the composition to the voice parts of a musical score, and not the figures to its performers.) The whole abounds with body movements and these, in turn, produce interacting "melodies." Obviously it is impossible for the actors to observe a "natural" demeanor, being wholly under decorative obligations. A certain amount of stylization is unavoidable where every pictorial line functions as a melody in a complicated contrapuntal score. The necessary compromise between the exigencies of counterpoint and verisimilitude accounts for what we are inclined to brand rashly as "mannered behavior"—for example, the pose of St. John in the right-hand corner.

Enacted by a living actor on the stage, St. John's attitude would rightly be called affected. But as a part of the lyrical picture pattern it is quite legitimate. His lowered head, joined with the line of the shoulder in a horizontal, and the two advancing arms forming its parallel—all this should be appreciated from the point of view of a "composer" who is primarily concerned with the visual relation of the figure to the oppressive bank of clouds and to the elegiac slant of the horizon. The desired counterpoint to these horizontals is the vertical cadence of the drapery. This in turn forms a parallel to the drooping arm of Christ. But both the verticals and the horizontals bring their stern power of expression into full play only when their interaction with the oblique line of the ladder is grasped. Likewise, the poses of the women—particularly the festoon of their seven hands—are conditioned by decorative rather than naturalistic exigencies. This is also true of the undulating hem of the cloak of Nicodemus, who is standing on the ladder to the left. These "coloratura runs" alleviate the rigid lines and angles prevailing in the upper section, as well as forming the needed transition from the harsh music above to the flamboyant music below.

This contrapuntal approach was completely abolished in Ribalta's *The Vow of St. Francis* (Valencia Picture Gallery, Fig. 62). Ribalta's creative imagination did not begin with a decorative mesh of fluctuating lines; it started from the separate tangible characters. Through them he achieves a simple and clear picture pattern which would tolerate no appended ornamental coloraturas.

Fig. 62.—Francisco Ribalta: *The Vow of St. Francis*, Valencia, Picture Gallery

The way in which St. Francis throws his arms about the Son of Man in a passionate embrace is physiologically and psychologically true. His eyes are closed in the rapture of emotional self-abandon. The whole action is free from affectation. Christ is no pitiful figure. Because He is just such a sturdy man as the friar He does not appeal to the beholder's sentimental regard. Like an older brother He puts the crown of thorns on the head of the friar. The whole conception breathes virility. Ribalta's voice sounds like one from another world if his St. Francis is compared with Campaña's St. John caressing the crown of thorns (Fig. 61). When that new voice was heard for the first time, those conversant with Mannerism must have felt as though a veil were removed from the authentic face of life and its furrows of passion and torment suddenly exposed.

In this respect, it may be repeated, the effect of Ribalta's *Vow of St. Francis* must have been similar to that created at the same time in Italy by Monteverdi's "Lament of Arianna" (1614), a song considered throughout the seventeenth century to be the *ne plus ultra* of terse emotional expression. Severo Bonini, Marco Gagliano, and other contemporaries have recorded the sensation created by its unprecedented "realism." In that monody, Monteverdi, with a minimum of means derived from the keenest observation of human behavior and speech habits, depicted in not more than four measures the agony of a deserted lover, with the words "Let me die, let me die!" The same resolved phrase recurs and recurs; as though groping for some unknown solace, it suddenly rises out of unrelated vagrant harmonies through an ascent of chromatic intervals, and ultimately precipitates into an abyss of despair.

As in Monteverdi's music, there was no longer a trace of the florid in Ribalta's picture.* Nowhere did the contour wax ornamental, the little emerging from the dark being plain. The coloration was drab. The angels on either side were no longer "putti" but real children. One of them is improvising suavely in the lower keys of the viola da gamba; the other is bringing to Christ a flower wreath, to replace the crown the Lord is giving away. This tender idyl occupies a relatively subordinate position.

THE CARAVAGGIO QUESTION Francisco Ribalta (about 1565–1628), the dean of the school of Valencia, was the greatest and most influential of the reformers of Spanish painting in the late sixteenth and early seventeenth centuries. Ribalta, like Michelangelo da Caravaggio in Italy at the same period, instigated the new realism by which Mannerism was overthrown in Spain.

That Ribalta was Caravaggio's Spanish counterpart is an undisputed

* Curiously enough, the Monteverdian *dramma per musica* was not accepted in Spain. Apparently its most characteristic feature was objectionable: the *recitativo* which, according to realist standards, was too much of a compromise between plain speech and song. The national musical drama of Spain, the *zarzuela,* is different from Italian opera in that its musical numbers are set off from each other not by *recitativos* but by spoken

fact. But the relationship between the Valencian and the painter from Lombardy is an unsolved problem. Once all the credit for the new movement was given to the latter; Ribalta's realistic approach to religious art was believed to have been only an offshoot from Caravaggio. The resemblance between Ribalta's and Caravaggio's manners is indeed great, particularly in two respects: first, in the use of so-called "cellar light"—sharp oblique beams falling in laterally and spotting out the figures from a dark background; and, second, in the substitution of somber glowing blacks and browns for the conventional bright vermilions, blues, and greens. It was to this toning-down of the decorative coloration of the cinquecento that both Caravaggio and Ribalta owed their classification as *tenebrosi* (tenebrous painters). Ribalta's alleged dependence on Caravaggio seemed all the more probable in the light of the whole preceding history of art in Spain, where for centuries every significant innovation had been adopted from France, Flanders, or Italy. It was, therefore, quite natural that Italian influence should continue at the beginning of the new era. In view of the proverbial backwardness of the Spanish school, it seemed unlikely that anything so incisive and far-reaching as Ribalta's revolutionary art should have arisen independently of the revolution begun by Caravaggio.

More recently (at the time of the first publication of this book) the theory of Ribalta's dependence was upset by newly disclosed facts which made it appear more than doubtful that he could have seen any of Caravaggio's decisive works in Rome. The discovery that Caravaggio was born as late as 1574* indicates that those of his paintings which were unqualified manifestations of his new revolutionary style† were executed at a time when Ribalta—according to documents that seemed to establish his birth at Castellon de la Plana in either 1551 or 1555—was already well in his forties and certainly no longer a student in Italy. Since then, however, the picture has again been changed by more recent research, and changed in such a manner that a visit of Ribalta to Italy at the time when Cara-

dialogue. (Calderón's *comedia armónica, Eco y Narciso,* is an early example.) A more authentic parallel to Monteverdi's form is the liturgic choral drama of Spain, for instance, *La Fiesta de Elche* (1639). See Otto Ursprung, "Musikkultur in Spanien," in *Handbuch der Spanienkunde* (Frankfurt, a.M., 1932), 351.

    * Longhi, in *Pinacoteca,* I (1928).

    † The paintings in the Contarelli Chapel of San Luigi dei Francesi (1597) and in the Cerasi Chapel of Santa Maria del Popolo (1600).

vaggio was decorating the Contarelli Chapel does not necessarily fall outside the pale of possibility. Delphine Fitz Darby's reconstruction of Francisco and Juan Ribalta's biographies* has definitely established the fact
that Francisco was born about 1565 and that he received his early training
in Madrid from one of the members of the school of the Escorial, perhaps
from El Mudo. If Ribalta paid a visit to Italy, as to which no evidence has
ever been advanced,† it would seem most likely that he went there after
his graduation from his Madrilenian master; in other words, sometime
after 1582, the date inscribed upon Ribalta's diploma picture, *The Nailing of Christ to the Cross* in the Hermitage in Leningrad.‡ Inasmuch as he
was still in Madrid in 1596 or 1597 when his son Juan, who eventually
became his father's assistant and collaborator, was born, Ribalta could
indeed have gone to Rome between 1597 and 1599. For he is not referred to as being in Valencia, whither he had moved from Madrid and
was to spend the rest of his life, until 1599. Had he been in Rome, he
would have come just in time to witness the hanging of Caravaggio's all-
important paintings of the life of St. Matthew in the Contarelli Chapel.
But, I repeat: there is no evidence of his having gone to Italy at all, and
Ribalta's art rather refutes the whole idea. Like Rembrandt, whose early
realism often reminds one of Ribalta, he may have refused to take the
trip which the Romanists considered indispensable for the education of
a budding genius. If he did not go he was in a much better position to continue painting in his un-Italianate manner.

* Delphine Fitz Darby, *op. cit.*

† A replica of Caravaggio's *Crucifixion of St. Peter,* of 1600 or thereabouts, in the
Colegio del Patriarca at Valencia, is said to be by Ribalta; but except for an oral local
tradition this is quite without foundation. The influence of Correggio, on the other
hand, which is apparent in Ribalta's retable of *Santiago* at Algemesí, need not necessarily be explained from a study of Correggio's original work at Parma, but may just as
well have been transmitted by El Mudo, whose *Holy Family* (1575, Escorial) is replete
with Correggio reminiscences. It was Palomino who, early in the eighteenth century,
invented the legend of Ribalta's education in Italy. But his romantic story of Ribalta
going there because his beloved, the daughter of his master, refused to marry him unless
he first went abroad for study is quite incompatible with the historical facts recently
disclosed. Mrs. Darby (*op. cit.*, p. 69) suggests rather plausibly that one of Palomino's
papers may have been misplaced and that he intended to account not for Ribalta's
but for José Ribera's departure for Italy.

‡ The important inscription reads: *Francisco Ribalta Catala lo pinto en Madrid ano
de MDLXXXII.*

There is no question as to the Caravaggiesque character of Ribalta's art. The only question is: Was it a derivation from Caravaggio or an independent parallel creation of the master of Valencia? The last-named alternative represents, I believe, the truth. The striking resemblance of Ribalta's and Caravaggio's styles is enigmatic only if one fails to recognize that both painters exploited the same source and, advancing independently in similar directions, ultimately arrived at the same stylistic conclusions. This common source was *Il Giorgionismo,* the Venetian manner of chiaroscuro painting which was inaugurated early in the sixteenth century by Giorgione of Castelfranco.*

That Caravaggio was a Giorgionist at heart was news not even to his contemporary critics. Concerning the *tenebroso* manner of the paintings in the Contarelli Chapel, Baglione, in his Caravaggio biography (1644), quotes Federigo Zuccari as saying, *"Io non ci vedo altro che il pensiero di Giorgione"* ("I do not find anything here except Giorgione's idea").

But Ribalta's art was also intimately connected with the following of Giorgione. His *St. Matthew and the Angel* (Fig. 54) follows in more than one way Romanino's version of the same subject (Brescia, St. Giovanni) and Savoldo's in the Metropolitan Museum.† In other words, Ribalta is connected with the same class of *Giorgioneschi* with which Caravaggio's early history has been recently linked.

Among the past masters of Venice, Ribalta's favorite was Sebastiano del Piombo, Giorgione's nearest pupil and friend. "It is common knowledge that Ribalta was very fond of him," says Cean Bermudez.‡ Moreover, Ribalta's painting *Christ Carrying the Cross* (1612, London, National Gallery) owes much to Sebastiano's well-known picture of the same title in the Prado. There is even more conclusive evidence in Ribalta's little triptych of 1617 in El Prado, which bears the telling inscription *Sebastianus del Piombo invenit: Franciscus Ribalta Valentiae traduxit* (invented by Sebastiano del Piombo, translated by Francisco Ribalta of Valencia).

---

* The relationship between Caravaggio and the school of Giorgione has been investigated by Nikolaus Pevsner in an article entitled *Die Lehrjahre des Caravaggio,* in *Zeitschrift für bildende Kunst,* Vol. 62 (1927–28), 278ff.

† Reproductions of Romanino's and Savoldo's paintings appear in Dr. Pevsner's above-mentioned article on pages 238 and 287.

‡ *Diccionario,* IV, 170.

Both Ribalta and Caravaggio erected their respective art styles upon foundations laid by Giorgione and his followers because of their common opposition to the Mannerism of the Michelangelo exploiters, and their common desire to restore a purely painterly art by emancipating painting from sculptural viewpoints. To accomplish this, Giorgionism—always the most radical opponent of Michelangeloism—furnished the most reliable weapon.

The evolution of Giorgionism in Italy gained impetus from such paintings of Giorgione as the triple portrait in the Pitti known as *Il Concerto,* and *Le Concert Champêtre* in the Louvre (both about 1510). In the one, the liquid dusk of an interior, in the other, the throbbing brilliance of the open country, make the solid forms melt into the setting. Before moving to Rome, Sebastiano del Piombo continued to develop the luminarism of his great Venetian master, as can be seen in his Saints *Louis* and *Sinibaldo* of 1507, in St. Bartolommeo di Rialto in Venice.* To any follower of the Michelangelo tradition the representation of a Saint in a niche would have signified pre-eminently a sculptural assignment. The niche would have been considered a matter of secondary importance; at best, an enframing contrast to make the figure stand off with greater plastic precision and clearness. In Sebastiano's paintings the figures are of secondary importance. The liquid gloom in the niches, the dusk in which the Saints are half submerged, the reflected lights quivering across the gloom, the colorful shadow cast by each figure upon the lighted section of the hollow—these are of primary interest. From such a semi-nocturnal painting it was a small step to the next phase—the complete nocturne of Lorenzo Lotto's *Nativity* (1521, Venice Academy), in which almost all the central-Italian conventions, valid in the past, were reversed. Instead of the conventional figure composition there is now only an atmospheric ambient—the black of night from which a few scattered specks of light glimmer. Such early endeavors to further Giorgione's chiaroscuro at first went unnoticed, however; this sketchy generalization did not comply with the then valid requirements of monumental design.

The decisive word in the matter was spoken by Correggio, the progressive painter of Parma. His *Holy Night* (*La Notte*, 1530, Dresden)

* Duncan Phillips, *The Leadership of Giorgione* (Washington, D.C., 1937), 145.

challenged Michelangelo on his own ground. In this monumental composition of life-size figures the most consistent use of chiaroscuro blends
with the most tangible corporeality; it enhances the plasticity of the
figures rather than obliterates it. The Madonna and the shepherds are
so thoroughly rounded and modeled that they seem to be present in the
flesh, though only in so far as they enter into the focal center of the light—
another point of inestimable consequence. Perhaps the most significant
contribution that Correggio made to Giorgionism was his discovery that,
beyond its illusionistic functions, liquid light-dark was an organizing
means. The entire pictorial structure of *The Holy Night* is organized by
the flow of light through dark rather than by the position of figures and
objects in the picture space and their bilateral balance. Furthermore, this
new composition system ministered to a novel mode of narration. Correggio made the pictorial narration pointed and succinct by using the light
as a means to accentuate the essentials, and the dark as a means to efface
the negligibles.

Evidently it does not take a Caravaggio to account for Francisco Ribalta's artistic evolution. The Venetians of the early sixteenth century
exercised a growing influence upon the cinquecento art of Spain, and so
did Correggio, whose influence upon Luis de Morales has already been
pointed out. Correggio's influence upon El Greco, in turn, is plain to anyone who compares the former's *Holy Night* with the latter's *Nativity* in
the Metropolitan Museum. And the style of Ribalta, who during his early
Madrilenian period must have seen some of El Greco's work, was, in the
last analysis, the style of El Greco stripped of mysticism and brought down
to earth.

It is noteworthy that Ribalta's art gained more and more influence in
Spain during the seventeenth century, in contrast to Caravaggio's, which
did not last in Italy as long as it did in the countries north of the Alps.
The waning of Caravaggio's influence at home has been considered something of a mystery, whereas it is no mystery at all. His consistent realism
was bound to succumb in Italy to an eclectic revival of the idealism of the
Renaissance, because Italy had always been surreptitiously biased in favor
of "idealism." In Spain, however, Ribalta's consistent realism was bound
to bear fruit a hundredfold, because there it was at home. Spanish painting
from its earliest stages had striven for naturalism. The attacks of formalism

and eclecticism from which it suffered off and on, and which invariably threw the development off its normal track, were due to foreign importations.

Ribalta was at once the emancipator of Spanish art from foreign influence and the originator of an art distilled from the very essence of Spanish sentiment. In Spain *verismo* was considered not, as in Italy, a *maniera barocca,* but an *estilo nacional,* the flower and the fruit of age-old propensities of the Spanish race and temper.

With all the facts that I have marshaled, let it be understood, I am only correcting the current misconception that "the new pictorial problems which arose in Spain with the waning of Romanism, particularly the new doctrines of lighting, were provoked by Caravaggio."* If such an error continues to be accepted, the history of Spanish art and the laws that actuated its evolution are in danger of being permanently misinterpreted. The history of Spanish seventeenth-century painting pivots on Ribalta's achievements.

That the trend inaugurated by him may eventually have been braced and intensified by Caravaggio's art is undeniable. I readily admit the possibility of a belated influence of Caravaggio even upon Francisco Ribalta, at least during his later period, and, surely, upon his son Juan, who died at the age of thirty-one years in the same year as his father. But even though the more daring *tenebroso* manner of Juan Ribalta's *Nailing to the Cross* (1615, Valencia Gallery) reminds one definitely of Caravaggio, it need not necessarily have been inspired by him. It may just as well have developed from the indigenous manner of his father, Francisco.

JOSE RIBERA On their study trips to Italy, the followers of Ribalta were naturally attracted by the kindred art of Caravaggio. This is particularly true of Jose Ribera (1588–1653), Ribalta's greatest pupil, who went to Italy when he was quite young and stayed there for more than forty years. The Italians hardly knew him by his real name; because of his short stature they called him "Lo Spagnoletto," the little Spaniard.†

* Valerian von Loga, *op. cit.,* 136.

† August L. Mayer, *Jusepe de Ribera,* second edition (Leipzig, 1923); Hugo Kehrer, *Spanische Kunst von Greco bis Goya* (Munich, 1926), 146–178; E. Harris, *Spanish Paint-*

In Rome, where he arrived shortly after the untimely death of Caravaggio, Ribera quite naturally studied the paintings of that great conqueror of Italian Mannerism. At the time no student of art could help
being drawn into the heated arguments for and against Caravaggio with
which the air of all the Roman studios was thick. For the younger artists
it was a point of honor to be familiar with Caravaggio's *St. Matthew* pictures in St. Luigi dei Francesi, *The Crucifixion of St. Peter* and *The Con-
version of St. Paul* in St. Maria del
Popolo, *The Madonna of Loreto* in
St. Agostino, *The Entombment* in
St. Maria in Valicella, *The Madonna dei Palafrenieri* in St. Peter's,
and the numerous smaller paintings
in the palaces of the Roman clergy,
such as the *St. Catherine* owned by
the Cardinal del Monte, an echo of
which is audible in Ribera's *St. Ines*
(Fig. 63). Other famous works of
Caravaggio were in Naples, where
Ribera established his permanent
residence about 1615: *The Seven
Works of Charity* in Monte della
Misericordia, *The Resurrection* in
St. Anna dei Lombardi, and *The
Scourging of the Lord* in Santo Domenico Maggiore. In fact, by the
time Ribalta reached Naples, Caravaggio's style ruled the city. In view

Fig. 63.—Jose Ribera: *St. Ines*, Dresden,
Picture Gallery

of the impact of the influence to which Ribera was exposed in those most
impressionable years of his career, it is all the more remarkable that he
did not become an outright *Caravaggiesco,* as did so many of his Italian,
French, and Dutch contemporaries—Saraceni and Gentileschi, Valentin
de Boullogne, Honthorst, van Baburen, Terbruggen, and Rombouts.

ing (Hyperion Press, Paris and New York, 1937), Plates 48ff. Several important articles
by Elías Tormo in *Boletín de la Sociedad Española de Excursiones,* Vol. XXIV.

If one omits from consideration Ribera's realistic approach to any kind of subject matter, which he undoubtedly acquired with the *tenebroso* manner from Ribalta before going abroad, the Italian influences discernible in Ribera's technique are none other than those which for decades had fashioned the development of painting in Spain—Titian, Paolo Veronese, Tintoretto, and Correggio. Probably it was the eclectic school of the Caracci which made those ancient masters a new experience for Ribera, a synthesis of the Venetian tradition of coloration with the colorful clair-obscure of Correggio being the aim of the Caracci. Ribera, a lifelong resident of Italy, could not, of course, remain wholly immune to certain Italian ideals. In the Neapolitan milieu, his rugged realism mellowed with time. He learned to comply with the Italian requirement of beauty. The drab coloration of his Spanish master gave way to a luminous palette rich with those colorful transitions which eventually enabled Ribera to convert even the vulgar models he liked so well into visions of russet gold or pallid silver. Nevertheless, he remained throughout his life a faithful disciple of Ribalta's principles.

His early paintings were more radically realistic than those of Ribalta. Ribera was the first Spanish painter of the seventeeth century who indulged in profanity and specialized in depicting physical ugliness. One of his early paintings, *The Workman* (Rome, Corsini Gallery, about 1625), exhibits the repulsive physique of a half-naked laborer, obviously a model from the Neapolitan slums. Here Ribera focused every technical device on portraying the model's characteristic uncouthness—his hideous face, his fat stomach, his rags, and his unwashed hands. Ribera never quite renounced his pleasure in what is physically ugly. It survived in his very last painting, *The Clubfooted Dwarf* (1652, Louvre). In general, even his saints are ugly, and so are the compositions in which they appear—particularly the early ones. Throughout the 1620's and 1630's—at least until 1637—he shunned beauty in the conventional sense, even when the communication of some profoundly spiritual idea was his aim. In an etching of 1621, and in a painting of 1623 in the National Museum of Naples, he represented *St. Jerome Hearing the Last Trumpet*—a pictorial paraphrase of the Saint's words: "Incessantly that terrible trumpet pierces our ears; Arise ye dead! Come forth for judgment!" The two pictures differ in the general arrangement of the figures and the particular pose of St. Jerome, but in both instances his aged body with its sagging desiccated skin is as unlovely as is the jerky composition, developed from harsh angles and strident diagonals with no regard for equilibrium.

Still, while Ribera never wholly relinquished his ultra-realistic approach, he turned gradually from mere external exactitude to spiritual and psychological interpretation. Of this change the half-length *St. Jerome,* in the Prado (about 1652), is a perfect illustration. The beholder, forgetting to inquire either into the skillful simulation of physical life or into the masterful construction of the pattern, is conscious only of a mysterious soul permeating from matter. An unearthly light envelops the body. Even the darkness that bisects the face is translucent.

Ribera's later style may be defined as a synthesis of external verity, animation, and strict, even beautiful, composition. This was a sign not so much of an individual artist changing his manner as of the transformation of the whole period style in the 1640's when the Early Baroque was giving way to the High Baroque and Zurbaran and Velasquez, as well as Ribera, were entering the classical phase of their respective manners.

In accordance with the uncompromising realism of Ribera's early period, the compositional order of his paintings was at first fortuitous, as though he did not wish any significance to be attached to a pictorial unity. He preferred unattractive patterns even as he preferred unattractive models. Nothing more jagged and disagreeable could be imagined than the zigzag pattern of *The Holy Trinity* (1632, Escorial; somewhat later replica in the Prado)—a haphazard disarrangement of Albrecht Dürer's well-balanced woodcut which El Greco had copied, fifty-five years earlier, for *The Holy Trinity* of the high altar of Santo Domingo Antiguo in Toledo. God the Father is not in the center but in the upper left-hand corner. The dead body of His Son is dangling from His lap toward the opposite corner. The loin cloth is so dragged out of place by the angels that it cuts a discordant diagonal across the surface. The picture frame is not granted the function of a permanent architectural setting—limiting the painting and making it obey orders—any more than is a window through which the spectator by hook or crook snatches a glimpse of a fleeting apparition.

Shortly after 1637—at the time of Ribera's growing appreciation of physical beauty—a sense of the significance of lucid pictorial construction replaces his early undisciplined manner. A star witness of the change is the *St. Ines* of 1641 (Fig. 63), whose composition has been discussed in the previous chapter (pages 157–58). Likewise, *The Liberation of St. Peter* (1642) and its companion picture in the Dresden Gallery, *The Apparition of the Angel to St. Francis,* are compositions carefully balanced within the frame and dominated by the sweep of long, consonant curves. In addition, the faces and hands are spirited, and the color chord of deep blue and amber intensifies the decorative charm of the whole. Every form bids for a pleasant effect of harmony and none is left to chance.

Perhaps because he realized that this fluent *bel canto* design was "foreign" and not in keeping with his realistic intentions, Ribera ultimately abandoned it for an even more severe and simple structure composed of straight lines, triangles, and squares. *The Adoration of the Shepherds* (1650, Louvre) is his last word in geometric simplicity. But the sobriety of its pattern should not be dissociated from the profound solemnity of Ribera's naturalism at that time. Composition and subject matter were now in perfect accord. Nature was never revered more devoutly and less sentimentally. The integration of body and spirit was never made to speak with greater sincerity than in Ribera's most mature art.

FRANCISCO ZURBARAN The broad and solid foundations constructed by Francisco Ribalta of Valencia and his fellow pioneers of Seville—Francisco Herrera *el Viejo* and Juan de las Roelas—support the classical realism of Francisco Zurbaran (1598–1664) and Diego Velasquez (1599–1660). Born almost within the same year and reaching almost the same age, they also shared similar aims in art. Both evince the same unsentimental objectivity, the same aversion to the elegant and false bombast of the Mannerists—Zurbaran out of considerations peculiar to the ascetic art of the monastery, Velasquez out of considerations peculiar to the aristocratic art of the royal court. Both were equally immune to foreign, particularly Italian, conventions. Both refused to paint anything unless a model was before them. In other respects, however, Zurbaran differs from

Velasquez as Michelangelo differs from Titian, or, more generally, as a sculptor differs from a painter.

Both artists investigated nature with grave intensity, as though it had never been done before. But the objective verity for which Velasquez was striving was, in the last analysis, a purely optical verity. His aim was to reduce everything visible to color spots of accurate value relations. In other words, his was the objectivity of an impressionist. Zurbaran traveled the opposite road, proceeding like a sculptor. To him the objective representation of life spelled accurate modeling and concise design. The chiaroscuro, which he employed like Ribalta, does not diffuse the forms; it consolidates them.

To some extent Zurbaran must have been instructed by his masters in Seville in the manners and the compositional rhetoric of the Italians. We know next to nothing about his first teacher, Pedro Diaz de Villanueva, a pupil of Morales;* but there was also Juan de las Roelas, from whom Zurbaran learned as much on the side as he did from Ribalta, Herrera, and Ribera; and Roelas did not entirely dismiss the picturesque charms of Italian art. Yet, despite such instruction, anything less rhetorical or picturesque than Zurbaran's angular picture patterns could hardly be imagined. His *Purísima with Saints Anne and Joachim* (1630, Edinburgh) looks like a relapse into the style of the Primitives rather than an imitation of the Italian Baroque. He had no knack for fluent pictorial narration. The subject most congenial to his talent was the single effigy conceived as a statue—*St. Francis* or other individual saints, martyrs, church fathers, and friars. His "compositions" often amount to nothing better than collocations of several perpendicular figures in a row. In his cycle of *The Life of St. Buenaventura* (executed in 1629 in cooperation with Herrera *el Viejo* for the Colegio San Buenaventura in Seville) even the most common conventions of "good composition" were disregarded. Note the crude manner in which the oblique line of the death bier cuts through the picture of the *The Funeral of St. Buenaventura* (Louvre). The expression is entrusted exclusively to the virile portraits of the dead Saint, Pope Gregory X, King Alfonso X, the Archbishop of Seville, and the other mourners.

* José Cascales y Muñoz, *Francisco de Zurbarán* (Madrid, 1911), 197.

Moreover, Zurbaran was not a colorist. Light and dark were to him what they are to a sculptor—chiefly descriptive of bulk and recession—while color was an adjunct which one might employ or omit. On rare occasions he may touch one to the very quick by little more than a patch of burning crimson set in black, like a lake of fire deep in the crater of a volcano—for example, in the effigies of *The Church Fathers* in the Museum of Seville. The images of *Christ on the Cross* (Fig. 64), on the other hand, are almost in monochrome, and *The Madonna with the Carthusians* from the Cartuja de St. Maria de las Cuevas (Seville Museum) resembles a carving which is without color to begin with but has been coated with white, pink, and bright blue as an afterthought. Everything in Zurbaran's art points to an ascetic personality to whom anything flavoring of the luxuriant and the brilliant was fundamentally repulsive. Perhaps his religious fervor made Zurbaran revive the old Spanish traditions. In his paintings, to an even higher degree than in Ribalta's, the sculptural instinct was reborn with *sosiego* and a predilection for sharply designed linear ornamentation.

Fig. 64.—Francisco Zurbaran: *The Dead Christ*, Seville, Provincial Museum

Am I stretching the bounds of psychology too far if, on the other hand, I interpret the exacting scrutiny of Zurbaran's draughtsman-like manner as the sign of a thrifty mind? Something of the dearth of his native province Estremadura and of the hardship to which its inhabitants have always been exposed is integrated in his extremely sober art. And the contrast of his economical manner with the extravagant impressionism of Velasquez is amazing. Study the two painters in their embroidery patterns or other curious designs upon garments. Metaphorically speaking, Velasquez is a spendthrift. He reduces to shapeless color hazes the pink flowers woven into the silver robe of *The Infanta* (Fig. 72), squandering, as it were, a wealth of available, actual form for the sake of a luscious effect of flowing light. Zurbaran, on the other hand, allows not one of a hundred lines to go to waste. The embroidered orphrey on the dalmatic of his *St. Lawrence* (Leningrad, Hermitage)* and the brocade patterns of the dress worn by his *St. Elizabeth* (Montreal, collection of the late Sir William Van Horne)† are accounted for thread for thread and form for form. It seems only logical that the strength of his art lay not in the planning of grandiose compositions but in the precise rendition of isolated effigies. He tried several times to achieve the impossible by imitating the compositions of other artists. The pattern of the above-mentioned *Madonna with the Carthusians* was derived from an engraving of *The Death of St. Augustine* (1624) by Schelte a Bolswerth‡ and *The Apotheosis of St. Thomas Aquinas,* done in 1631 for the College of St. Thomas at Seville (Seville Museum), employed the standard two-story pattern used for "glorifications" by Annibale Caracci and other Italian eclectics.§ But so far as "great composition" is concerned, Zurbaran's attempt to vie with the Bolognese Academy resulted in a failure. It is the details that count. Every one of his heads is a stirring likeness: Emperor Charles V; the archbishop, Diego Deza; the rector of the college, D. Diego Ortiz; and St. Thomas himself, for whom D. Agustin Abreu Nuñez de Escobar is said to have posed. Yet rather than to men of flesh and blood these faces seem to belong to statues of granite posed on a bare iron scaffolding instead of on radiant clouds.

VELASQUEZ   The artistic development of Diego Velasquez y Silva is understood most clearly if it is divided into three major periods (not including the years of his apprenticeship in Seville from 1611 to 1617 under Herrera *el Viejo* and Francisco Pacheco). The events articulating the three periods are two sojourns in Italy. His first voyage to Genoa, Venice, Bologna, Rome, and Naples (from the late summer of 1629 through the

---

* Hugo Kehrer, *op. cit.,* 201.   † *Ibid.,* 205.   ‡ *Ibid.,* 190, 191.
§ For example, Annibale Caracci's *Christ in the Glory with Saints* in the Pitti Palace

winter of 1630) terminated the first period (1618–29) which begins with Velasquez's marriage (April 23, 1618) in Seville to Juana de Miranda, daughter of his teacher, Pacheco. It includes his early activity as an independent master in Seville and as court painter to the youthful King Philip IV, in Madrid. Velasquez paid a short visit there in 1622, but the coveted permanent appointment did not materialize until the following year. The second period (1630–49) was terminated by the artist's second sojourn in Italy from January, 1649, to June, 1651. The third period extended from 1650, when Velasquez was in Rome, to his death in Madrid on August 6, 1660.*

From the work of his first period, produced partly in Seville, partly in Madrid, no one would have ventured to predict that the artist was to become *le peintre le plus peintre qui fut jamais* (the most painterly painter that ever was). Neither his early *bodegones* (genre paintings) and likenesses nor the few religious subject pieces that came off the young Sevillian's easel before 1629 foreshadowed the astounding coloristic manner of his later periods.

At first he was concerned with the simplest class of subject matter, men or women picked from the populace of Seville and grouped unpretentiously in drab interiors: *The Breakfast,* which shows apprentices sharing their master's frugal meal (about 1617, Leningrad, Hermitage); *Three Musicians,* standing around a table set with some dishes and food (Berlin, Kaiser Friedrich Museum); *Two Youths in the Kitchen* and *A Sevillian Water Vendor* (both in the collection of the Duke of Wellington). His chief objective at this time was pure and simple form, defined in so far as possible in unbroken, bent surfaces of cold light and ponderous dark.

Obviously some of these early bodegones are in the tradition of Fray Juan Sanchez Cotan (1561–1627), that remarkable artist of Granada whose prosaic still-life painting (Fig. 13) for all its resemblance to Caravaggio's work nevertheless evolved quite independently in the south of Spain, even as did the religious prose of Francisco Ribalta in the east. Young Velasquez must, however, have seen some of Caravaggio's pictures, if only by way of reproductions. While it is evident from *The Adoration of the Magi* and *The Virgin in the Glory with Saints* in the Bologna Pinacoteca.

* *Velazquez,* Phaidon Press (Oxford University Press), Introduction and work catalogue by Enrique Lafuente.

Fig. 65.—Velasquez: *The Adoration of the Magi,* Prado

(1619, Prado, Fig. 65) that as yet he had no conception of the magnificent pageantry displayed in Rubens' painting of the same subject (1609, Prado), which had been in Spain since 1612, the same picture proves beyond doubt that he was well acquainted with Caravaggio's *Madonna of Loreto* (Rome, St. Agostino) and had assimilated Caravaggio's "cellar light" as well as his vernacular rendition of biblical subject matter. Velasquez's Virgin and three Kings are people of plain-spoken hardy peasant stock. Likewise, *The Three Musicians,* in Berlin, are the next of kin to Caravaggio's *Gamblers* (Paris, Collection of Edmond de Rothschild) or at any rate to the class of "musician picture" which originated with *The Luteplayer* of Caravaggio, in the Hermitage, and was soon imitated all over Europe. Judging by *Christ and the Pilgrims of Emmaus,* in the Metropolitan Museum (Fig. 66), the Caravaggio influence persisted until the beginning of Velasquez's second period. While that painting is unthinkable without the model of either Caravaggio's own dramatic interpretations of the same episode or one of their several imitations, such as the Rubens painting of about 1610, in the collection of the Duke of Alba, the flower-like coloration is quite uncommon for the first period. And so is the most unusual conception that the two conversing Disciples remain unaware of the Lord's presence at their table. This seems too mature and mystic a thought for Velasquez's early period. It seems more plausible if one assumes that the painting was done about 1630, either in Rome under the direct inspiration of Caravaggio's pictures in the Palazzo Patrizi and the Palazzo Borghese (now in the National Gallery of London) or in Madrid.

The early portraits painted by Velasquez in Seville and Madrid are in the sober manner of Francisco Pacheco. I say this with all due reservation. The youthful genius knew how to instill energy and character into a portrait, whereas his teacher, employing the same technique, recorded the external identification marks of his sitters. Pacheco's quarter-length portraits in the museum of Seville look like so many passport pictures when they are compared with some of the earlier Velasquean heads, the so-called *Pacheco* in the Prado or *The Poet Góngora* (1622) in the Museum of Fine Arts at Boston. These are unforgettable revelations of integral characters. One

Fig. 66.—Velasquez: *Christ and the Pilgrims of Emmaus*, New York. Courtesy of the Metropolitan Museum of Art

senses the power of a new manner of speech, even though at first it concerns almost exclusively hands and heads. The criticism of the young
artist's jealous colleagues in Madrid was not entirely unfounded. They
whispered to his royal employer that the new sergeant painter was good
only for face-painting. But Velasquez was perhaps no less justified when
he snapped back that he had yet to be shown the Spanish painter who
could paint a face.

A similar critical reaction may have entered the mind of Peter Paul
Rubens when, on his second visit to Madrid in 1628, he probably induced

Fig. 67.—Velasquez: *The Topers,* Prado

his young colleague to devote more attention to large-scale composition
and, incidentally, to meet certain other requisites of international reputation, such as the nude. Without the insistent persuasion of the Flemish
champion of historical and mythological subject pieces, who wished to
see his Spanish friend abreast the international trend, Velasquez probably
would not have painted *The Topers* (*Los Borrachos,* 1628–29, Prado, Figs.
67, 68), his first large-scale composition and the first of his pictures to contain nudes—that is, bodies stripped of their clothing rather than "nudes"
in the academic sense. The very subject is Flemish rather than Spanish.
Drunkenness was frowned upon in Spain; in Flanders it was considered
a manly virtue. One wonders how the canvas ever attained its present
name, *borracho* being an abusive word of the vilest kind. The original

Fig. 68.—Velasquez: *The Topers* (detail), Prado

title was *Bacchus Crowning His Companions.* The naked youth wreathed with vine leaves reminds one once more of Caravaggio—see his *Self-Portrait as Bacchus* in the Uffizi—but the added expression of merriment falls quite outside Caravaggio's line of thought. In fact, this was the first time that wassailing and authentic laughter were chosen as a theme in any Spanish mythology painting (Fig. 68).

Rubens was firmly convinced of the provincialism of Spanish painting, and it is therefore highly probable that it was he who urged Velasquez not to delay his study trip to Italy. There alone he would learn what he most needed. It was all very well to know the sixteenth-century Venetians in the royal palaces in and near Madrid, but, after all, art had advanced in the fifty-odd years that had elapsed since Titian's death. Rubens demonstrated this by his replicas of some of the Titians in the king's collection. In the opinion of the astonished monarch the replicas were better than the originals.

It is a safe assumption that in Italy Velasquez was determined to see as much as possible of Italian painting in little more than a year. Specific traces of what he saw, however—counted by the dozen in the paintings done by others, including Rubens himself—are not apparent in the subsequent work of Velasquez. This is the more remarkable in the light of Italy's often devastating influence on the Spanish painters of the preceding periods.

Velasquez shipped two canvases from Naples to Madrid in 1630: *The Smithy of Vulcan* (Prado), a study of figures—chiefly nudes—in an interior, exposed to two different sources of illumination, the cool daylight outside and the warm glow of the furnace and the red-hot block of iron on the anvil; and *Joseph's Brethren with the Blood-Stained Coat* (Escorial), a study of similar figures exposed to the outdoor light that floods the open hall through which they are dispersed. Neither of these two paintings shows either servility to classical antiquity or admiration for the splendid dramatic "action pictures" of the Italian Baroque. They may owe their luminous coloration to the influence of Ribera, whom Velasquez visited in Naples, and again they may owe nothing to the Spanish expatriate. Whatever Velasquez learned, in addition to what he had already learned from the work of the Venetians in the royal Spanish collections, was so thoroughly assimilated that it is impossible to point out any specific source of influence.

It is nevertheless undeniable that Velasquez's style underwent a complete transformation during his stay in Italy. The nudes, with which the above-mentioned paintings abound, are executed with far greater freedom and breadth than those of *The Topers*. After the petty tradition that prevailed in Spain, in Italy Velasquez's eyes suddenly became sensitive to larger connections, to the scope of a complete whole. He learned to subordinate details to masses. Quite unlike *The Topers*, the picture of *Joseph's Brethren* is not an aggregate of individual figures. A total movement pervades the whole. This is true not only of the more fluent presentation of the actors and the dramatic expression of their gestures and faces; it is true above all of the liquid luminarism which submerges the nudes in the bright atmosphere and distances everything in the picture space. And if these innovations may be attributed to any one influence, it was Venice enlisting another disciple of Giorgionism, a disciple who advanced the Venetian chiaroscuro far beyond the range of Ribera.

The first multi-figured composition that Velasquez painted after his return to Spain was at the same time the first example of "open-air" painting in history—*The Surrender of Breda,* also known as *The Lances (Las Lanzas,* 1635, Prado, Fig. 69). Leaving the "black" period far behind, Velasquez now saw before him a twofold problem: the perception of the phenomenal world in terms of pure color rather than of form; and the organization of a canvas as one arranges a bouquet of gay flowers, matching and contrasting their luscious tints. A brightness of ochre and white on the extreme left contrasts with the brownish, dark horse on

Fig. 69.—Velasquez: *The Surrender of Breda* (also known as *The Lances*), Prado

the extreme right. A merry sparkle of white, sky blue, pink, orange, and silvery gray stands out against a background of richly graded blue and green. Amidst the reddish brown, greenish blue, and tan uniforms of the vanquished army on the left, a youthful officer, exposed to a flood of light, exhibits a white gilet embroidered with vermilion, which contrasts beautifully with his blue breeches and with the brilliant orange sash worn by the Dutch commander Justin of Nassau. Dark modeling shadows, which would have muddied the pure luster of the color scheme, are avoided wherever feasible. Replacing the traditional perspective design in creating a sense of distance are color gradations and color relations. The checkered flag, behind the horse and the self-portrait in the right-hand middle ground, appears once more in the center background; but

Fig. 70.—Rubens: *Meeting of the King of Hungary and the Cardinal Infant at Nördlingen,* Vienna, Museum of Art History

what is pink in the former is heightened to orange in the latter. Incidentally, Velasquez purloined the compositional pattern from Rubens' *Meeting of the King of Hungary and the Cardinal Infant at Nördlingen* (1635, Fig. 70), one of the canvases which had been devised for the decoration of the city of Antwerp in honor of the new governor of The Netherlands, Don Ferdinand, brother of the king of Spain. This coincidence establishes the year 1635 as the date of Velasquez's painting.*

Las Lanzas is no apotheosis of war and victory done in the Baroque manner. It is a sustained record of Spanish chivalry, a commemoration of the *caballerosidad* of the Marquis of Spinola, who allowed the enemy to leave the fortress fully armed, their flags flying. Velasquez depicts neither

* Until recently *The Surrender of Breda* was mistaken for a work of the third period. The *terminus post quem* is 1632, the year in which work was started on the decoration of the Salón de Reinos of the Buen Retiro palace, of which the canvas formed an im-

a battle nor a triumph. He shows the two commanders meeting on equal footing amidst their troops, the victor anxious to relieve his enemy's embarrassment by laying a friendly hand upon his shoulder. It is a record of Spanish chivalry written in portraits—the most objective and, perhaps, the most gentlemanly portraits the world had so far seen. But he has made them part and parcel of a total vision. No longer are there isolated heads; rather, viewed with the rapid glance of an impressionist, there are masses of heads. Further, the individual heads fuse into groups; the individual groups fuse with the vast bright landscape of a noonday in summer. The atmospheric unity, obtained in defiance of so many different colors, perhaps best demonstrates his superb skill.

The gradual evolution of this colorful manner is evident in the single portraits of the second period. After early unsuccessful attempts and experiments with a landscape background—an example is the *Cristóbal Suarez de Ribera* (1620, Seville, St. Hermenegildo)—Velasquez reverted to the old and the conventional arrangement used by Moro, Sanchez Coello, and Pantoja; namely, the full-length, black-clothed figure in front of a drab wall (*Duke Olivares*, 1623–24, London, George Lindsay Holford Collection). In certain early portraits of the second period Velasquez dis-

portant part. *Terminus ante quem* is April 28, 1635; on that day the Florentine ambassador Serrano saw the picture in its place (Elías Tormo, *Velázquez y el Salón de Reinos*, in *Boletín de la Sociedad Española de Excursiones*, 1911). On the ground of an investigation of the portraits in the Breda picture, Juan Allende Salazar and F. J. Sánchez-Cantón narrowed the possible date of the painting to the years 1634 and 1635 (*Retratos del Museo del Prado*, Madrid, 1919, 202–204). But the year 1634 must be eliminated, since the painting of Rubens on which Velasquez broadly patterned *The Lances* cannot have been brought to his attention before 1635. This, therefore, must be the year in which *The Surrender of Breda* was painted, on the tenth anniversary of the conquest (June, 1625). Even though the two paintings in question are approximately the same size (Velasquez: 307 cm. by 367 cm.; Rubens: 328 cm. by 388 cm.), it is nevertheless unlikely that Velasquez knew the original Rubens canvas. He probably saw its reproduction in one of the very elaborate volumes of copper engravings of Rubens' decorations made by Theodor van Thulden at the expense of the city of Antwerp, the *Pompa Introitus Ferdinandi*, published in 1635 and the following years. Evidence of the popularity of these volumes of engravings in Spain is found in a famous painting by Valdés Leal. In one of his *Geroglíficos de las Postrimerías* (Seville, La Caridad) a folio volume of van Thulden's *Pompa Ferdinandi*, open at the title page, lies at the feet of Death, who is putting out the candle.

engaged himself from his initial color phobia. But his advance toward colorism in portraiture was slower than one would expect from the historical compositions of the time. *Don Diego del Corral* (1631–32, Prado) still wears black and stands in front of a solid wall. Closer inspection reveals, however, that the black is broken up into any number of grays—greenish gray and yellowish gray predominating. The wine-red tablecloth and the crimson cross of Malta affixed to the breast counterbalance the ruddy flesh tints in this subtle chamber symphony. Not long after this Velasquez broke away from the colorless conventions of the typical Madrilenian court portraits. The coloristic manner asserts itself in the full-lengths of *King Philip IV in Hunting Attire* (about 1634–36, Prado) and his brother *The Infant Don Ferdinand.* The figures stand out from a bright sky enframed by trees; and if the natural colors are at first muffled with gray, the equestrian portrait of the young *Prince Balthazar Carlos on Horseback* (1636, Prado) attains the full brilliance of *The Surrender of Breda:* a crisp blue in which the landscape, the horse, and the little horseman seem to float.

Then comes another great surprise. The experience of the second Italian journey, in 1649, transformed this flowery colorism into what may be defined, roughly and somewhat paradoxically, as a coloristic monochrome. The nuclear work of 1650, the color scheme of the portrait of *The Pope, Innocent X* (Rome, Doria Gallery), is like symphonic variations on the single theme of crimson. The two *Views of the Medici Gardens* (Prado), also painted during this second stay in Rome, reveal a similar preoccupation with monochrome effects in connection with the *plein air* problem. Concerning these small canvases, critics are generally agreed that the painterly disregard of the solid forms, more precisely their translation into elusive color hazes, anticipated the impressionistic tenets of the late nineteenth century. Not until Camille Pissaro did any painter again venture to envisage a landscape so exclusively in terms of a single bright-gray opalescent with a few pale flecks of cool rose, olive green, cobalt, black, and white.

This "impressionism in monochrome" was carried to yet another peak in *The Maids of Honor,* painted in Madrid in 1656 (*Las Meninas,* Fig. 71). The problem the painter assigned to himself was that of depicting recessional things in a spacious interior by means of infinite tonal gradations of gray, applied in pure surfaces and spaced through nothing but the interrelation of chromatic values. Vermilion, green, blue, yellow, and other colors are used to offset and determine a multitude of shifting values of gray and, at the same time, to blend them in a harmony ranging from the deep black in the painter's robe to the radiant silver of the Infanta's hair. What local colors were left were converted to gray. The emerald-green skirt of the kneeling maid looks gray except as it emerges into full light, and

Fig. 71.—Velasquez: *The Maids of Honor,*
Prado

Fig. 72.—Velasquez: *The Infanta Margarita,*
Prado

so does the dark sapphire blue of the dress of the midget woman in the right-hand corner.

In the large *Portrait of the Infanta* (about 1660, Prado, Fig. 72) the coloration is even more alienated from the color phenomena that it conveys. Not a single color is what it seems to be. On coming closer, the beholder discovers that what looked gray at a short distance is actually flakes of purple and pink. What appeared to be a golden brooch consists of irregular patches of white, brown, ocher, and pale blue. The dominant reds run their gamut from deepest carmine to palest coral pink. Brilliant crimsons are brilliant only because they are imbedded in a glowing blue that no one notices until he studies the painting at close range. The magnificent drapery in the upper left-hand third of the canvas—seemingly crimson—is made up for long stretches of dabs of white, light gray, lemon yellow, chocolate brown, and pale green. The whole effect is sheer sorcery.

But what seems like sorcery actually represents the scientific discovery that the reality of matter is one thing and the reality of pictorial form quite another. The realm of the palpable for which the other realists were striving was not the realm of optics which Velasquez explored. What he found was that realism resides in the painter's eyes rather than in the objects he paints and that ocular reality obeys its own laws.* Thus Velasquez wrote *finis* to the realists' age. There was nothing more to say.

* José Ortega y Gasset (*Sobre el punto de vista en las artes, op. cit.,* 113): *"Velázquez detiene su pupila. Nada más. En esto consiste la gigantesca revolución."*

The Age of Calderon and Murillo

CHAPTER EIGHT

ROMANTIC PAGEANTRY   The majority of the historians of civilization have failed to stress the significant difference between the Spain of the sixteenth century and that of the seventeenth. Spanish writers, especially, regard the two centuries as a single *Siglo de Oro*. The truth is, at least in the fine arts, that during the seventeenth century Spain asserted her independence of other countries and became superior to them, in sharp contrast to the sixteenth century when, as we have seen, her borders were wide open to alien influences.

Another point usually overlooked is the difference between the art of the first half and that of the second half of the seventeenth century. In the opinion of the rising generation of artists born between 1600 and 1630, the sober realism of the Early Baroque, which overthrew Mannerism and culminated about 1640 in the High Baroque of the painters born in the last decades of the cinquecento, had had its day. The elementary work was done, and the repertory of forms created by the founders of the *estilo nacional* was outworn. The younger artists, who were at their best after 1660, believed that it was not enough to paint simple, direct prose. They focused their talents on brilliant pageants resplendent with theatrical glamor, romantic illumination, and grandiose, euphonious phrases. "When you set up my picture," the younger Herrera is reported to have said of his *Transfiguration of St. Francis* (Seville cathedral, about 1660), "let the unveiling be accompanied by flutes and cymbals." Murillo or Mateo Cerezo might have attached similar conditions to the hanging of any one of their paintings.

199

These are the exponents of the new art: Alonso Cano (1601–67), Jacinto Espinosa (1600–80), Pedro de Moya (1610–66), Juan Carreño (1614–85), Bartolome Esteban Murillo (1617–82), Francisco Herrera *el Mozo* (1622–85), and Juan de Valdes Leal (1630–91). Mateo Cerezo (1635–75) and Claudio Coello (1635–93) are the last representative painters of the Late Baroque.*

The novel objectives of these artists may perhaps be pointed out by contrasting a few paintings of Murillo and his seniors with respect to his and their conceptions of certain sacred themes.

When Ribera painted *Jacob's Dream* (1633, Prado), he omitted the fabulous golden ladder upon which, according to the Scriptures, the angels descended from heaven. Rather, he painted a man sound asleep under a tree. A faint intimation of cherubs in the shapes of the amber morning clouds was all that his realistic mind was willing to concede to the fanciful note of the plot. To Murillo, on the other hand, its rational aspect was irrelevant. In his painting of the same subject (Leningrad, Hermitage) Jacob was reduced to the insignificance of a stage prop. This painter's interest and that of his public lay in the miraculous pageantry—the romance of heaven opening its gates; a nocturnal forest clearing suddenly pierced by a vision of silver clouds that cast their magic reflections around; and a celestial ballet of winged children dancing up and down the magic ladder.

The literary fountainhead of this generation's stream of thought was Calderon, the mystery-loving, courtly and aristocratic, florid poet. Not earth-bound and realistic but soaring to the metaphysical world, Calderon's plays bear little, if any, reference to a workaday life. They are steeped

* On these artists see M. Gómez Moreno, "Alonso Cano," in *Cosas granadinas de arte y arqueologia* (Granada); L. Tramoyeres Blasco, *El pintor Jerónimo Jacinto de Espinosa* (Valencia, 1916); August L. Mayer, "P. de Moya," in *Allgemeines Lexicon der bildenden Künstler* (Leipzig) XXV (1931), 205; D. Berjabo Escobar, *El pintor D. Juan Carreño de Miranda* (Madrid, 1924); S. Montoto y Seda, *Murillo* (Barcelona, 1932); August L. Mayer, "F. Herrera el Mozo," in *Allgemeines Lexicon (op. cit.)* XVI (1923), 539; José Gestoso y Pérez, *Biografía del pintor sevillano Juan de Valdés Leal* (Seville, 1917); C. López Martínez, *Valdés Leal* (Seville, 1922); Aureliana de Beruete y Moret, *The School of Madrid* (London and New York, 1909), for Cerezo; and C. Pérez Bustamente, *Claudio Coello; noticias biográficas desconocidas (Boletín de la Sociedad Española de Excursiones,* 1918).

in allegory and magic. His *autos sacramentales* (sacred plays) are brimming with specters and demons. "All manner of supernatural powers—acting either as *deus ex machina* or as *diabolus ex machina*—confuse and disentangle, disturb and harmonize, his spiritual plays, enshrouding and interpenetrating the didactic plot with mysterious symphonies of an essentially musical construction. Peals and responsories, hymns, music, thunder and lightning pour forth over the children of the senses from both Heaven and Hell—the Christian as well as the heathen, the real as well as the imagined. Punishment and reward, temptation and redemption come to the mortals by way of storms, earthquakes, drums, trumpets, or other pompous noises and lighting effects."* Calderon's sacred shows were grandiose fantasias, melodramas; in fact, Calderon was the real instigator of the zarzuela, the specifically Spanish form of the opera.† In a large measure he was the instigator of all grand opera—that highly imaginative fusion of poetry, music, painting, sculpture, architecture, and histrionic art which was deemed the highest and most important form of art at all the courts of Europe from the mid-seventeenth century on, and which became the greatest single influence in the formation of the Late Baroque style.

In our sophisticated day and age, when operatic performances are considered only as social entertainments, it is difficult to realize the significance of the opera in the era of the composers Giovanni Andrea Bontempi (1624–1705) and Marcantonio Cesti (1618–69). At that time the greatest architects and painters were employed as stage designers, receiving for their services remunerations up to 300,000 *thalers* for the *mise-en-scène* of a single opera.‡ At that time even Pope Clement IX wrote an operatic libretto and eventually other *librettisti,* such as Pietro Metastasio, vied with Homer and Dante for public favor. In Venice alone no fewer than

* Karl Vossler, "Calderon," in *Corona* (July, 1931), 47 (author's translation).

† *Ibid.,* 47. The name "zarzuela" for any Spanish opera dates from the performance of Calderon's *El Golfo de las Sirenas* at the royal castle of Zarzuela on January 17, 1657.

‡ That was the cost for the staging of Bontempi's *Paride* in Vienna, in 1662. A similar sum was paid for the staging of *Il Pomo d'Oro* during the wedding of Margarita of Spain and Emperor Leopold I, in 1667. The production cost of Calderon's *El Golfo de las Sirenas,* at Zarzuela in 1657, was only 16,000 ducats.

three hundred and fifty operas, with music by forty different composers, were created and performed in the short space of sixty years (1640–1700). These *operas* of the late seventeenth century, with their typical medley of *aria di bravura,* ballet, instrumental interludes, barcaroles, sicilianos, battle symphonies and marches, sweet cantilenas, and what not, were as different from the *musical drama* of Claudio Monteverdi as were the sentimental and showy paintings of Murillo, Cerezo, and Coello from the direct and austerely realistic paintings of Ribalta, Zurbaran, and Velasquez, the chief difference being the new sense appeal and the obliteration of what was simple and realistic by what was extravagant and fanciful.

Calderon in his *autos sacramentales* is what Murillo and his contemporaries are in their paintings. In their pictures, as in his plays, the world of reality is curiously blended with a world of lofty ideals. The poet uses flowery phrases where the painters use flowery colors, and similarly they show a peculiar zest for a vague, light-irradiated atmosphere. The glittering veil of symbols and allegories with which Calderon shrouds the world of matter brings into play that same oscillating twilight which is present in the vaporous paintings of Murillo. The latter employed the advanced luminarism of Velasquez, but he made it serve another end. The light of Velasquez clarifies the visible objects; the light of Murillo transforms reality into sheer romanticism.

Calderon most strikingly resembles the painters of his time in his sense of distance, his desire to bring into play the perspective relation between things that are chronologically distant from each other; for example, his association of the past with the future, the Old Testament with the New. This is very like the preoccupation of the late seventeenth-century painters with striking spatial recession, which, as I have pointed out earlier, was a distinguishing trait of the entire European Baroque. It should be noted that Ribera, Zurbaran, and Velasquez managed to uphold the national ideal of planarity, at least in a decorative measure, but that the generation following them felt more and more tempted to produce magic illusions of depth and distance.

To become aware of the innovations made in the field of space presentation during the Spanish Late Baroque, one need only compare *The Crucifixion of St. Andrew* by Juan de las Roelas (about 1606–09,

Seville Museum), with the same subject by Murillo, painted some seventy years later (Prado). The older artist held the main action within the bounds of the dark foreground and made its uniform darkness contrast with the uniformly lighted background. As a result, the effect of separate planes predominates despite the rearward echelons of several rows of actors on foot and on horseback. As a whole, the pattern of the Roelas picture may be likened to an upright wheel, through whose rim and spokes one catches a glimpse of distance (St. Andrew in this simile standing for the hub, the cross for the spokes, and the onlookers, including the angels above, for the felly). Murillo, on the contrary, plunges the beholder's vision into the depth. He removes the action from the footlights to the background. This he lights up to the fullest brilliance, thus contrasting its dazzling effect with the dark *repoussoirs* he has so shrewdly arranged in the corners of the foreground. The function of these foreground figures whose backs are turned to the spectators is merely optical; they gaze, point, and move into depth, but they play no particular character parts in the drama. The invention of meaningful characters, the great problem of the Cervantes generation, no longer troubled Murillo. He employed a multitude of anonymous people merely to enhance the stunning illusion of depth. His stage is full of indifferent extras.

It may be assumed that this departure from the High Baroque signifies that the rising generation was no longer puzzled with the grave research problem of the older masters. The Late Baroque was the age of consummate technical dexterity. First and last, its artists were virtuosos of the brush.

Murillo's development shows both the waning interest in the poignant truthful manner of narration and the growing importance of the technician's point of view. His historical significance has been a matter of controversy. It can be a matter of controversy only if the painter, in the technical sense of the word, is not judged apart from the interpretative narrator, the genre novelist. As a technician Murillo ranks among the greatest. His ultimate vaporous manner is the consummation of Giorgionism. As an interpreter, however, he was from the start superficial as compared with Ribalta, Ribera, Zurbaran, and Velasquez, and with advancing age he went from bad to worse. A survey of Murillo's development through his three periods (*frio, cálido,* and *vaporoso* are the Spanish distinctions) produces this impression: the more dazzling the "painter" the more disappointing the "narrator." As long as his colors were like Ribera's, his narratives were emotionally unencumbered and his compositions severe, somewhat like those of Zurbaran. But as his palette waxed more

colorful and flowery, his sacred stories were more extravagantly staged and his initial sense of structure thus lost. Ultimately his narrative was more or less consumed by the pyrotechnics of the illumination— but unfortunately not enough to efface the cheap sentimentalism which some of his critics have mistaken for "mysticism."

The Spanish Late Baroque was the age of the clever stage directors. Let me once more use Murillo to illustrate my point. In aim and execution his *Vow of St. Francis* (1674–76, Seville Museum, Fig. 73) is quite different from Ribalta's picture of the same title (Fig. 62). With only a few shifts in arrangement the whole mood has been refashioned to please a more extravagant taste.

Fig. 73.—Murillo: *The Vow of St. Francis,* Seville, Provincial Museum

In contrast to Ribalta's Christ, whose expression is intensified by a concomitant physical effort, the Lord in Murillo's picture stoops to His subject with the effortless grace of a dancer. Murillo was not concerned with Ribalta's grave consideration: "How does a man who has both feet and an arm nailed to the cross support the weight of his body while using the free arm to put a crown on the head of another man standing below?" Murillo treated the nude with a view toward its euphony. The Savior's feet, nailed to the cross as they are, would be an indelicate sight; so the painter tactfully shrouds them in darkness. Accordingly, Ribalta's St. Francis has been replaced by a self-assured actor versed only too well in sentimental roles. In his impeccable pose nothing survives of that breath-taking impulse of heart which actuated the advance of the friar in the older picture. Murillo's Saint merely strikes a fetching pose beneath the cross, taking care that his right foot is nicely poised upon the globe. His cassock is not patched with odds and ends of cloth, and his eyes are not closed in the ecstacy of the moment. He does not nestle close to his Lord, for the latter—every inch a courtier—seems anxious to avoid too close contact with his underling without seeming unkind. Murillo's Jesus gives an elegant sideward swing to His hips so that a gulf separates His chest from the friar's head. Whatever happens here happens according to etiquette. In conformity with such aristocratic demeanor, the Lord even refrains from awarding His crown to Francis. Instead, He touches the man's shoulder with an effeminate hand, and there is a languishing eye-to-eye dialogue.

In addition to this reinterpretation of the action, one should also notice the new manipulation of the proportions, the lighting, spacing, composition, and other problems of form. Ribalta's severe bilateral symmetry has been discarded for a more elastic pattern, dominated by diagonals. A pair of winged cupids (in lieu of Ribalta's two separate, and somewhat older, angels) is perched on a cloud in the upper right-hand corner, slightly behind the main group. Because of other dominant diagonals—the interlocking glances of the Lord and the Saint, the slanting position of their arms, and the oblique inscription plate on top of the cross—the beholder's eye is forced to link those putti with the globe in the lower left-hand foreground upon which St. Francis rests his foot. The fact that the diagonal recedes at the same time dilates the spacing of the whole.

Murillo attempted to substitute something more elegant for the pithy action of Ribalta's painting. He altered the proportions of both the canvas and the forms it contains. The earlier canvas, packed to the brim with form, was square and ponderous. Murillo favored more graceful proportions. He so regulated the flow of light that it rallied in a slim inverted triangle, hinged upon the central perpendicular axis of the composition. Cutting across the figures, the illumination makes their mass seem less than it actually is. Moreover, the painter provided for ample space around his actors. Their dulcet duet needs an efficient sounding board and a surrounding filled with the sweet scent of golden-hued vapors. Where these become incandescent as by magic, they reveal visions of ruins and a distant city. The whole is a fanciful operatic scene.

The mutations of taste may be further illustrated by a number of pic-

tures of the Savior on the Cross. As compared with Zurbaran's three
paintings in the museum of Seville (Fig. 64), or the *Crucifixus* of Velasquez
in the Prado, the sentimentalism of Murillo's *Christ on the Cross* (Leningrad, Hermitage*), representing the latest period of the Sevillian romantic,
borders on the coquetry of the Rococo. Anthony van Dyck was godfather
to its mannerisms. They evolved, it is true, from less affected beginnings.
The *Crucified Christ* in the Czernin Gallery at Vienna†, painted some
twenty years earlier, was not playful. The change from its quiescent style
to one more agitated can be caught from an otherwise indifferent item:
in the Vienna picture the inscription plate on top of the cross was a plain
square board, in the painting in the Hermitage it has become a scroll
twisted by the wind.

Needless to say, this evolution was not confined to Murillo alone. He
exemplifies a general trend that extended far beyond the Andalusian
school. I could as well have illustrated the whole matter with the paintings of Mateo Cerezo, the North Castilian who was born and died in
Burgos and received his training in Madrid. The picture for which he is
best known is his *Cristo de la Agonia* (Burgos cathedral), whose twisted
body emulates that of the carved *Cristo de la Expiración* in Triana, by
Juan Antonio Gixon. The languor of the uplifted face is enhanced by the
sentimental hues of half-light through which the city of Burgos, resting
against snow-covered mountains, looms in the distance. One knows Cerezo
after having seen any one of his bizarre saints. Velasquez would probably
have turned away in dismay from Cerezo's *St. John the Baptist* (Kassel
Gallery) who, with the familiar stage swagger of an opera star, seems to be
winding up an aria on high *C*.

MURILLO'S PAINTINGS OF THE IMMACULATE CONCEPTION The Franciscan
enthusiasm of the Spanish Church and the ideal of chivalrous courtship,
as exemplified in St. Ignatius Loyola's consecrating his arms to the
All-Purest during his vigil in the shrine of Montserrat, have made "the

* August L. Mayer, *Murillo (Klassiker der Kunst*, XXII, Berlin and Leipzig, 1923),
191.
    † *Ibid.*, 99.

Immaculate Conception" one of the most Spanish themes in the art of Spain. *La Purísima Concepción* is that "great wonder in heaven" of which the Revelation of St. John speaks in the beginning of the twelfth chapter: "A woman clothed with the sun, and the moon under her feet, and upon her head a crown of twelve stars; and she being with child cried, travailing in birth, and pained to be delivered."

The iconographical development of the picture of the Immaculate Virgin through the seventeenth century affords another revealing clue to the development of the romanticism of the Spanish Late Baroque. As one regards, in proper chronological succession, one representative example of the Purissima after another, one's imagination is lured away, step by step, from the tangible verity of the earlier versions by young Velasquez (London, L. Frère Collection) and Zurbaran (Edinburgh, National Gallery), for example, to the fanciful visions of maidens floating in radiant clouds by Murillo and Valdes Leal. The Calderonic view asserts itself more and more as one's vision is ultimately removed to a domain neither quite real nor quite imaginary, a domain of pictorial expression comparable to the opera and the ballet as distinguished from the spoken drama.

The pregnancy of the Apocalyptic *Immaculata* was the first realistic feature to be discontinued by the painters of the seventeenth century. Next, Mary, at first a royal matron, was juvenated until she ultimately became an entracing lass of fourteen or fifteen. At the same time, the solid bank of clouds, on which at first she stood like a statue, was transformed into floating mists, and the whole setting, at first a simple river landscape or a seascape, lost its earthliness, turning gradually into a vague illusion of radiance. The composition, moreover, was stripped of its original tectonic symmetry even as the plastic solidity of all the forms was dissolved by a hazy brilliance.

Murillo's numerous Purissimas illustrate the development of Spanish painting during the second half of the seventeenth century. This new trend may be illustrated by citing a few characteristic compositions, arranged in chronological order of appearance.

The early *Purísima of the Franciscans** (about 1655–60, Seville Museum) retains the statuesque realism of the first half of the century. The

* *Ibid.,* 73.

majestic body of the Virgin—reminiscent of the ponderous type created by the sculptor Juan Martinez Montañes (see his statue in the Seville cathedral)—is set off by a contour keen and hard as steel from a cloak unpliant and solid as an architectural conch. Despite the exuberance expressed in the pose as well as in the illumination, the whole conception is fundamentally that of a sculptor. The large cylindrical areas, alternately light and dark, contrast palpably with each other, not as yet dissolved in hazy vapors. The arms and the advancing leg, in particular, are modeled with great determination.

The *Aranjuez Purísima** (about 1665, Prado), which shows the Virgin for the first time with her head lifted heavenward as in rapture, represents a decided departure. A more ethereal, "painterly" interpretation has overcome the earlier sculpturesque style. The clouds are no longer treated as a solid pedestal, and the cloak is now a filmy thing, broken up by swiftly changing specks of light and shade. The stance as well as the mass-outline of the Virgin have likewise lost some of their statuesque significance. The arms no longer form a sculpturesque contrast. Instead of being separated from the chest by means of an interpolated beam of light, they are one with it. The change in the depiction of the eyes and their sockets illustrates, perhaps better than anything else, how the "tactile" ideation has given way to a "retinal" ideation. A hazy half-shadow, covering the forehead, the eye-sockets, and the nose, makes all these parts fuse in a single visual impression. Formerly such forms were plastically more differentiated; the lids were bulging convex surfaces heavily modeled in keen light and set off from the thick shadows hovering between the lids as well as under the jutting brow-bones.

From this point Murillo advanced to more lavish extravaganzas. The *Purísima* of 1668† in the Sala capitular of the cathedral of Seville, emerges from a background of rosy angels. The new motive provides a rhythmically vibrant pattern. Accordingly, the surfaces of the Virgin's robe quiver with scintillating half-light and half-dark. The entire contour is just as restive.

The girlish *Purísima of the Capuchins* (1674–76, Seville Museum, Fig. 74) fairly melts away in the delicate mists that surround her. Her silhouette

* Mayer, *Murillo,* 75.
† *Ibid.,* 83.

is less accentuated, at points becoming quite evanescent. Again the background is alive with little cherubs. But instead of forming a homogeneous mass, they come as two separate sparkling bouquets; indeed, lilies, palm fronds, and flower buds are scattered in between. A third group of angels in the upper left-hand corner is dimmed so that the coveted unilateral sway from left to right may not be endangered. Murillo, aiming at a swifter, more transient, movement, relinquished bilateral symmetry even in pictures as solemn and formal as these.

The *Purísima* in the Hermitage at Leningrad* (about 1680) should be in-
Fig. 74.—Murillo: *The Purísima of the Capuchins*, Seville, Provincial Museum
cluded in this group, although, because of the missing crescent, the subject was an *Assumption of the Virgin*. It is an enchanted *Jubilate*, a florid rhapsody in terms of bubbling specks of colored light. The bright background is ablaze as with flames, and the Virgin's form is flamboyant. The simple silhouette is gone. In an enthusiastic gesture of greeting Mary's arms protrude from the mass of the body, as does her cloak. The cloak is no longer joined to the background, as in the *Purísima of the Capuchins* (Fig. 74), but stands out as flakes of dark from flakes of light. The last vestige of the tactile style has become obliterated in this "painterly" vision. It is as though so many trills of a silver flute were ringing from every brush stroke. And, if the sustained and solid surfaces of the early *Purísima of the Franciscans* remind one of steady melodies sung in whole notes, the sparkling effervescence of *The Assumption* reminds one of coloratura runs sung in sixteenths, and intertwining with the *cantus firmus* at all points.

It would indeed be interesting to study how the repertory of Late Baroque forms continued to evolve in the paintings of the Immaculate

* *Ibid.*, 173.

Conception for which Mateo Cerezo was famous in his day. Unfortunately, however, none of them is extant. Instead, I shall turn to Juan de Valdes Leal, Murillo's rival, who dissolved solid form still more completely by means of his impressionistic brushwork.

VALDES LEAL If the Virgins of Murillo and Valdes Leal are considered together, the transition from an initial tactile manner of form construction to an ultimate retinal manner of form destruction is acutely perceptible. In his early works Murillo's forms are like a smooth mirror of undisturbed water, yielding a perfect and finite reflection of the tangible object. Gradually, with the greater development of his painterly vision, the surfaces become like water ruffled by a breeze. But in the paintings of Valdes Leal the surfaces are furious waves whipped by a gale.

Valdes Leal's *Purísima* (Seville Museum) was painted in 1671, at the time when the artist was engaged in decorating the cathedral of Seville for the canonization of St. Ferdinand. The iconographical arrangement bears a certain resemblance to Murillo's *Purísima of the Capuchins*, but not so the painterly execution. The very notion of solid form is shattered by the geyser of cherubs and clouds on which the Madonna ascends—an insubstantial vision of white, azure, and pale yellow. Valdes anticipated the Rococo of Churriguera. The background is an evanescent haze of light blue, yellow, and pink. In the upper left-hand section an angel is accented by a black sash and a white lily. A crimson cover flung over a chair glitters in the lower left. Amber palm fronds are dispersed in the lower center. A cherub draped with salmon red follows on the right. Another in sky blue is seen above him. The so-called preparatory sketch for the painting, once in the Marcel Nicolle Collection in Paris, is even more Rococo; indeed, its painterly texture is so gossamery that it has often been classified as a variant by some eighteenth-century Spanish painter.

A few critics confess that they are more deeply impressed by the art of Valdes Leal than by that of Murillo. I admit that Valdes was a more exciting *painter,* in fact, an extremely fastidious colorist. Note how he drapes his female figures in emerald green touched off with carmine, or in amber highlighted by splashes of green. The women who tempt St. Jerome (in the painting in the Museum of Seville) are a constant inspiration to any colorist. On the other hand, this same picture reveals Valdes' unfortunate inclination for the far-fetched and extreme. If Murillo inclined toward sentimentality and sweetness, and Valdes Leal did not, then the latter was always straining for effect. The conventional Temptation of St. Anthony must be outstripped by a *Temptation of St. Jerome,* and its sultry mood receives yet another bizarre and unpleasant touch in the adjoining *Scourging of St. Jerome,* where a hectic and impassioned angel is meting out punishment to the naked Saint with a cat-of-nine-tails. Valdes' subjects are often of the weirdest kind, and he specialized in painting the severed heads of martyrs. All this may mark his art as unhinged and therefore "modern," but his queer thoughts as well as his turbulent brushwork mirror his unbalanced personality and the violent bursts of temper from which the gentler Murillo had much to suffer. Valdes' pupil Palomino gives a vivid description of how his erratic master would suddenly leap toward a canvas upon which he had traced a composition, dash off a few apparently unrelated brush strokes, and having done so would just as unexpectedly turn to something else. But such eccentricities of temperament and technique are not sufficient to exalt Valdes Leal at the expense of his rival. One may not casually dismiss Murillo, the last great representative of the school of Seville, for Valdes Leal, its most bizarre mind. Whatever the objections to Murillo, compared with Valdes Leal he was in far greater measure a master of *la grande peinture.* What he had to say was said, for the most part, with a clear voice and was finite. Above all, he was quite free from pettiness. In the last analysis, Murillo's art has the compelling grandeur which emanates from a perfectly pure mind. And precisely that is the last thing that could be said of Valdes, who was a genius, but manifestly an unhealthy genius.

SENTIMENTAL BODEGONES V aldes Leal's fastidious selection of out-of-the-way subjects of unfamiliar Christian iconography introduces another feature of the Late Baroque development. Valdes and all the other painters of the Calderon generation as well were subtle variety hunters. They were not satisfied with exploring the forms of the phenomenal world and

representing them simply for ocular enjoyment, but were bent on endow-
ing their paintings with some added sentimental appeal.

This is perhaps more apparent in the bodegones than in the sacred
pictures of the time, because in a Crucifixion or a Last Supper the undercurrent of thought and sentiment cannot be so fully disregarded as when
the subject is a still life of vegetables, a beggar, or a group of musicians.
The bodegones of Fray Juan Sanchez Cotan, Herrera *el Viejo,* and Velasquez kept clear of sentimental implications, but those of Murillo and his
contemporaries overstepped the frontiers of pure painting and vied with
the poet and the novelist.

The early bodegonistas of the Baroque were intent on revealing no more
than the objective forms. Fray Sanchez Cotan, in the still life of 1602
(Madrid, Alphonse of Bourbon Collection, Fig. 13), disclosed the authentic plasticity of large and small fowl, a branch of lemons, a bunch of beets,
and a few sticks of celery by reconstructing their space-communicating
surfaces as though he were anticipating the cubism of Picasso. Cotan did
not tell any particular story, either here or in the *Kitchen Still Life with
the Cook* (Paris, Sedelmeyer Collection), where the cook is a bit of pictorial form no more important than the fish and the sausages.

Some of the early bodegones are plain portraits. An example is the
Two Minstrels by Herrera the Elder (Vienna, Liechtenstein Gallery, Fig.
75), showing a blind musician with a guitar and his bright-
eyed companion. In this sim-
ple pictorial statement all the
distinctive marks of the conventional genre subjects are lacking. Nothing about the models,
nor the mode in which they
are presented, makes our lips
curl into a smile. There are no
caustic comments on debased
ragamuffins, no picturesque
costumes, no novelistic action.
Plain portraiture was mixed

Fig. 75.—Francisco Herrera the Elder: *Two Minstrels,*
Vienna, Liechtenstein Gallery

with plain still-life painting in the early bodegones of Velasquez. But without doubt these were exercises in pictorial forms and nothing more. So long as we expect to be entertained by any particular plot, *The Musicians* (Berlin, Kaiser Friedrich Museum) or *The Two Youths in the Kitchen* (London, the Duke of Wellington's Collection) will impress us as stiff and uninspiring. Fundamentally, these bodegones are studies of certain pictorial problems: for example, that of defining in terms of spherical surfaces such round objects as heads, arms, hands, glasses, a chopping board, a guitar, and so on.

In contrast to this artistic purism of the realists, the concomitance of sentimental notions is the distinctive feature of the bodegones of the Late Baroque. Murillo, in his appeal to our poetic imagination, expects the beholder to read his paintings as one reads a book. In general, all the genre painters after 1660 dwelt on witty, pointed anecdotes and satirical annotations. Some of them specialized in a single limited class of farcical subject matter. In Rome, Herrera *el Mozo* satirized the funny louts on the fish-market until he was known all over the place by the nickname "The Fish-Spaniard" (*Lo Spagnuolo degli pesci*).

The characteristic finesse of the Late Baroque is also reflected in the intricate representation of the forms themselves. The still life with which every Murillo painting abounds is never as simple as the still life in the paintings of Zurbaran or Velasquez. The younger generation sought more difficult tasks. Note the pottery, the baskets full of melons, oranges, lemons, and grapes, the distaffs and what not, which appear as by-matter in Murillo's Sevillian street scenes of boys nibbling fruit or throwing dice. Any professional copyist will testify that, as compared with these precious little tidbits executed with so much subtlety, the plain jars, bottles, and other kitchen ware in the bodegones of Velasquez are as easy to do as child's play.

The same exhibition of what is complicated and difficult distinguishes the figures in Murillo's genre paintings from those of the earlier realists. For example, Murillo's street urchins are far more complicated creatures than any other youngsters depicted on any Spanish canvas before the year 1660. This is the result of the painter's peculiar gift of capturing not only the pliant forms of the child, which appeal to the eye, but the transcience of his emotions as well, which appeal to one's sentimental contemplation.

Everybody knows Murillo's *Toilet Making* idyl (Munich, Fig. 76). Now whether our attitude toward the artist be friendly, hostile, or indifferent,

Fig. 76.—Murillo: *Toilet Making*,
Munich, Alte Pinakothek

there is no denying that the image of the boy is a masterpiece of child psychology, and that only highly developed observation could grasp its elusive complexity with such assuredness. The boy is doing at least three different things at once. He is suffering the scalp treatment that his grandmother is meticulously giving him, he is chewing his hunk of bread, and he is toying with his little dog. All these occupations are passing swiftly through his little mind, resolving there into a single, somewhat vague, mood to which the child gives himself listlessly, as any child would. Admittedly, the repertory of forms available to the more ancient masters was neither rich nor flexible enough to master such an intricate psychological medley. To the Late Baroque, however, it was a fascinating challenge and accessible only to an elaborate technique. The bravura of observation had to be matched with an unprecedented technical bravura. Murillo possessed it.

On the other hand, such subjects were uninteresting to any painter of the Late Baroque unless they were set in an extravagant scenery. Yet extravagance was risky. For, unless technical deftness is controlled by critical tact and self-discipline, it always tends to emancipate itself from its original objective and to become an end in itself. Such was the case with Murillo.

Though the friends of Andalusian folk life will never tire of admiring for their intimate observation his *Three Boys Throwing Dice* (Munich) —a painting of his last period—they cannot very well deny that an overdose of attractive stage devices, lighting effects in particular, makes it not a faithful image but rather a flattery of life, an exhibition of technical bragadoccio. Everything is just too pretty for words. The shower of golden half-tones upon the face and the body of the boy in the center renders even a street Arab charming and presentable, if need be, at court.

And if this was true of the sunny scenes of "The Great Theater of the World," to which all these romanticists ministered alike, it was no less true of its gloomy aspects. Valdes Leal romanticized the stench of the sepulcher even as Murillo romanticized the slums. Those monstrous allegories known as *The Hieroglyphs of Death (Los Geroglificos de las*

Fig. 77.—Juan de Valdes Leal: *The Hieroglyphs of Death,* Seville, La Caridad

Postrimerias, Seville, La Caridad, Fig. 77) are not so far removed as they may seem from Murillo's merrymaking. They are still life too. The only difference is that Valdes Leal applied his hypersensitive observation and stupendous craftsmanship to thoroughly repulsive subjects. The scene is laid in a tomb. Two coffins are open, one of them containing the decaying body of a bishop, the other that of a knight of Santiago. Moreover, the pictures are sweeping moral sermons stuffed with allegories as well as with breath-taking realistic details. Vermin crawl on the white silk of the bishop's mitre and chasuble. The purple linings have peeled off the rotting wood of the caskets. From the mists above a mysterious hand emerges holding a balance burdened with further allegorical *nature morte.* That the painting should not only be perceived visually but also read intellectually becomes clear from the added inscriptions. *Ni más, ni menos* ("Neither more nor less"), it says on the scales; and a scroll at the bottom is incribed with the legend *Finis gloriae mundi* ("The end of the glory of the world").

CLAUDIO COELLO With the weak and imitative followers of Murillo the decline of Spanish painting became rapid. The last phase of the Late Baroque was a period of shallow and mendacious Mannerism. The *St. John Evangelist* in the Metropolitan Museum, attributed to an unknown follower of Alonso Cano, is typical of innumerable effigies of coquettish, capering, and overacting ballet dancers who went forth in the guise of saints from the Spanish studios of the late seventeenth century.. The deterioration from the crest to the lowest trough of the Baroque style is evident if this pathetic ham actor with his ridiculous attitudinizing is contrasted with the *St. Francis in Ecstasy* by Zurbaran in the Museum of Fine Arts in Boston.

The general decline is just as evident in genre painting as it is in ecclesiastical art. Moreover, the genre pictures of Murillo's pupil Pedro Nuñez de Villavicencio—for example, his *Boys Playing Dice* (Prado)—betray the early signs of the French Rococo. These are not honest peasant lads at all, but rakish young aristocrats of the kind François Boucher was soon to paint exclusively, masquerading as "shepherds" in peasant costumes borrowed from the ballet wardrobe. For, with the waning political power of the kingdom, Spanish art was rapidly losing its native traits.

The time was approaching when foreigners were appointed as court painters to Philip V (grandson of *Le Roi Soleil*) and Charles III: Andrea Procaccini came from Rome; Jean Ranc and Louis Michel Van Loo from Paris; Giovanni Battista Tiepolo from Venice; Anton Raphael Mengs from Dresden. Toward the end of the seventeenth century Spanish civilization also surrendered to the French. In 1783 all men in Spain were forbidden by a royal statute to wear the traditional Spanish dress. Instead, they were forced to wear the military suit and the tricorne of France.

The decline of Spain's native art cannot, of course, be attributed to the growing influence of Italy and France. Other reasons account for its

decadence. During the late seventeenth century the number of outstanding native painters began to shrink in an appalling measure as compared
with the multitude of renowned artists abroad, say in Holland.

The last of the outstanding native painters of the school of Madrid of
the late seventeenth century was Claudio Coello. His retable with *The
Homage of St. Louis to the Holy
Family* (Prado, Fig. 78) leaves no
doubt that in his time simplicity
was obliterated in complexity, in-
timacy in showiness, and honest religiosity in pompous rituals.

Here Mary and her young Prince
are receiving a foreign king. While
she lifts the infant's filmy diaper
most royally between her thumb
and index finger, she casts her eyes
in decorous modesty upon the basket of fruit which St. Anne is presenting. St. Louis is garbed with
everything that an opera king

Fig. 78.—Claudio Coello: *The Homage of St.
Louis to the Holy Family,* Prado

wears for such an occasion, except the crown and the scepter, which
make a very handsome still life upon the ruffled oriental rug. He bows
as if he were performing a step from a minuet, almost bending his knee.
The picture represents a typical operatic "reception at court." The stage
setting—a bewildering maze of trees, scraps of Baroque architecture,
Persian rugs, and draperies—mirrors the influence of the stage settings
devised by Ferdinando and Francesco Galli Bibiena for the Hapsburg and Farnese court theaters at Vienna and Parma. Their sceneries
were the last word in make-believe. In what way the architectural parts
are supposed to be structurally interrelated, or how the dais, upon which
the Holy Family is enthroned, is linked with the walls, piers, and arches
that emerge laterally and behind, are questions without reasonable answers. Interest lay here in a brilliant ensemble of props and wings pic-
turesquely spun over with clinging vines, flowers, and silk hangings. The
more jutting or recessional the parts, the better for the light and the

scintillating color harmony composed of hundreds of delicate nuances of azure, pink, gray, black, and gold.

As an illustration of the extreme theatricalism rampant in Spanish painting when Claudio Coello was its leader, no better example could be found than his retable *La Sagrada Forma* (Fig. 79), completed in 1687 for

the sacristy of the Escorial. The painting contributed even more to the artist's world fame than did the elaborate street decorations and arches of triumph which he devised in honor of the wedding of Charles II and Marie Louise of Orleans. Cean Bermudez devotes a footnote of no less than seventy-nine lines to its description. It represents the transfer by Charles II of a sacramental wafer of mysterious origin to the sanctuary of the Escorial. The last Hapsburg monarch on the Spanish throne is kneeling in front of the altar amidst a host of princes and retainers, while the prior of the monastery exalts the monstrance with the sacred relic. Allegorical figures hover

Fig. 79.—Claudio Coello: *La Sagrada Forma,* Escorial

near the ceiling: Religion, Divine Love, and the House of Austria—a woman clad in yellow, bearing the imperial mace and the Hapsburg eagle in her hands. The multitude of the clergy fills the depth of space.

If a last glance is cast back from Coello's painting at *The Maids of Honor* by Velasquez (Fig. 71), for example, it is painful to note in what measure the clarity and simplicity of the Velasquean style have perished. Rest has been replaced by unrest. Instead of a tectonic frame of steady perpendiculars and horizontals, we face a proscenium of irregular design. Its moldings advance and withdraw, zigzagging and jerking hither and thither. Above, a varicolored stage curtain, cut across frequently by inscription scrolls, is being gathered by cupids into picturesque clusters. The picture contained within the frame is no less agitated. Velasquez reduced his forms to areas almost geometrical in appearance; consequently the steady rhythm of his composition is like deep, quiet breathing. Coello's picture is disturbed by the loud clatter of petty and ragged fields of dark and light; the upper third of the hall is split up by six lighted window areas, seven darker embrasures, as many motley compartments of the ceiling, and three flying angels. The lower part is likewise occupied by numerous recessional rows of flaming tapers, rows of heads, and rows of bodies—an intricate interaction of human figures, alternately dark and light, large and small, moving depthward and sideward. Whereas Velasquez extends the action beyond the confines of his canvas by showing the images of the king and queen reflected in a mirror on the rear wall of his stage setting—thereby merely *suggesting* the presence of spectators outside the pictured scene—Coello actually allows the action to overflow from the stage into the house; his own portrait and the likenesses of other dignitaries emerge tangibly in front of and from under the canvas. Nothing, I think, could better demonstrate the boisterousness of the Late Baroque style in contrast to the fine reticence of the High Baroque.

REVIEW The development of art has often been likened to the deliberate swing of a pendulum. If we look back upon the evolution of Spanish art, it is generally true that every important departure was either caused or quickened by the opposition of the new leaders to the preceding period style, which had either exhausted its means of expression or overstressed its tendencies. When the naturalism of the fifteenth century grew too realistic or, rather, too unmindful of the higher requirements of the sublime, the pendulum turned to swing in the opposite direction, the idealism of the Renaissance being the result of the reaction. Again, when the antinaturalistic decorative tendencies of the first half of the cinquecento were overstressed by the Mannerists of the second half, Ribalta and the whole generation of Cervantes turned back in the opposite direction, refuting the style of El Greco and thus, in a sense, returning to the solid earth of the quattrocento Primitives. Yet again, the opposition to the excessive sobriety, the economy of means, and the severity of Zurbaran and Velasquez forced Murillo, Cerezo, and Coello back into a romanticism whose

sentimental appeal, decorative extravagance, and flamboyant design remind one more of El Greco than of Ribalta. La Bruyère's famous axiom,
Les extrèmes se touchent, referred to this to-and-fro development under
the combined action of momentum and gravity, progress and reaction.

The simile of the swinging pendulum needs one qualification, however,
if it is to be entirely fitting. It never swings back exactly to the point from
which it started to move. The point to which it swings back always lies on
another, more advanced, plane. To clarify this, let me point out these
facts: The positive artistic contributions of the preceding epochs were
never wholly cast away by the following epochs. No matter how contempti-
ble the art of the quattrocento was to the formalistic taste of the cinquecento, the former's close approach to the nature of the phenomenal world
remained an indispensable hypothesis for the idealistic style of the latter.
Juan de Juanes was deeply indebted to the fifteenth-century school of
Valencia. And this is true of all subsequent masters. El Greco was no less
deeply obliged to the Venetian school of Titian, Velasquez to El Greco,
and Murillo to Velasquez. If any new period had started a wholesale destruction of the art of the past, instead of utilizing in fullest measure its
finest contributions, Spanish art would have lost every vestige of continuity.

In comparison with the High Baroque of Ribera, Zurbaran, and Velasquez, the Late Baroque was another "idealistic" phase. Its idealism was
distinguished from the fanciful idealism of El Greco and the Mannerists
by a substructure of "spirited realism," contributed by Velasquez and his
colleagues. The paintings of the contemporaries of Murillo cannot be
described as manifestations of outright realism, as we have seen. Yet none
of the artists of the Calderon age lost contact with living nature as El
Greco did.

In view of these facts, it is not surprising to learn that when, after a
short period of stagnation and foreign domination, another great phase
of Spanish art began, the pendulum swung back to the impressionism of
Velasquez but reached it on a more advanced plane, a plane conditioned
by the understructure which the romantic Late Baroque had created in
the intervening period.

In regard to this last great phase of Spanish art—from the late eighteenth
through the early nineteenth century—it is necessary to say in advance that
its representative was not a school but the single genius of Francisco Goya.

The Age of Napoleon and Goya

CHAPTER NINE

GOYA LEGENDS AND GOYA FACTS Francisco de Goya had indeed more in
common with Velasquez than with Murillo or Coello. He resorted to
Velasquez to liberate himself from the decorative juggleries of the Late
Baroque and the Rococo of Giovanni Battista Tiepolo of Venice. On
the other hand, Goya was not the objective, detached observer Velasquez
had been. His temper was at once subjective and emotional. Yet, his emotionalism did not stir him, as it did Murillo, into catholic religious trans-
ports. Goya's was neither the ardent art of the Catholic Reformation nor
the theatrical art of the Calderonean age. His was the aggressive art of the
revolution and the age of Napoleon Bonaparte. His ecclesiastical paintings
were, for the most part, rather indifferent productions. It was the cankered
social and political conditions of his age that roused the scorching oratory
that thunders from Goya's worldly etchings and paintings. The tenor of
that art was social criticism.

It is all very well to break forth into eulogies over Goya's clever technique, the beauty and strength of his coloration, the imaginative quality
of his picture patterns, and what other esthetic charms his art may possess.
But the full significance of his art is not disclosed unless it is studied
against the background of Spanish history.

Goya's name has been enveloped in many sham traditions which it has
taken a long time to brush away. The stuff and nonsense about Goya's
life and character, fabricated by Matheron (1858), Brunet (1865), and
Yriarte (1867), and kept alive by others as late as 1914, leaves one with the
impression of an incorrigible plotter and cynic "willing to pass the time
of the day with the biggest scoundrel"; "a roystering bully who was always

ready for a fight or a dissipation"; a libertine of the worst kind who when staying at Rome "one black night scaled the walls of a convent in order to abduct a young and charming nun."* Fortunately the student who is interested in facts rather than in fiction may now consult the works of scholars who have begun to remove from Goya's face the silly make-up of a third-rate village comedian.†

The life of Goya spanned a long period, from 1746 to 1828. Moreover, two thirds of it fell within the *ancien régime*. The demoniac art that is brought to mind by the mention of "Goya" did not evolve until nearly the beginning of the nineteenth century. Up to the age of forty-five we may speak of Goya the courtier; after fifty, the rebel. The courtier and the rebel are two distinct persons.

Goya the courtier, the fashionable society painter, had little in common with Goya the rebel. The former had a host of legitimate children and wrote thoroughly unromantic letters to his friend Martin Zapater.‡ His early life may have been spotted with a few temperamental escapades, but it was not at all what the French romanticists and their uncritical exploiters tried to make one believe.

Goya's artistic talent did not emerge, as fiction has it, when the infant was found drawing with a chunk of coal on a plastered barn wall—according to one author it was a pig, according to another it was the village blindman. That anecdote harks back to fifteenth-century chroniclers, first being told of Giotto and thereafter of many other budding artists; in fact, it runs through art biography like a red thread.

Goya was not uncommonly young when his talent was discovered; he was fourteen. In Saragossa, where his father was an artisan, the young art student attended regularly the classes held by Jose Luzan, who was apparently a sound instructor. Goya was as well liked by the distinguished Saragossans as he eventually was by the distinguished Madrilenians.

* Hugh Stokes, *Francisco Goya* (London, 1914), 72, 86.

† Valerian von Loga, *Francisco Goya* (Berlin, 1921, 2d ed.)., Aureliano de Beruete y Moret, *Goya* (3 vols., Madrid, 1917–19; English ed., London, 1922); *Catálogo ilustrado de la Esposición de pinturas de Goya* (Museo del Prado, Madrid, 1928); Daniel Catton Rich, *The Art of Goya; Paintings, Drawings, and Prints* (Art Institute of Chicago, January to March, 1942); Charles Graydon Poore, *Goya* (New York, 1939).

‡ F. Zapater y Gómez, *Goya, noticias biográficas* (Saragossa, 1868).

It was logical, after his apprenticeship was over in 1766, to move to Madrid. There one of his fellow townsmen was making a successful career: Francisco Bayeu, a pupil of Anton Raphael Mengs, was easily the most influential artist at court. Goya became Bayeu's assistant and later married his sister.

The romantic biographers give another reason for Goya's removal to Madrid. They would have us believe that he had to flee from Saragossa because he was involved in a religious feud. Next they make him flee from Madrid to Rome, allegedly because he was implicated in another public scandal. Inasmuch as he was awarded the second prize from the Royal Academy of Fine Arts in Parma on June 27, 1771,* I prefer to believe that the young painter was sent to Italy at the expense of the Academy of San Fernando. Of course so simple an explanation again fails to make a good novel. So Goya's biographers picture him as having been found in an alley of Madrid with a dagger in his back. Thereafter they make him wander through southern Spain, earning his living as a bullfighter. Ultimately, to motivate his departure from Rome, they concoct the hair-raising incident mentioned above—the abduction of a nun, followed by renewed persecution and flight. Had he been forced to escape from Madrid, surely the way across the Pyrenees through France would have been shorter and safer. Moreover, if Goya had really arrived in Italy as a fugitive, it would be inexplicable that the Academy of Parma, so closely linked with the royal court of Madrid, entered Goya's name in a public contest; that the pope, who was likewise well informed about Madrilenian events, patronized him; and that the Russian ambassador invited the young artist to the court of the empress, Catherine II.

On his return to the Spanish capital in October, 1775, Goya's every effort was bent toward winning academic as well as public recognition. In fact, the steps he took to insure it come very close to "social climbing." He sided with the classicist Mengs and his coterie, and thus netted himself an important commission for the royal tapestry looms (beginning in October, 1776). This in turn opened the road to a position at court. In 1779

---

* The record is quoted in *Gazette des Beaux Arts,* 1860, II, p. 216. Goya was awarded the prize for an entirely academic painting, *Hannibal Greeting the Plains of Italy from the Height of the Alps.*

Goya applied to Charles III for the title of *pintor de cámara*. He failed
to get the job, but he was voted into the Academy (1780). The new title
launched him as a fashionable metropolitan painter who was patronized
by the duchesses of Osuna and Alba. The Infante, D. Luis Antonio, and
other princes, dukes, generals, high state officials, and leading financiers
had their portraits painted by him. In 1789 he was called upon to paint
King Charles IV and his queen. In 1795 he was elected president of the
Academy. In 1799, when he was appointed *primer pintor de cámara*, Goya
reached the top.

THE PAINTER OF THE TAPESTRIES During most of this early period,
until 1792 or thereabouts, Goya's art was suave and well-mannered. It displayed the propriety becoming to one employed by the top-ranking aristocracy of the eighteenth century. The forty cartoons for the royal tapestry
looms speak for themselves.

From the splendid decorative qualities of these flawless productions it
would be difficult to predict that ultimately Goya would emancipate Spanish art from the aristocratic idiosyncrasies and the foreign fashions of the
ancien régime. Goya did not originate that genre-like conception of Spanish folk life which the public of today considers the most significant feature
of his cartoons for the tapestries. In the selection of his subject matter
Goya merely imitated Francisco Bayeu. It was not Goya but Bayeu who
in his own tapestry designs first substituted the typical Madrilenian country life for the sham imitations of Flemish, Italian, and French *tableaux
vivants*. They had been the vogue among the eighteenth-century eclectics
of the Academy and particularly among the design-makers for the looms
since the founding of that royal institution in 1720—first under the sur-
veillance of Andrea Procaccini, a student of Carlo Maratta, and afterward
under the management of Mengs, who employed all the foreign *blageurs*
in the capital—Mariano Maella, Jose de Castillo, and the three Gonzales-
Velazquez brothers.

Indeed, a careful comparison of their tapestries leaves no doubt that
Bayeu's ideas were more radical than Goya's. Goya appears as a defender
of aristocratic ideals which Bayeu dismissed. Bayeu depicted the life of

the middle-class people; Goya preferred to depict the genteel life of high society.

In this regard his famous tapestry cartoons, most of which are now assembled in the Prado, follow more closely than Bayeu's the brilliant coloristic trend that was flowering in Venice among such painters of *mœurs* as Pietro Longhi and Giovanni Antonio and Francesco Guardi. The Venetian genre painter whose snapshots of society life young Goya approximated most closely was Gasparo Traversi. Inasmuch as Traversi died in 1769 or thereabouts, Goya could not have met him personally when he visited Italy. But I do believe that Traversi's paintings left an indelible impression on young Goya's mind. Traversi has precisely that which is most characteristic of Goya's genre pictures. Transcending the more general depiction of milieu in which Longhi and the two Guardis specialized, Traversi studied, from the standpoint of an amused observer, the people and the conditions in which they lived. He was perhaps the only one of Goya's contemporaries in all Europe whose pictorial comments were ironical, sarcastic, and even malicious.*

Nothing in the tapestry cartoons reveals that they were painted on the eve of the Great Revolution. In them everyone is leading a life of joy, and social problems seem to be non-existent. The enchanting playgrounds of Madrid are set for picnics and rural frolics, for young folk to play blindman's buff or toss a stuffed jumping jack into the air, for the girls to play badminton, for the boys to walk on stilts, inflate toy balloons, and fly kites.

All is painted in the sunny unencumbered tints of the Rococo palette. Although the tapestries extend over a fifteen-year period (1776–91), they exhibit relatively few traces of a stylistic evolution. Certain changes in the manner of the execution were merely necessary adjustments to the technical requirements of weaving. The early cartoons were too dark and went too painstakingly into the details of form. The exigencies of the weaver's technique eventually compelled Goya to use a limited range of colors and to reduce his lights and shades to a few broad flats.

The rich coloration of some of the tapestry cartoons eludes description. Never was painted anything more lusciously decorative than *The Lady*

---

* Longhi, in *Vita Artistica*, II (Rome, 1927); Pevsner-Grautoff, *Barockmalerei in den Romanischen Ländern* (Wildpark-Potsdam, 1928), II, 205.

with the Red Parasol (El Quitasol) or *The Coach Passing by the Crockery Market (El Cacharrero)*. Here a dominant bright blue appears unbroken in the huge coach wheels, and it is combined with white in the crockery in the foreground as well as in the attire of the page who is hanging onto the two footmen in the rear of the coach. The footmen and the coachman are dressed in a daring light pea-green. The lemon-colored mantilla of the woman holding the china cups and the coral-red coat of the hatless cavalier gazing into the coach complete the bewitching color symphony. Anything less playful or less brilliant would have been unwelcome at a time when Spain was still under the spell of the Rococo slogan, *vive la joie!*

THE ETCHER   Even as Goya was toying with the superficial semblance of life, and the aristocracy was pretending not to notice the distant rumblings of the revolution, the enemies of the Old Order were arraying themselves at the borders of Spain.

Did Goya disregard what was happening? Was he unaware of the fire sale of the *ancien régime* conducted in France by Robespierre, Danton, and the other managers of the New Order? He saw it all. But somehow he was at first afraid to face the facts outright. When a fermentation process has started to transform a man's outlook on the world, it must have time. An artist like Goya could not suddenly leap from the dainty puppet show of the tapestries into the brutal reality of the *Desastres de la guerra*. As an animal takes refuge from an approaching elemental catastrophe in a safe hide-out, so Goya hid his thoughts in the dream-fancies of *Los Caprichos*— the first in a series of books of etchings which were to win for him a niche in the graphic arts beside Albrecht Dürer and Rembrandt.

So far Spain had produced no *peintres graveurs*, that is, print-makers who envisage the world and express their views of it primarily in the graphic language of black-and-white. With the exception of Jose Ribera, none of the leading Spanish painters of the seventeenth century ever touched a burin or a copper plate. In the eighteenth century Francisco Bayeu, Jose del Castillo, and certain other academicians eked out their incomes by making printed copies of the most popular paintings in the Prado, and thus Goya himself started.

His early technique was patterned on the prints of Giovanni Battista Tiepolo and his son Tiepoletto. The title of *Los Caprichos*—"Motifs as I see them"*—is reminiscent of a series of ten etchings by Tiepolo, *I Vari Capricci*, of 1749, whose fanciful subjects and treatment somewhat resemble Goya's. Tiepolo derived his bright and sketchy manner of etching from the technique of Rembrandt, whose influence had earlier come to Venice by way of Giovanni Benedetto Castiglione. But while Tiepolo, like all the other eighteenth-century students of the great Dutch etcher, was interested exclusively in his sunny and impressionistic prints, Goya was drawn to those dark prints of Rembrandt which the collectors of today admire as much as the Rococo age neglected them. The sixteen plates which Goya etched after paintings of Velasquez in 1788—among them his masterpiece, *Las Meninas*—were done in Rembrandt's dark glowing manner. Simultaneously Goya tried the mezzotint, which was winning international fame for England, and the aquatint of the French. These more recent intaglio processes enabled him to produce a more liquid and luminous chiaroscuro. Compared with what he created after 1792, Goya's early prints as well as his early canvases were merely experiments with fashionable technical processes.

With his graphic short-hand comments on the events of the day, *Los Caprichos*, Goya joined the ranks of the "enlighteners." The silly diversions of the Rococo age had lulled Reason to sleep. *Reason*—the favorite cry of the French revolutionists—Goya was going to arouse in Spain, where the aristocracy and the people had not yet heard the new message, where Reason was still asleep. Goya would preach in a universal idiom and make the Spaniards wake up and face the real issues reasonably. Then the superstitions that were burdening their minds and hindering social and cultural progress would swiftly dissolve into thin air. This, I think, is the authentic meaning of the inscription on the original frontispiece (now Plate 43): *El sueño de la razón produce monstruos* ("When reason dreams it produces monsters").† It is the exhortation of an enlightener:

* *Capricho*, often signifying a *motif*, always implies a personal, unconventional approach. Francisco de los Santos so used the word, for example, in saying that a certain religious painting by Tintoretto abounded with magnificent *caprichos* (*Descripción del Escorial*, Madrid, 1681, p. 39).

† The original inscription (on the sketch in the Prado) reads *Ydioma universal*

"What are you afraid of? You have believed in monsters that exist nowhere except in your dreaming imagination. Awake and realize that they are superstitions!"

Goya's etchings were not flippant comments but a single cry of warning. Today, even though we may no longer heed his warning, we still hear his cry. The tone of suffering and dismay which characterizes the *Caprichos* is quite unlike the superior attitude that Daumier afterward exhibited in his sarcastic utterances on politics and society.

Goya's etchings were obviously not intended for the multitude. Their subtleties were comprehensible only to his friends. To realize this one should read one or the other of the *Sainetes* by Ramon de la Cruz, short plays which were very popular about the middle of the eighteenth century. These make merry over the everyday life of the Madrilenians in terms intelligible to the mob. A few themes from the *Sainetes* are used again in the *Caprichos*—the unresourceful physician, the inadequacy of school teachers, and so on. All the more striking is the difference in the attitude of Ramon de la Cruz, who caters to the crowd, and Goya, who addresses the intelligentsia. Furthermore, Goya's criticism is always bitter. It completely lacks that good-humored sympathy with his subjects which is characteristic, I think, of the playwright who, though satirical, cannot afford to insult his lowbred audience. Goya's satires are little concerned with what was popular with the people; in fact, the most popular subjects of the day, the theater and the bullfight, are missing.

On the other hand, Goya was too much the son of "medieval" Spain to shrug his shoulders and detach himself from the Spanish superstitions. The original frontispiece shows him asleep at his desk, besieged by bats, owls, monkeys, cats, and all the other monsters of which he was warning the nation. Even while he was ridiculing them, they held him in their grip.

Goya's departure from the niceties of the tapestries toward a critical, mordant, revolutionary outlook came in the wake of a physical crisis which coincided in point of time with the decisive events of the great French Revolution. He was seriously ill in 1792 at the time when Louis XVI was

dibujado y grabado p' F. de Goya año 1797. In this year the whole series was ready for publication; work on it had begun in 1793.

forced to parade, wearing the red cap of the Jacobins, in front of the jeering Parisian mob. In the following year Goya had to beg leave to withdraw to Andalusia to recover his shaken health. There the first sketches for the *Caprichos* were made when Louis Capet was put to death. Goya suffered another grave accident in 1794, the year when the reign of red terror was at its height in Paris, Marie Antoinette was beheaded, the Christian religion abolished, and the Cult of Reason established. Exactly what his accident was has never been explained, but it is certain that it permanently impaired his health. His hearing was affected and within a short time he suffered the tragedy of complete deafness, the psychological effects of which made him "hate himself." After the crisis was over, Francisco Goya was no longer the same man. He was fully aware of how deeply these events influenced his art. In a letter to D. Bernardo Yriarte, dated January 4, 1794, we run across this startling passage: "I have commenced to draw in order to occupy my imagination which my ailment has deadened" (. . . *para ocupar la imaginación mortificada en consideración de mis males*).

The decisive outcome was that Goya ceased to be a *painter* in the old sense of the word. No longer was he willing to accept the phenomenal world as a mere representational assignment. Goya became the first great artist-dissenter of modern times, a mordant critic of his age, the earliest of all graphic editorialists. Henceforth he rejected picture-making as a useless pastime. Even when he painted ostensibly historical pictures, such as *The Skirmish at Puerta del Sol* (Fig. 84) and *The Execution of the Rebels* (Fig. 86), or mythologies such as *Saturn Devouring His Children,* he was transmitting "emphatic messages"—*caprichos enfáticos.*

LOS CAPRICHOS On every page of the *Caprichos* Goya ridicules the monstrosities engendered by superstitious minds. He satirizes certain religious practices (*53,** 70*) and exposes clerical misdemeanor (*13, 49, 79, 80*); he brands the reign of vice (*59*) and the outrageous rapaciousness of the so-called society (*77*); he chides the conventional marriages (*2, 9, 14*) and

* Italicized numerals refer to the original numbering of Goya's prints and thus also to the pagination of the *Caprichos von Goya,* 83 facsimile reproductions, edited by Valerian von Loga (Munich, 1922).

their consequences (*57, 75*). He sharply criticizes the education of children who are either scared out of their wits by the bogeyman (*3,* Fig. 88) or all but flogged to death for having broken a pitcher (*25*).* He lays bare the vices of the female sex, the dressiness of the young and the old (*17, 31; 55,* which is likely a caricature on the old duchess of Osuna). He lampoons the rampant fashion craze. He shows women carrying chairs upon their heads (*26*), the implication being that with dresses as short as they are, they ought to sit on their heads. One of the numerous preparatory drawings that was rejected before publication jeered at the vanity of the male sex in a similar fashion, showing men who wear their trousers as sleeves and their shoes where other people have ears.† Goya voices his disapproval of the annual carnival (*6,* Fig. 89). He accuses the girls of shamelessly exploiting their suitors (*19, 20*) and the men of ruthlessly "breaking a girl's wings" (*21*). He thinks ill of flirtation (*5 ,7, 27, 35*) and pandering (*15,16,28, 31*), and warns of the consequences: kidnaping (*8*) and deadly duels (*10,* Fig. 80). He denounces the girls who venture out on a stormy night (*36*) and comments, not without pity, on others who are arrested on a charge of vagrancy (*22*), locked up in jail (*32, 34*), and publicly disgraced (*23, 24*). He derides the foolish weaknesses inherent in mankind in general: indolence (*73*), gossip (*48*), avarice (*30*), greed (*72*), and stupidity (*29, 37, 38,*

Fig. 80.—Goya: *Love and Death,*
Los Caprichos, 10

* The enlighteners of the late eighteenth century emphasized the significance of child education along the lines of J. J. Rousseau's *Emile*. Goya was probably familiar with Johann B. Basedow's *Elementarwerk* (1774), a standard book on the subject, because of its famous plates, etched by Daniel Chodowiecky.

† Reproduced in Pierre D'Achiardi, *Les Dessins de Goya* (Rome, 1908), CLXXX.

41, 42, 46). He scoffs at the autocracy of the recruiting officers (*76*) and the arrogance of the ministers (*33*).*

Above all, Goya never tires of mocking at witchcraft, demons, vampires, hobgoblins, elves, and similar monsters (*43, 45, 47, 51, 60–62, 64–69, 71, 74*). He reviles women who trust their father confessors too much (*52*), or pluck a hanged man's teeth (*12*) because of their magic power to insure the fidelity of husbands or lovers. Only a few of the etchings are humorous genre pictures without a satirical sting: the house on fire (*18*), the tavern scene (*78*), the smugglers (*11*). Some allegorical etchings are easy to comprehend—for example, *56*, the "ups and downs of luck." The symbolism of others is difficult to decipher or is altogether obscure (*54, 58*).

Other etchings remind one of the satanic fancies carved upon the medieval choir stalls of the cathedrals of Saragossa, Toledo, and Avila, with which Goya was as familiar as he was with the designs of the Dutch painter Hieronymus Bosch. In these the beasts look and act like men, and the men like beasts (*63*). Throughout the series Goya unloosed a veritable witch's sabbath of animal symbolism—jackasses young and old, teaching as well as being taught at school and at home (*37, 39*), listening to a concert (*38*), acting as physicians (*40*), having their portraits painted (*41*), or riding on the backs of human beings (*42*), for "every useful society member bears his burden." Another *capricho*, labeled "Chinchillas" (*50*), shows a blindfolded ass feeding two aristocrats whose brainless skulls are padlocked and who are straight-jacketed by their escutcheons. The fur of a chinchilla is as priceless as a nobleman's coat of arms; nevertheless, these dangerous rodents have an unfortunate way of honeycombing the ground with their burroughs until whole cities and provinces above collapse. The terse satire of the etching was the result of an extreme condensation of an occasional sketch of beggars receiving alms at the church door from the charitable members of the congregation after the service.†

Nor does Goya shrink from satirizing himself: he pictures himself as an

---

* *Capricho 33* is based on a pun; *El conde palatino* may mean "the count of the Palatinate," "the palace count," or "the palate count." Goya illustrates the third meaning: the minister Urquijo pulling the teeth of his underlings.

† The sketch is reproduced in D'Achiardi, *op. cit.*, XXVIII, 50 A.

ass on a sick bed (*40, 58*); as a monkey who sings or paints to amuse his boss, the royal ass (*38, 41*); as a wanton bird pursuing a girl around whom other birds are swarming like moths around a candle (*19*). He shows a sheep-headed judge (*46*) and a wise owl who sticks to the letter of the law, unperturbed by human destiny (*75*). Besides bats, cats, dogs, and goats, his symbols include lewd swine (*57*); uncanny beings, half-man, half-bird of prey (*72*); beasts that are half-kangaroo, half-mule (*63*). The exploited suitors are depicted as decoy birds plucked of their plumes (*19, 20, 21*). A silver-tongued parrot is acting as defense counsel (*53*).

In an advance advertisement intended to promote sales* Goya apologized to his friends "for having chosen only such subjects as enabled me to ridicule and brand certain prejudices, impostures, and hypocrisies that have become sanctified by time. I deny that any one of my prints alludes to any particular living person; for such would imply misjudgment of the ends of art as well as of the means entrusted to the artist. I beg the public's indulgence for not having been able to avail myself either of definite instances or even of studies from life. Though the perfect imitation of nature is no less difficult to achieve than admirable when it is achieved, my work nevertheless merits estimation, since it departs completely from nature and conveys to vision such forms and movements as to this day have existed only in the imagination. Like poetry, art may select from the world whatever is fitted to its ends. The artist may reassemble in a single phantasm certain circumstances and character-marks which in nature are distributed among separate individuals. It is from such a sage and ingenious combination that he takes the title of an inventor and ceases to be but a slavish copyist."

To the historian of art the closing passages sound familiar: art departing from nature; art presenting forms which exist only in the imagination; the right of fancy to weld natural fragments into new entities; the artist as an inventor—these are the expressionistic theories of medieval art reborn. Goya must have realized that, like his *Caprichos*, the Gothic phantasms carved on the *sillerias* of the Spanish churches were the esoteric utterances of heresy and mutiny.

Goya was the first to yield again to their influence. Curious though it

* Published by Valentin Carderera in *Gazette des Beaux Arts*, XV (1863), 240.

may seem, those medieval manifestations of a heathen rather than a Christian imagination had been known ever since they were first carved. The Primitives, the Mannerists, the realists, and the artists of the Baroque—all had seen them. But none had used them to inspire his own art. If there was a reverberation of the Gothic in Goya's art, no external link can explain precisely why he resorted to it and how he could express in the medieval repertory of form the sentiments relevant to his own age—the age of the French Revolution.

The most plausible explanation of this mystery lies in the parallelism of the conditions under which both the heretical Spanish Gothic art and the dissenter-art of Goya came into being. Like Goya's, the Gothic art was the mouthpiece of an age muzzled and repressed until the unbearable intellectual tension caused a general explosion.

Around 1300 the oppression of intellectual freedom resulted in heresy. A similar oppression of free thought in the period before 1800 led to social criticism. In the art of Spain the explosion was more violent than elsewhere in Europe because there the Middle Ages had never quite vanished. The Spanish Gothic flowed directly into the Spanish Baroque. To a long-range observer it may even appear that the broad stream of Spanish medievalism flowed right into the Napoleonic era.

Whenever revolution has rocked Europe in the past, the concomitant moods have appeared in the popular terms of "graphic" art. Before the invention of woodcut and copper engraving the agitators and critics used carving as a medium of propaganda. On the bridge between the Middle Ages and the age of humanism, heresy manifested itself in grotesque images carved on the arm-rests, backs, and misericordes of the choir stalls, and, less frequently, in the marginal designs and culs de lampe of the illuminated manuscripts. The revolutionary movement from the feudal social order to the democratic, attendant on the Lutheran Reformation, was advanced in printed broadsides. Shortly before 1500, when every believer in Chiliasm was expecting the second coming of Christ, Albrecht Dürer published his graphic illustration of The Apocalypse, a haunting sermon in pictures showing the necessity of preparedness. When, with the first success of the Lutheran Reformation, the German peasants rose against the feudalists, Hans Holbein's Dance of Death upbraided the ruling classes as well as the ruled, pointing out the equality of all human beings before death, from the pope down to the beggar. In the seventeenth century the terrors of the Thirty Years' War registered in Jacques Callot's etchings, *Les Misères de la guerre.* And again, about 1800, when the French Revolution was casting its heavy shadows over feudal Spain, Goya printed the *Caprichos,* which were an Apocalypse and a Death's Dance rolled into one.

THE PORTRAIT OF THE ROYAL FAMILY For a short time it appeared that Spain could steer clear of the revolution. Charles III was as enlightened a ruler as could be found in the eighteenth century. But no sooner had he abolished the supremacy of the clergy, established an efficient government, and introduced freedom of speech and opinion than the black forces of reaction moved against his good intentions, undermining the liberal regime until everything reverted to the old status.

Succeeding to the throne in 1788, Charles IV and his queen, Maria Luisa of Parma, re-established the ancient Spanish order, sanctified through many centuries—the unapproachable hierarchy of the throne and the altar on the one hand, and the unheeded *misera plebs* on the other. This was an easy accomplishment, for the traditional inertia of the Spanish people aided their spiritual shepherds in thwarting every good intention of Charles III. To make things worse, his weak successor was governed by a cynical wife. Maria Luisa's favorites as well as all the other important scoundrels in office recaptured their shaken positions and behaved as they pleased.

The author of the *Caprichos* (which at that time were known only to a few of Goya's intimate friends) belonged to that very court. Shortly before his appointment as *primer pintor de cámara,* he had secretly jeered at the duties of an official portraitist. Plate *41* of the *Caprichos* gives his idea of what those duties were: to "monkey around" with a jackass until, on the canvas, he looked like a lion—"neither more nor less."* But Goya could no longer work under cover. About the year 1800 portrait painting in

* *Ni más, ni menos,* is the inscription under Plate *41,* which shows Goya as a monkey portraying a lion for an ass. The inscription under the original sketch (Prado)

his opinion ceased to be synonymous with flattery. Goya had become a realist. He spoke out openly (it would not be true to say courageously, for his venture was too bold and too honest to be understood by the imbecile lot who occupied the throne and the space around it).

Shortly after his appointment (October 31, 1799) he painted *The Family of Charles IV* (Fig. 82). The change in his manner since the time of the

Fig. 81.—L. M. Van Loo: *The Family of Philip V,*
Prado

tapestries, with its turn to keen directness, is astounding. All the decorative, theatrical details have been discarded. The large group portrait is the recast *Meninas* of Velasquez (Fig. 71). Here, too, the painter is seen standing behind his large canvas in the left corner. But whereas the court painter in the age of Philip IV was not only entitled to represent himself on an equal footing with the members of the royal family but also to reduce the images of the royal couple to a faint reflection in the mirror, such an insult to royal dignity was not permitted in the days of Charles IV. Emphatically the king and queen hold the center of the stage and the painter must render his own image as inconspicuous as possible. This

reads, "So you won't starve" (*No morirás de ambre*). The satirical idea as such was not invented by Goya. David Teniers had represented apes acting as artists (picture in the Prado) and so had Jean Simeon Chardin (see *The Monkey Painter,* in the James Simon Collection, Berlin).

change in the arrangement is significant—the Hapsburgs were monarchs; the Bourbons were despots.

In coloration the painting is a glorious example of Velasquean impressionism. From a distance every form seems to be defined with the utmost precision, but at close range the whole is a weft of indistinct color hazes. Its harmony surpasses even Velasquez. A conceit of black lace over a silk robe of yellowish white is worn by the queen; a sparkle of stars, crosses, and ribbons of blue, white, and coral are showered over the chocolate-

Fig. 82.—Goya: *The Family of Charles IV*, Prado

brown suit of the king; vibrant hues of olive green, citron, azure, brown, and gold are employed in the raiments of the princes and princesses. This entire chord glows from a background floating in silver gray and golden ochre. The composition, on the other hand, reveals the Spartan temperance for which the classicism of J. L. David was simultaneously pleading in France. This sober alignment of eleven perpendiculars (disregarding the persons whose heads alone are visible) is indeed far removed from the sociable and flattering postures curling like so many festoons through a spacious hall in Louis Michel Van Loo's large *Family of Philip V* (about 1740, Prado, Fig. 81).

The sobriety of the arrangement is matched by a realistic character depiction which is nothing short of ruthless. The arrogance and ugliness of the queen is rivaled only by the pathetic foolishness of the king—an empty shell, a boxer deprived of brains but possessed of a terrific appetite. The sergeant painter could not very well slap his royal chief on the back with the sardonic remark attributed to Lenbach when he was painting the portrait of a certain German captain of industry: "Go on, show some spirit! Or is posterity to say that Lenbach stooped to paint a man without brains?" Such an admonition, moreover, would have had little effect on a monarch who later told Napoleon that his entire life, day in, day out, summer and winter, rain or shine, consisted of hearing mass, going hunting, eating, and sleeping. "In the evening Manuel Godoy (the omnipotent minister) told me whether matters were going well or ill. Then I went to bed and began again next morning unless some important ceremony compelled me to rest."* The head of Maria Josefa, the king's aged sister, emerging from the background on the left, resembles a scrawny vulture. Not in vain had Goya dealt with animal physiognomy in the *Caprichos.*

But most startling of all is the stodgy small-town mood pervading the whole. A great deal of truth lies in the witty remark of a French critic: "These people have the appearance of the family of a little retailer whose lottery ticket drew the big prize." Neither the king nor the queen ever realized the gross blasphemy inherent in the painting. To them it was the epitome of royal dignity, expressed in the proud language of Velasquez.

THE DISASTERS OF THE WAR The *Caprices* of 1794, as I have said earlier, were Goya's shelter from events in France. *The Disasters of the War,* his second series of etchings, on which he began work in 1808, are a frontal attack on what happened in Spain under Goya's very eyes.

In 1808 Napoleon attempted to pocket Spain as though it had been so many neglected square miles of real estate. The Spanish people had always been loyal to their sovereigns so long as they were allowed to remain Spaniards. Since the distant times when the Moors were expelled, they had not surrendered to a foreign conqueror. Therefore the nation rose to a man in self-defense when the Napoleonic army, with the connivance of the so-called national government, invaded Spain, besieged Saragossa and

* De Bausset, *Mémoires de Napoléon* (Paris, 1829), I, 233.

Madrid, forced the king to abdicate, and established Joseph Bonaparte on the throne.

Most of the eighty etchings* known today as *Disasters of the War* were not published until thirty-five years after Goya's death. The published volume consists of two parts, which Goya had planned to publish under separate titles—*Fatal Consequences of the Sanguinary War against Bonaparte in Spain* and *Emphatic Fancies* (beginning with Plate 66).† The first part, constituting about two thirds of the present whole, originated between 1808 and 1810. Three plates are dated 1810 (*20, 22, 27*); a few others may have been added even a little later. The second part criticizes the political conditions after 1814, when Ferdinand VII, abolishing the constitution of the Cortes of 1812, completely undid liberal progress.

In contrast to the *Caprichos*, nothing is dissembled or allegorical in the first part of *Los Desastres de la guerra*. In these war pictures Goya faced brutal truth. Very few of them were drawn from memory or imagination. Most of them were sketched directly from life, on the battlefields of Aragon and Castile, or in the alleys and streets of Saragossa and Madrid. In 1808 Goya visited the war zone. Forty-six sheets of the sketch book which he had taken along with him constitute the unmitigated record of his personal impressions (Prado). Four of the subtitles emphasize the reliability of the pictorial records by statements such as these: "I could not stand the sight of it" (*26*), "I saw this," and "I saw that" (*44, 45*), "It occurred just so" (*47*).

Perhaps Goya at first planned a pictorial history of the glorious patriotic adventure. This is suggested by the fact that he depicted certain incidents which he could hardly have seen with his own eyes, but which are recorded in the history of the Spanish War of Independence: Maria Agustina, the heroic maiden of Saragossa, who loaded the cannon after every man of the squad was dead (*7*, Fig. 83); the burning of the town of Torquemada by the troops of Lasalle (*41*); the lynching of the Marquis of Perales by the mob in Madrid (*28*). If this was his first plan, the sight of the real thing

* Originally there were 81. A print glorifying the worker, entitled "This is the Truth," has recently been discovered. Two other *caprichos enfáticos* are appended in Hugo Kehrer, *Los Desastres de la guerra*, 82 facsimile reproductions (Munich, 1921).

† *Fatales consecuencias de la sangrienta guerra en España con Bonaparte y caprichos enfáticos.*

changed it. His etchings were to be history, indeed, but not the traditional brand of history; there would be no panegyric of patriotic deeds *ad maiorem belli gloriam,* but an unmasking of war's unspeakable horrors.

Once more, the great dissenter refused to bow to tradition; instead he created an entirely new idea. Hitherto, in all the history of art, war had

Fig. 83.—Goya: "How brave!" *Los Desastres de la guerra,* 7

been glorified in terms of flags flying, clarions calling, cannons roaring, and heroic warriors showing their prowess on prancing steeds. That glory was debunked in Goya's etchings. *Los Desastres* are the earliest manifestations of pacifism in art.

Only one etching in the entire series of eighty shows the mêlée of a real battle (*17*, "They cannot agree"). And in only one other is the subject of a purely military nature (*8*, "Charging Cavalry"). The remaining etchings of the first part deal only with lamentable episodes of the guerrilla: duels between French soldiers and Spanish peasants (*2, 3,* Fig. 91); women armed with spears, short sabers, daggers, and rocks, battling in the most cruel fashion against their military oppressors (*5*). Only twice does Goya sound something like a note of heroism—the prowess of the woman at the cannon (*7,* Fig. 83) and the bravery of an infuriated civilian defending himself with a hatchet against threefold odds (*3*). The complete absence of a heroic element makes the remaining pictures deadly and disheartening. If the artist occasionally rises to a philosophic generalization, it is only to end in bitter pessimism: "To be killed—that is what you were born

for" (*12*); "Bury the slaughtered remains of those who were dear to you—
and keep silent" (*18*, Fig. 92); and "If nothing worse happens to them
than to be crippled in a battle, then there is hope that they will be killed

Fig. 84.—Goya: *The Skirmish at Puerta del Sol*, Prado

Fig. 85.—Goya: "And there is no remedy,"
Los Desastres de la guerra, 15

the next time" (*24*). Death, death, and again death is the tenor of Goya's
indictment. How romantic were *The Hieroglyphs of Death* by Valdes
Leal (Fig. 77) as compared with the true face of death unmasked by Goya.
In twenty-seven of the eighty etchings, corpses are scattered on the ground.
Three etchings represent nothing but so many piles of them (*22, 23, 63*).

In four pictures one or two living persons are added for contrast: parents in search of their dead son (*18*, Fig. 92); a starving pauper (*48*); a priest in despair (*60*); a man, still wrapped in his ghastly graveclothes, staggering away from the killed, among whom he was laid by mistake (*62*). The survivors carry the bodies to the cemetery (*20, 21, 56, 64*) or cast five at a time into a single grave crudely dug in the field (*27*); the wounded and crippled are removed to the hospital (*24*), where painful surgical operations are being performed (*25*). Goya exposes the terrible fate of friars lynched by civilians (*46*), civilians lynched by the Napoleonic soldiers, who strap them to posts and shoot them through the stomach (*15*, Fig. 85) or through the back (*38*). He shows men garroted for having been found with weapons on their persons (*34, 35*); men hanged by the most cruel methods (*14, 31, 32, 36*). He shows the plundering and the mutilation of the dead (*16, 33*), and mangled bodies hanged or impaled on trees (*37, 39*). The indictment rises to a particularly savage pitch as Goya sketches the sad lot of womanhood in the war. No fewer than nine prints represent rape (*4, 6, 9, 10, 11, 13, 19, 31, 41*). The butchering of entire families by Napoleon's *grande armée* is recorded (*26*). Amidst the savagery men and women lose their minds (*65, 68*).

Nor does Goya omit the more general disasters of the war. The entire populations of certain towns flee as the enemy draws near (*42–45*). A house is blown up by a bomb and the dead inhabitants, as well as the debris of floors and furniture, land in the basement (*30*, Fig. 94). Goya also narrates the silent tragedies that occurred among those who could not leave the imperiled cities in time: a dead mother leaving an orphan behind (*50*); lone women or men dying because there is no one left to care for them (*52, 53*); men and women wailing in the street (*54*); beggars in the suburbs (*55*); miserable half-starved creatures hiding in alleys or under the arcades of the bull ring (*57–58*). A single deed of charity, which Goya may have witnessed in Saragossa, is recorded as an exception (*49*). The rich still pass by the beggars (*61*), and on the whole those behind the front are doomed no less than those who go to battle. A group of six, gathered around a pot of peas (*51*), and another five, who divide what is contained in a small cup (*59*), conclude the tragedy at home.

The second part of the book deals with the most cruel realization of all—

that the whole patriotic struggle was in vain. Under Ferdinand VII, who
was crowned king of Spain after the fall of Napoleon, reaction set in anew.
The *Caprichos Enfáticos* deplore and chastise the new rise of feudalism and
clericalism: the superstitious devotion of the populace to dead relics has
not changed (*66, 67*); again the blind are leading the blind to destruction
(*70*, Fig. 93).

In the first part Goya had sometimes grouped the pictures as sequels,
two or three following upon one another like antitheses or parallelisms,
with subtitles to clarify the interrelation. For example, under an etching
depicting a brutal assault (*4*), he says, "Women inspire courage," and
under the following one (*5*), where a mother is piercing the abdomen of a
soldier with a long spear, he says, "And they are beasts." A woman is defending herself literally with tooth and nail against her assaulter, who
wears a corporal's uniform. Another woman armed with a dagger is steal-
ing in from the rear, and it is certain that the brute is doomed (*9*). "They
are unwilling," says the subtitle; "And so are these," says the next one
(*10*), though this time it is the men who are victorious over defenseless
women. The lynching of the Marquis of Perales (*28*) is associated with
the lynching of a common soldier by the mob (*29*). A terrible alignment
of eight men strangled on the garrote (*35*) precedes a similar picture of
three men hanged on trees—an unending defile of gallows into infinity
(*36*, Fig. 90). The text under the first-named etching reads, "We do not
know why this happened"; under the next it reads, "Nor this, either."
The plundering of the monastery of Cuenca (*47*) follows upon the killing
of its inhabitants (*46*). The beggars outside the city are succeeded by those
in the city (*57, 58*), and so on.

In the *Caprichos Enfáticos* this mutual interassociation of ideas has been
carried even further. The last twelve etchings lash the reactionary policies
like the illustrations of twelve stanzas of an ode on vicious government.
In these Goya answers the question that he asked time and again in his
pictures of the war: "What was all this for? What are the results?" "Nothing!" This answer is inscribed on a scroll in the decomposed hand of a
veteran whose skeleton a pack of ghastly phantoms (symbolizing the reactionary forces of the Church) are frightening out of its grave (*69*). The
blind lead the blind (*70*, Fig. 93). A monk, with a bat's wings instead of

ears, is writing the new book of "laws against the commonweal" (*71*).
Vampires suck the life of the nation (*72*). The mob is dancing around the
golden cat (*73*). The royal fox solemnly declares that "Humanity is to
blame for what Spain is suffering" (*74*). Overjoyed by this message, the
vulture Church dances a mad farandola amidst the host of the crazy kings,
dukes, jackasses, swine, and the other "charlatans" (*75*). Once again
Goya asks, "Is there no hope? Will not the people expel the carnivorous
vulture?" (*76*). "Shall the rope break on which the monks are trying to
walk?" (*77*). "Will the valiant horse kick and defend itself successfully
against the cunning of the curs, foxes, wolves, and hyenas?" (*78*).

Goya closes on the strain of mysticism with which he opened his horrify-
ing sermon. The first plate of *The Disasters*—a man of Goya's personal
features kneeling in prayer in the seething darkness—represented "Humanity sadly foreboding what is to come." In the last two etchings of the
Caprichos Enfáticos light is seen emanating from Truth resurrected.
"Truth died" (*79*). "Will she rise?" (*80*). Her halo is radiant.

Two events of the war in Madrid so deeply stirred the patriot Goya
that he monumentalized them eventually in two large canvases: *The
Skirmish of Puerta del Sol* and *The Execution of the Rebels on the Third
of May, 1808*. Goya was an eyewitness of the battle of Puerta del Sol. A
color sketch, now in a private collection in Madrid, was apparently dashed
off on the spur of the moment. Technically it is a bit crude as compared
with the painting in the Prado (Fig. 84); yet it is electric with an animation curiously lacking in the latter. In the sketch only two main incidents
are referred to. In the center of the foreground a mameluk of Murat's
troops has been shot from his white horse. While he is still hanging to the
horse's back, one foot caught in the stirrup, an *espada* stabs the animal
from in front, and another man, approaching from the rear, is about to
slash open the dying man's abdomen with a dagger. To the left another
Spaniard, dressed in white, is knocking another mameluk out of the sad-
dle into the open arms of the mob. The larger painting offsets these two
motifs not only with elaborate anecdotal details but also with the local
scenery. The necessary enlargement of the figures impairs their spon-
taneity.

Creative imagination had a much greater share in the other canvas, *The*

Execution of the Rebels, which was completed in 1814 (Fig. 86). Some of the motifs which Goya incorporated in this canvas had already appeared in the earlier etchings. Plate *15* of *The Disasters* (Fig. 85) furnished the firing squad, the butchered monk who lies face down in the foreground, and the lighting effect—patterned as a wedge of brightness which pierces

Fig. 86.—Goya: *Execution of the Rebels, May 3, 1808,* Prado

a larger area of dark as it slants in from the left. The graphic exigencies of etching compelled Goya to be brief of expression; the large canvas called for more details. But since Goya's etchings retain their inherent monumentality even when enlarged to ten or fifty times their original size, the "graphic" conciseness was not lost in the process of transferring the etching to the painting.

The pictorial grouping was manipulated in accordance with the antithetical principle so often employed by Goya in *The Disasters of the War.* The entire right-hand third of the canvas was reserved for the display of the military machine. It is a dull mass: a sevenfold parallelism of so many lunging fusileers. There is neither a face nor an individual expression among them; each is but a robot's uniform and rifle. The opposite third on the left is a perfect antithesis. It contains seven individuals, two of them dead, five still alive; and each of these is a separate personal drama—the fanatic who with arms upraised appeals to the soldiers, and the impassive monk next to him who gives himself to prayer. Three other men standing behind the leader mirror less courage, but each in a different shade and degree. One has his eyes fixed on the barrels in anxious expectancy, the next is stopping his ears, looking away, and the third buries his face in his hands and shrinks in horror. The military and civilian parties, thus diametrically opposed, are linked by the central architectural setting which looms from the pallid dawn and rises to what is the apex of a compositional pyramid. Beneath it we discern three onlookers in a suggested multitude. From their faces and gestures the two dominant moods of the picture sound once again—senseless fear and impassivity. Perhaps the most significant utterance in the whole drama comes from the weird and unremitting shriek of the hideous yellow light of the lantern in the center.

THE LATE WORKS   The unfortunate results of the war taught Goya that for a dissenter like himself the only course to take in a country where frank patriots were unwanted was to cease talking about this mad world. He performed his duty as a court painter in executing the portraits of Joseph Bonaparte and Ferdinand VII, as he had painted portraits of Charles IV. But after 1815 only on rare occasions did he paint or draw anything that savored of political or social propaganda. His impressionism gained new strength and a broader scope from subjects that were emotionally indifferent.

The History of the Bullfight (La Tauromaquia*) gave him a chance to apply his keen realism to a subject where accuracy was essential but where no satire was involved. The Tauromaquia is a series of études in light and movement. Of course, had there been nothing else to recommend it but the interesting treatment of light and dark and its subtle compositions, the book of etchings would hardly have become so popular in Spain, where every child is an aficionado, a fan and expert in the rules and tricks of the game, and judges its pictorial representation accordingly. For all their daring impressionism, the prints of the Tauromaquia are exact records, no less exact than The Disasters of the War—records of how the different suertes had changed from the days of the Moors to the days of Goya. It is really a biographical history of the great national game. Goya

* Hugo Kehrer, Tauromachia von F. de Goya, 43 facsimile reproductions (Munich, 1923).

depicts what happened to this, that, or the other banderillero, picador, and matador. He tells of the skill of Pepe Hillo and his tragic death in the arena. He immortalizes the daring stunts of Fernando del Toro, Rendon, and Pedro Romero. He shows how Martincho tempted the bull to attack him while he, with his feet manacled, sat on a chair or stood on a table. Another breath-taking picture describes the accident by which the mayor of Torrejon lost his life (Fig. 95).

About ten years later, at the age of seventy-nine, Goya took up the subject again in four lithographic prints. *The Bullfights of Bordeaux,* published in a set of one hundred copies in 1825, are more imaginative and in the broad manner of Goya's old age. He learned the lithographic process from his friend Cardano, who had brought the recent discovery back from Paris in 1819. It enabled him better than any other graphic technique to preserve the freshness of the first sketch in the finite expression of black-and-white. But, except for the one set, he made no effort to make money out of the sale of his etchings or lithographies. For whose benefit should he publish them?

The lonely man had lost all interest in business matters. Disillusioned and embittered, the aged Goya retired to his country home near the Puente de Segovia. The people called it *la quinta del sordo*—the deaf man's cottage—and they went out of their way to avoid seeing its owner. There he lived, shut off from the world, alone, save for the company of a housekeeper. Not a sound pierced the ears of the deaf hermit.

But as the world without became more and more mute, his soul lived, all the more, from within. It was in these late years that Goya again resorted to his dreams and visions, depicting them in sepia drawings of the broadest execution, in etchings, and in murals.

Goya's last book of etchings* has been known both as *Proverbios* (proverbs) and as *Sueños* (dreams). Some of the prints resume subjects last treated in the tapestries (*Jumping Jack, Folk Dancing,* and other typically Spanish genre themes); others deal with social issues of the time (*The Barren Branch,* Fig. 87) or with events connected with the Napoleonic Wars (*The Phantom; The Débâcle,* Fig. 96)—themes made familiar by the *Caprichos* as well as *The Disasters.*

* Hugo Kehrer, *Proverbios von Goya,* 21 facsimile reproductions (Munich, 1920).

Goya's original name for these prints was *Disparates* (absurdities, non-sense, strange things). That name, better than any other, defines the significant stage which this series of etchings represents in the evolution of the artist's satirical work. In the *Caprichos,* it will be remembered, a modicum of jocundity was admixed which permitted glimpses of the

Fig. 87.—Goya: *The Barren Branch, Disparate*

brighter side of even the most cutting caricatures. *The Disasters of the War* were so deeply steeped in bitterness that Goya's sarcasm could only make one laugh on the wrong side of his month. The *Disparates* represent yet another, final, stage. In them Goya burlesques his bitterness. The paradoxical predominates, and consequently the bottom is knocked out of any argument, no matter how grave it be. Although his blood runs cold, he laughs at the absurdity of it all.

The more recent title, *Sueños,* is more suggestive of the authentic source from which Goya's visions welled forth. Moreover, the graphic idiom through which they appeal to the beholder—the scant reference to the scenery in terse, rugged patches of black-and-white—lends to these "strange things" that indeterminate, evasive quality of dreams to which Leonardo da Vinci referred in one of his aphorisms: "Men shall walk without moving, they shall speak with those who are absent, they shall hear those who do not speak."* On the other hand, these graphic images of dreams are animated by an intensified sense of touch, a trait probably characteristic

* *The Notebooks of Leonardo da Vinci, op. cit.,* 1106.

of the deaf man. An uncanny sense of corporeality is communicated by *The Dancing Giant,* a bit of typically Spanish imagery: "the towering mountain leading the frightened mountaineers a dance." Everywhere in these etchings space has become a haunting experience, seeming to expand beyond the boundaries of ordinary nature. In *The Sack Race* there is an added suggestion of soundlessness as people encased in sacks move insanely through space—an infinity of it, limitless yet muffled, insulated against any tonal reverberation. In still other instances Goya seems to deny the existence of tridimensional space. The "ridiculous disparate" (Fig. 87) depicting a number of men and women huddled together on the limb of a dead tree is as unspatial as a Chinese painting.

At the time when he was inventing and printing these nightmare prints Goya was also decorating his home with large murals (now in the Prado). Some of the subjects resemble the *Disparates,* and their painterly execution is quite as weird. Others deal with episodes from Spanish folk life: *Two Men Fighting with Cudgels; Women Laughing; Men Eating; People Listening to a Reader; Two Old Friars; A Young Wench;* crowds of inebriated men and women singing inarticulately during *The Pilgrimage to the Miraculous Fountain of St. Isidro.* Still others have biblical or mythological narratives for subjects: *The Fates; Judith and Holofernes; Saturn Devouring His Children* (inspired by a Rubens painting in the Prado). A fourth group comprises grotesque fancies: *Witches Riding through the Air* and *The Witches' Sabbath.*

A mere classification by subject matter is irrelevant. It is the style, the manner of execution, which makes the murals that Goya painted for *la quinta del sordo* truly extraordinary. How any human being could endure *living* in an environment thronged with such titanic visions is beyond comprehension. Such distortion of the natural forms, such blocking-out of crude masses, would be enough to drive an ordinary man crazy. In these latest works Goya was neither a realist nor an impressionist. The faithful follower of Velasquez has here become the creator of expressionism. Neither in his fantastic subjects nor in design and coloration do these murals belong to the playful, unencumbered, and joyous eighteenth century from which Goya came, or to the scientific, pedestrian nineteenth century which he heralded in *The Disasters of the War.* To recognize how he forecast what Picasso eventually was to accomplish in his *Mural of Guernica,* note Goya's deliberate misshaping of the organic forms: a foot painted in terms of a yellow quadrangle or an entire body in terms of a regular hexahedron. Indeed, Goya's last work belongs in essence to the twentieth century.

Life in the Spain of Ferdinand VII finally became intolerable. In 1824 Goya spent a few months in Paris, where he first saw the paintings of John Constable and Eugene Delacroix. He then established himself in Bordeaux, where he died April 16, 1828. He paid a final short visit to Madrid in the spring of 1826. The king had promised him a pension if he would let himself be painted by Vicente Lopez. The latter's *Portrait of Goya,* in the Prado, reminds one of the artist's spiritual brother, Beethoven.

The body of Francisco de Goya y Lucientes rests in Madrid in San Antonio de la Florida, a hermitage that he himself had adorned, exactly thirty years before his death, with frescoes depicting a resuscitation.

THE RESTORATION OF THE SPANISH TRADITION The art of Goya was profoundly Spanish. Not only in his selection of native motifs, the dramatic realism of his narration, and other features that pertain to subject matter was Goya's art Spanish but also in his use of the artist's media, his patterns of composition, in short, all features that pertain to pictorial form.

The last representative painter of Spain restored the tradition described in the first part of this book, a tradition which had fallen into oblivion during the second half of the seventeenth century and the subsequent period of French and Italian supremacy. In Goya's paintings, etchings, and lithographs, one again encounters the "planar" mode of composition so typical of the Spanish style in earlier epochs. He restored the "inflexible" design, and again apprehended reality in terms of "allover surface patterns."

Technical necessities with which the artist had to cope aid in explaining the planarity of Goya's compositions; for example, the requirements of weaving which have already been discussed. On the other hand, Goya's compliance with the exigencies peculiar to certain technical processes cannot account for his personal style. Surely the aquatint technique did not effect the planimetric style of Goya's etchings. Rather, he adopted the process, invented by J. B. LePrince and publicized in 1791, because he found it admirably suited to his desired planimetric forms of expression. The aquatinter covers his plate with a coat of grainy resin which, when bitten in acid, produces flat shade areas not unlike those of a wash drawing. In his four sets of etchings Goya used the new process with increasing success.

The earliest aquatints of the *Caprichos* clearly show Goya's intention to neutralize the extravagant depthward perspective, fashionable with

Fig. 88.—Goya: *The Bogeyman,*
Los Caprichos, 3

G. B. Tiepolo and the other Rococo painters, by the means peculiar to the newly invented graphic process. An example is *The Bogeyman* (3, Fig. 88). Beginning with the specter in the right-hand foreground, who is seen from the back, and ending with the mother's rearward tilt and the white object behind her, there is a rapid diagonal recession into the depth of the picture. But the two aquatinted flat tones of black, plus the unbroken white flats of the paper, transform the perspective recession of the figures and objects into a pattern of collocated planes. So, in defiance of the so-called naturalistic progress of the eighteenth century, Goya's picture pattern has become akin to the patterns of the Spanish Primitives, at least in one important feature: it reaffirms the original Spanish tradition of planar perception.

In the later prints of the *Caprichos* Goya discarded the depthward perspective of the Rococo style for completely planimetric compositions in which the setting, the lighting, and the grouping are oriented in planes running parallel to the proscenium and the footlights. An excellent example of this is the satire on girls who accept any prospective husband (2, Fig. 89). The lateral movement of the figures and the altar steps is funda-mentally different from the diagonal recession of the figures and the setting in *The Bogeyman* (see Fig. 88).

Fig. 89.—Goya: *At the Hymeneal Altar, Los Caprichos, 2*

As time went on, Goya consistently flattened every· individual bulky form whether or not it fell within the aquatinted areas of the picture surface. The two wenches sweeping their mating birds out of the love nest, and the two old women behind them—in other words, a depthward succession of three rows of figures—have been reduced to a single planar brightness in *Capricho 20*. Later, in *The Disasters of the War,* Goya went still farther in translating even the foreshortened figures into planimetric patterns. Among the unhappy women who are imploring the pity of their assailants in *Desastre 19,* the one prone in the center is composed of unbroken flats of white and black. An even more interesting example is the dead soldier in the front right-hand corner of *Desastre 17.* Here a bold foreshortening has been all but obliterated in a flat speck of white paper. Henceforth Goya adhered to the principle of "planar" composition even if the essence of the expression seems to have called for a perspective flight away from the beholder, as in *Desastre 36* (Fig. 90). The defile of the gallows into the distance is highly expressive, but it is subordinated to the action in the front plane, as an accompaniment is to the leading melody.

In the most forceful pictures of the *Caprichos* and *Desastres* the artist's "planar" ideation bears on the very linework. The lynching of a soldier (*Desastres, 29*) is represented by four or five flat silhouettes composed of

layers of parallel horizontal hatchings; the ground and the distant mob
are manipulated in precisely the same manner. Other outstanding illustrations of the planarity of Goya's pictorial expression are the tree in
Capricho 28; the bell tower and the huge arch in *Desastre 11;* and, above
all, the cannon, with Maria Agustina and three strips of dead bodies silhouetted against it, and the flat pyramidal eminence on the left in *Capricho 7* (Fig. 83).

The same picture well illustrates the inflexible rectilinearism of Goya's
design, which, like the planarity of his compositions, was more in harmony

Fig. 90.—Goya: "Who knows why?" *Los Desastres
de la guerra, 36*

with the ancient Spanish taste than the flexuous and curvilinear manner
of the early eighteenth-century Italian and French artists. All the great
native painters of the past, from Ferrer Bassa to Huguet, Morales, and
Zurbaran, would have approved of the rigid, angular, and terse linework
of Goya's etchings—the combination of triangles and flinty contours in
"How brave!" (Fig. 83) and "Who knows why?" (Fig. 90), or the mad
zigzag design of *The Ravages* (Fig. 94). Velasquez would have appreciated
the stiff parallel perpendiculars of the portrait of *The Royal Family* (Fig.
82), but the graceful Van Loo, who painted the portrait of *The Family
of Philip V* (Fig. 81), would have shrunk from them in disgust. Goya
avoided pliant curves, preferring angular forms even where he intended

to suggest such lissomeness as the flight of a butterfly, as in his *Satire on the Duchess of Alba,* "our lady of fashions" (*Caprichos, 61*). The witches, serving as an ornamental base,* are also blocked out as from the hardest kind of stone.

The designs of *The Disasters of the War* are even more wiry and barbed than those of *The Caprices*. The pattern of *The Fighting Peasants and Soldiers* (*Desastres, 2,* Fig. 91) consists largely of parallel horizontals and diagonals that intersect at angles as pointed as the teeth of a saw. It is no accident that one is constantly reminded of the most angular capital letters in the alphabet. The legs of the two peasants on the left are patterned like

Fig. 91.—Goya: "With reason and without it,"
Los Desastres de la guerra, 2

an *M,* the crossed gun barrels in the center like a *Z,* and the two soldiers taking aim on the right like a *V.*

Because of the realism of the subject matter the underlying compositional patterns, particularly in *The Disasters of the War,* are often not noticed by the beholder. Yet, in Goya's opinion, they were the very soul of his graphic messages. He was the first Spanish artist who again fashioned his pictures, as the Moors had fashioned their abstract wall decorations, from inflexible lines and planes of light and dark.

---

* In his comment of this print, bearing the enigmatic title *Volaverunt,* Goya says of the witches: "They are ornamental rather than useful. There are heads so full of gas that they need neither balloons nor witches to make them fly."

If one temporarily disregards the plot in Goya's etchings, it must be admitted that they resemble intarsia work or mosaic because of the way the sharply defined surfaces of black, gray, and white are fitted into the given picture planes. At times the plot itself is so gripping that one does not realize the significance of the pattern. In other instances the pattern is so fanciful that it almost effaces the narrative. An example is *Stormy Night (Caprichos, 36)*. Before one has time to identify the literal meaning of the various forms, one's imagination is captivated by the darting brightness of a mantilla, by the flamboyant darkness of a shock of hair which is like an echo of the former, and by the indeterminate shadows on the horizon toward the left. The idea of the "allover surface pattern" absorbed Goya more and more as he developed his highly personal style; his figures flattened out, his sceneries lost their initial elaborateness, his patterns became angular, flatly shaded abstractions. It is difficult to imagine how his contemporaries could understand what he was attempting. Goya's late art was too advanced for an age accustomed to judging pictures by their simulative qualities alone.

GOYA'S CONTRIBUTION TO THE SPANISH TRADITION B̲ut surely, beyond restoring the native tradition, an artist of Goya's caliber must have contributed something new, something completely his. When we analyze what it is that distinguishes Goya's "allover surface patterns" from those of the Moors, El Greco, and Velásquez, we find that Goya's surface patterns were conditioned by the particular moods they communicated. Quite apart from the figures and objects depicted by them, the patterns themselves are saturated with sadness or gaiety, with grim humor or deadly earnestness, with agitation or quiescence, with affirmation or denial. Whatever the mood of the message, it found an appropriate expression in an eloquent surface rhythm.

The forsaken mood of the picture of the husband and wife in search of their dead son (*Desastres, 18,* Fig. 92) not only emanates from the sentimental content but is aroused by the pattern itself—that lonely perpendicular staggering above the mounds of earth and corpses which heave and sink in the monotonous rhythm of waves. The upper edge of the picture weighs down upon the group of the parents; a fraction of an inch more clearing above their heads would have detracted from the oppressive mood of the whole. The parents emerge in the extreme right corner. For, no matter how desperate, they are actively pursuing their goal; hence the slight disturbance of the equilibrium to suggest tension and expectancy. The expression of hopeless forlornness in *Desastre 60* is different. The

Fig. 92.—Goya: "Bury and keep silent!"
Los Desastres de la guerra, 18

lonely priest has nothing to accomplish among the dead. "There is none to help him." Here, therefore, the solitary perpendicular occupies the middle, and the heavy clouds, sinking under the pressure of the darkness, close in on all sides as if to crush the priest with their load.

It is impossible in this brief chapter to discuss the fullness of Goya's patterned messages. I can only cite a few selected examples. *Kidnapping* (*Caprichos, 8*) is symbolized in a violent group contour, jagged and zig-zagging like lightning. In *Love and Death* (*Caprichos, 10,* Fig. 80), the man killed in a duel and the woman who tries desperately to brace him up are patterned like two sticks broken in the middle. It is revealing that the idea of their joint collapse came to Goya as an afterthought. In the earliest of several preparatory drawings* the woman stands upright like a pillar. Moreover, in contrast to the studies, it is only in the final impression that

* D'Achiardi, *op. cit.,* V, 10.

the frenzy of the woman reverberates in the irregular lines of the slanting
battlement and the rolling mountain contour. In *The Disasters of the
War* the scenery and the action are attuned to each other in a more penetrating manner. The "shattered" outline encompassing a group of "Sa-
maritans" who carry the dead from the battlefield is re-echoed, down to
minute details, in a group of mutilated trees (*Desastres, 20*). The pattern
underlying the plundering of the dead (*Desastres, 16*) reminds one of a
big octopus stealthily extending its slimy tentacles all over the picture surface. The notion of the blind leading the blind (*Desastres, 70,* Fig. 93) is

Fig. 93.—Goya: "They do not know the way,"
Los Desastres de la guerra, 70

expressed in a pattern suggestive of an uncoiling serpent. The panic-
stricken population fleeing from a burning city (*Desastres, 42*) is represented in the linear simile of an exploding rocket. Each of Goya's patterns
is as self-expressive as a metaphor is in poetry. He would not have had to
depict literally mothers and children, rafters, furniture, and the other
debris of a collapsing house. His chaotic pattern alone would tell the
message of *The Ravages* (*Desastres, 30,* Fig. 94). It is a veritable landslide
of areas light and dark, an insane jumble of crooked lines and angles.

    The idea of the self-communicative pattern persisted even in the non-
expressionistic pictures of the *Tauromaquia.* Here Goya's patterns

anticipate those amazing "snapshots" of fleeting moments which the Impressionists of the nineteenth century brought to the highest perfection; Edgar Degas, in particular. I refer only to *An Accident in the Bull Ring*

Fig. 94.—Goya: *Ravages, Los Desastres de la guerra, 30*

Fig. 95.—Goya: *An Accident in the Bull Ring, La Tauromaquia*

(Fig. 95). The bull has leaped over the barrier and caught the Alcalde of Torrejon on his horns in the midst of the terrified audience. The terror is expressed by the distortions of the unbalanced pictorial mass. The equilibrium is upset. A big gap on the left is outweighed by an area on the right bursting with the fear-crazed spectators. And, as the bull burdens the extreme right end of the pictorial scale-beam with his overbearing mass, the entire pattern becomes an expression of utmost suspense.

In the *Disparates* Goya was often more concerned with the abstract pattern of the composition than with the tangible objects and figures it embraced. This is certainly true of *The Débâcle* (Fig. 96), which symbolizes the fall of Napoleon in 1815. Because of the turbulent mass rhythm of the pattern, which causes everything factual to resolve into hazy gener-

Fig. 96.—Goya: *The Débâcle, Disparate*

alities, the beholder is aware of a hurricane rocking the huge tent, under which the multitude has sought refuge, long before he can single out the tumbling idol of the hero on the extreme left, or the frenzied priests and aristocrats who have climbed on one another's shoulders in order to support the collapsing canvas roof.

Guided by these few examples, the reader may learn for himself from the published works of the artist what new contributions Goya added to the Spanish tradition which he restored to life. Then he will come to realize, among other things, that Goya went further than did any other Western artist before Paul Cézanne toward perfecting the communicative pictorial pattern which, like music, needs no words to be comprehensible—in brief, that abstract art which, as an idea, originated with the Spanish Primitives.

PERSISTENCE OF THE PATTERNS AND PRINCIPLES OF SPANISH ART I have
marshaled evidence for the existence of a Spanish style since the beginning of the Middle Ages and have traced its growth and transformation
through subsequent epochs to the end of the era of Francisco Goya.
Although I am aware that the historians deem it improper to speak of
Spanish art prior to the founding of the Spanish State, it is nevertheless
my contention that Spanish art is far older than that. As a conclusion I
shall furnish proof that the same Spanish style which I have described on
the ground of the art of the more recent periods was already in existence
as early as the fifth century B.C.

My star witness is the magnificent stone bust in the Louvre, known as
The Lady of Elche (Fig. 97). It bears traces of Phoenician and Etruscan influences, to be sure. But these do not preclude the evident presence of an
original Iberian style any more than the signs of Flemish and Italian influences in the paintings of the Primitives of the fifteenth and the Mannerists of the sixteenth century pre-
clude the dominantly Spanish character of these later products of art.
Far more significant than the alleged foreign vestiges in the style of
The Lady of Elche is the Spanish
ideation which pervades her every
part. In its nature and decoration,
the bust is a close stylistic relative
of other well-known Spanish works
of art. As examples I shall cite only
Pedro de Mena's *Mother of Sorrows*
in the Victoria and Albert Museum
(Fig. 98) and the portrait of *Maria
Cristina de Bourbon,* the fourth
queen of Ferdinand VII, by Goya's
pupil Vicente Lopez (Prado, Fig. 99).

That *The Lady of Elche* is a characteristic piece of Spanish art is il-

Fig. 97.—*The Lady of Elche,* Louvre

Fig. 98.—Pedro de Mena: *Mother of Sorrows*, London, Victoria and Albert Museum

lustrated by the penetrating realism of the face. Such succinct fidelity to nature has very little, if anything, in common with the idealism of the classic Greek art of the fifth century B.C. Rather, it shows that the pre-Christian Spanish sculptor who executed the bust was just as keen on rendering a precise record of life as were his followers in the Christian epochs, and just as unconcerned as they as to whether the narrow nose, the sharp-edged lips, and the fleshy chin of his model were in keeping with the universal standards of sublime beauty. The bust must have appeared even more surprisingly Spanish when its original coloration was still intact; today a few traces of color on the lips and the eyes are the only remnants of the original polychromy.

In addition to showing the characteristic Spanish realism, the ancient portrait bust also exhibits those decorative features of the Spanish style which have been discussed at length in the earlier chapters of this book. Therefore, I need point out only the most obvious marks of identity: the glittering web of ornamentation that is spun across the surface and the angularity of the design.

The face of *The Lady of Elche* is the more delicate and smooth for the contrast of the lavish ornament by which it is set off. The ornamental bronze

Fig. 99.—Vicente Lopez: *Maria Cristina of Bourbon*, Prado

chains, buckles, and ear shields function exactly as do the stylized ringlets of hair and the brittle seams and puckers of the drapery in the bust by Pedro de Mena, and exactly as do the ornamental blue-and-silver mesh of lace, embroidery, and jewels in the portrait by Vicente Lopez. As a matter of fact, the very design of the ornaments on the wheel-like ear shields and the chains anticipates the *estilo plateresco* of the sixteenth century.

As for the Spanish fondness for angular grace, the retreat from the effect of pleasing curves is equally noticeable in *The Lady of Elche* and in de Mena's *Mother of Sorrows*. It is enough to compare the taut outlines that ensconce the faces from the temples down to the chin, or the straight lines which enframe the faces—the ear appendages in the former and the hood in the latter. The face of Queen Maria Cristina was by nature flabbier and its expression less impassive than those in the other two examples. Nevertheless, the entire pattern of the Lopez portrait is not supple as it would have been had it been painted by an Italian or French artist. The obtuse angular intersection of the veil with the forearm on the right brings into play that blunt rhythm, that expression of stubborn and superior reticence, which is so inbred in the temper of the Spanish race that without it neither the Spanish language nor the Spanish art would be what they are.

No, it is not fanciful and impermissible to associate, as I have done, by the underlying unchanging racial taste, the art of a century ago with that of the most distant past. The art of Francisco Goya was still basically the self-same Spanish art which we have encountered in the earliest examples. Indeed, in spite of its modernism, Goya's latest work was impregnated with a mystic otherworldliness similar to that which permeated the most primitive Spanish work.

Goya did not yield to the deadly influence of the Roman classicism which engulfed all the European countries save Spain at the beginning of the nineteenth century, throwing them back for almost a century into an unproductive sort of historicism. It was Goya who made the Spanish impressionism of Velasquez survive that fatal relapse. It was Goya, the only outstanding genius in European painting of his period, who kept the sacred flame alive. Had he not done so, it might well have become extinct and there would have been no revival in the late nineteenth century. It is of symbolical significance that Goya died in France. For it came to pass that from his paintings and etchings the luscious flower of French impressionism sprang—the school of Edouard Manet.

Already the painters of the twentieth century in Europe and the Americas have rallied around Pablo Picasso. With him another leader has risen from the soil of Spain. And again from his paintings the voice of mysticism has begun to speak through the veil of patterns fashioned like azulejos—abstract, angular, and planar. Picasso's art is quite new and unique. At least so it seems to the crowd. But those who know the art of Spain will not fail to recognize its intimate relationship to the art of the Moors, the art of the Spanish Primitives, the art of El Greco, and, last but not least, the art of Velasquez.

INDEX OF PERSONAL NAMES

INDEX OF PERSONAL NAMES

265

INDEX OF PLACE NAMES

INDEX OF PLACE NAMES